PANIPAT: 1761

PANIPAT: 1761

T.S. SHEJWALKAR

GYAN

Published by

Gyan Publishing House
5, Ansari Road
Daryaganj, New Delhi-110002
Phone: 011-47034999, 9811692060
E-mail: books@gyanbooks.com

Distribution Network
gyanbooks.com
India, USA, Canada, UK, Australia

ISBN: 978-93-7097-316-9 (PB)

First Published, 1946

2nd Impression 2025

Printed at: Gyan Press, Delhi.

PANIPAT: 1761

Arthur T.S. SHEJWALKAR

Deccan College Monograph Series

1

PANIPAT: 1761

BY

T. S. SHEJWALKAR

DECCAN COLLEGE
Postgraduate and Research Institute
POONA

PANIPAT: 1761

BY

TRYAMBAK SHANKAR SHEJWALKAR, B.A.

Reader in Maratha History, Deccan College Postgraduate and Research Institute, Poona

POONA

1946

To

the cherished memory

of

D. V. APTE

(1881—1943)

A deep scholar of Maratha History with whom the Author had discussed all that is printed here and than whom none would have been more pleased to see it in book form.

PREFATORY NOTE

The present volume initiates the Monograph Series of the Deccan College Research Institute, and it is no coincidence that the first volume in that series should deal with the Third Battle of Panipat. The history of this Institute is closely connected with that of the Peshwas whose religious benefactions were directed by Mountstuart Elphinstone, after the Battle of Kirkee, towards the promotion of Education among the people, and in consequence this Institute was founded in 1821, (on Saturday, 6th October) as the Poona Sanskrit College. Through the three stages of Poona College (1851) and Deccan College (1868) and the Deccan College Post-Graduate and Research Institute (1939) the Institute maintains the continuity of these benefactions, and the present year is significantly the 125th year after the original foundation when, besides this Monograph Series, two others, namely, the Dissertation Series and the Handbook Series are inaugurated. It is to be hoped that this long tradition of enlightened scholarship towards which both Indians and Europeans, particularly Englishmen, have so largely contributed, will be maintained rigorously in the future to heighten the common achievement.

The thanks of the Publication Committee in the present case are chiefly due to Mr. R. P. Patwardhan, M.A. (Oxon), I.E.S., Director of Public Instruction, Bombay Province, and Mr. D. R. Gadgil, M.A., M.Litt. (Cantab.) Director of the Gokhale Institute of Economics and Politics, Poona, for helpful criticism.

S. M. K.

21st March, 1946.

PREFACE

LET me explain the scope and purpose of this monograph and my design in writing it.

As the subject is an old one, generally known to most students of Indian history, I have thought of curtailing the narrative within minimum limits, leaving the bare anatomical structure behind. To fix the attention of readers on facts, I have avoided over-burdening this fragment of history with detail. Having no particular taste for the pageantry of history, I have eschewed all description with hyperboles surcharged with chauvinistic sentiments and thus left an open field to poets, dramatists and novelists.

Though so designed, the book is written for both the student and the general reader. As such it has assumed the form of a narrative and an essay combined. The appeal is to the reason, and not to the sentiment, nevertheless.

The work has entailed a reconstruction on the basis of the revaluation of the old material with the help of new material filling in the gaps, and a closer study of the positive background of geography. The result is a proper visualisation of the scene leading, in its turn, to a correct interpretation of the various sources and a restatement of the whole problem.

The battle of Panipat has naturally occupied a prominent place in the heart of the historically minded Marathas. Their interest in the affair was heightened by the genius of Vishvanath Kashinath RAJWADE, the founder of a school of historical research in Maharashtra. It has become a perennial theme for discussion ever since. RAJWADE was not noted for a sound judgment, however. His writings have provoked more polemical literature than any other man's in Marathi, and even Sir Jadunath SARKAR, writing in English, could not resist the temptation of having a fling at him.

This brings me naturally to the point when I should state the purpose of writing this volume. Had a person of Sir Jadunath SARKAR's competence and calibre, with all facilities at his command, dealt fairly with the subject, there would have been no valid ground for any one to dip pen in ink. He has devoted almost two hundred pages to the history treated in the present volume, in his *Fall of the Mughal Empire,* Vol. II. But all the shortcomings for which he had been criticised before by Maratha scholars are found repeated in this work. He has treated the subject from a wrong angle as a part of the history of the Mughal Empire. He has overlooked important relevant material. His interpretation of the material used is incorrect, not to say inadequate. He betrays insufficient knowledge of the Marathi language and inexpertness in using the material in that language. An unsympathetic critic must, at least, be fully and correctly acquainted with the subject he writes upon, and these conditions are unfortunately not found fulfilled by Sir Jadunath's very brilliant presentation in masterly English. The result is, the reader is carried away by the presentation, viewing things in a wrong perspective, unconscious of the errors committed or the incorrectness of the conclusions deduced. Sir Jadunath does not seem to believe in sticking to one ethical standard when treating the various parties in a struggle. It is true that nothing succeeds like success and the Marathas have failed in history. But historians, when passing judgment, should not forget the standard of conduct followed by the various parties in history. Ahmad Shah Abdali's strict discipline should not make us forget the methods of achieving it, nor should his victories efface the Afghan atrocities leading to that end. The Marathas could not establish their rule on a sound basis, and the foreign British succeeded where the indigenous Marathas failed. But this should not make us blind to the fact of Clive's forgery and cheating or the Bengal famine of 1770, carrying away more than a third of the Bengal population, a direct result of that rule. (It is curious to note in this connection that the Cambridge *History of India,* Vol. V, does not even mention this famine, a significant omission indeed!) The Marathas had the ambition of ruling over India, no doubt, but they were not prepared to forsake their standard of conduct to gain this end.

Instead of merely criticising others' works in detail ultimately leading to nothing, I thought it better to write out the whole piece myself in my own manner. The difference of opinion will be found, I hope, justified in the performance. In the world of Indian scholarship at present, the vogue of copying, imitating and adapting is current. This results in circulating the error in a wider area which later on comes to be called a universally accepted fact. Many scholars throughout the length and breadth of India are now-a-days trying to utilise the Marathi material and weaving it into the thread of their histories. An aggressive occupation of the historical field is going on before our eyes. But the danger underlying these efforts is scarcely understood by the scholarly knights-errant engaged in these adventures. It is high time some one should put a stop to their activities, for while it is easy to disseminate an error, it is not so easy to recall it back or to stop its ravages. As an humble effort in the cause of weeding out errors, I place this book before the public.

Though this monograph is complete in itself, it is not intended to supplant other works in the same field. This book is to be treated as an adjunct to the general histories of the period, without knowing which this work may not be properly understood or appreciated. As I have written my work with an eye on Sir Jadunath's volume, it has unconsciously assumed the form of a reply to his writing. In fact, where I have not differed from him I have almost followed him, especially in the portion mainly dependent on Persian chronicles studied from the MSS by him only. I believe there can be no higher tribute to a man's original work than that of following him.

Most of the ordinary readers will miss the graphic part of history they have up till now read in the accounts of Panipat. I thought of omitting them from my narrative because I have no belief in their truth or even probability. The idea of copying such details from the chronicles simply because no other light can be shed on these events or episodes, I think as faulty. By their repetition, a disservice is done to the cause of history. National sentiment is sure to be perturbed by this line of action, no doubt, but it is better to take that risk/than to be an agent in circulating palpable falsehoods. Those who have a liking for such stuff can have recourse to the original chronicles which should go as literary pieces, but not as history. They can be turned to sociological uses too.

The study of this subject I began a decade ago and many causes have retarded its progress. I had an intention of first stating the theory of the Maratha State in an independent monograph and then of writing this volume for the correct understanding of which it is absolutely necessary. Now I am stating the same in bare outline in the Introduction. Then again for various reasons, mainly but not exclusively personal, the work was written in parts and then held over. This fact has adversely affected its merit as a literary product. Had the work been written out in the first glamour of the subject and in the Panipat locality, it would definitely have been a more unitary piece of work. But the loss on the presentation side has been made up by gain on the thinking side. The battle could not have been satisfactorily described by me four years ago, when I could not visualise it properly. After that, the coming in of new material and even the hope of getting access to valuable material held over my design. Such rare material has been made available to me by the kindness of co-workers in the field of history, especially through the assiduity of Mr. G. H. KHARE of the Bharat Itihas Samshodhak Mandal. The thanks of all students of history would naturally go to him, in addition to those of mine. Other scholars who have helped me in furthering my project are Dr. G. S. GHURYE of the University School of Sociology in Bombay; Rao Bahadur K. N. DIKSHIT, the retired Director-General of Archæology, who acted as a host to me in my northern tour; the authorities of the B. I. S. Mandal, Poona; and many others too numerous to be individually mentioned. The readers' thanks should also go to Dr. S. M. KATRE, Director of our Institute, for the drive he has shown in pushing the work through and for its general and artistic get-up, and to the Press for their excellent workmanship.

21st March, 1946.

T. S. S.

LIST OF ABBREVIATIONS

Acton—Lord Acton's Lectures on Modern History (1907).
Ait.—Aitihasika (= historical).
Ait. Tip.—Aitihasika Tipane in Itihasa Sangraha Magazine.
BISM—Bharata-Itihasa-Samshodhaka Mandal.
BISMQ—Quarterly of BISM.
Bhau Bakhar—Bhausahebanchi Bakhar.
Bhau Kaifiyat—Bhausahebanchi Kaifiyat.
BDCRI—Bulletin of the Deccan College Postgraduate and Research Institute.
Dirom—Narrative of the Campaign in India by Dirom (1793).
Fall—Fall of the Mughal Empire by Sir J. Sarkar, Vol. II, 1934.
Hingne—Hingne Daftar, Vol. I, 1945.
IHQ—Indian Historical Quarterly, Calcutta.
IS—Itihasa Samgraha Monthly.
JIHQ—Journal of Indian History Quarterly, Madras.
Kashiraj—An account of the last battle of Panipat. Edited by Rawlinson (1926).
Purandare—Purandar Daftar volumes.
Raj.—V. K. Rajwade's volumes.
Shinde—Shindeshahi Itihasachin Sadhane.
Satara—Satara Historical Society's volumes of letters.
SPD—Selections from the Peshwa Daftar.
Shrivastava—Life of Shuja-ud-daulah, 1939.

Note—Please see the critical analysis of sources at the end of the book for more information.

INTRODUCTION

SHIVAJI founded the Maratha State for doing good to the Maratha people. But he was also conscious of his role in Indian history as a defender of the Hindus against the onslaught of Islam. At the same time he was no crusader against Islam as an alien faith; he only wished to divest it of its political role in India. In the first part of his life, he was not sure of his line of action or final goal. He made up his mind finally after his return from Agra in 1666. The establishment of an independent Hindu State as a rallying point for all Hindus became his aim thereafter. Compromise with Muslims or service under an Islamic State he found incapable of rousing the Hindus from their age-long stupor. These would neither defend Hinduism in the long run, nor allow the Hindus to grow to their full stature. Only a direct challenge to the Islamic idea of State—that Islam only is to live and grow while others must wither away and die—was the surest way of defending Hinduism and the Hindus. Aurangzib wished to unite India under one sceptre, that of Islam under the Mughals. Shivaji girded his loins to establish an independent Hindu sovereignty in India free from the shackles of the Mughal octopus. He succeeded in his determination and crowned himself as the Chhatrapati in 1674. He forged new weapons to gain his ends at the cost of his enemies. While his subjects were well protected, he made the enemy subjects pay for his wars against their state by the imposition of the Chauth, to escape which the only remedy was to come under his rule. Aurangzib revived the Jizya in the Mughal dominions after a lapse of a hundred years, to propagate Islam and weaken the infidels. Shivaji hurled back the missile with the aim of meeting the new menace by his demand for Chauth from the enemy lands. Aurangzib pulled down the temples and desecrated the Hindu shrines. Shivaji replied by reviving the temples turned into mosques by the Muslims in the south. While Aurangzib's manner was aggressive and bigoted, Shivaji's was defensive and moderate. This distinction should be borne in mind when judging Shivaji and Aurangzib, a distinction which marks the modernity and secularism of the one and the medievalism *cum* ecclesiasticism of the other. Not understanding this difference, Toynbee in his *Study of History* (3.203) has classed Shivaji with Ivan the Terrible, Saladin and Suleyman the Magnificent as champions of alien (non-western) civilizations. Shivaji was not only a champion of old-world Hinduism, but its modernising reformer also. He not only endowed temples or patronized Hindu learning; he also (and primarily) built new forts on the sea-coast for protecting his newly-established navy on the European model, and sent his own ships to Arabia for direct trade. He would not turn his new state into a closed, hermit-kingdom, after the manner of Japan in the sixteenth century, but left it open to all foreign influences in all walks of life, after due regulation to guard his independence. Had Shivaji's ideas and ideals been properly understood and followed by his successors, there would have been no occasion for a Panipat in 1761.

Shivaji was a bold soldier and a clever general, an able engineer who knew the art of fortifications better than the engineers themselves, and, above all, had studied geography with the minutest detail with the help of specially prepared charts, as Abbe Carre, the French padre, reports. Can any one doubt Shivaji's modernism with this testimony? Shivaji not only revered Brahmins, but employed them in building his state with the whip of a task-master, too. He made them crown him as a true twice-born warrior and received back into his own caste men like Netaji Palkar, who had been living in Afghanistan as a full Muslim for ten years. His bold stand electrified the whole Hindu society from the Indus to the Brahmaputra. Sikhs, Rajputs, Jats, Bundelas, and even the distant Ahoms of Assam rose against Aurangzib and made his reign one long line of more or less successful rebellions. In the south, Shivaji built up a strong state guarded by long lines of impregnable forts and newly-built ships, which withstood Aurangzib for a quarter of a century, and ultimately sent him to his grave in 1707.

With all their personal drawbacks and vices, Shivaji's immediate successors could tide over the Fundy tide of Mughal invasion because the men trained under Shivaji knew the basis of his state. With the passing away of these men, a new twist was given to the basis of the Maratha State which ultimately led to Panipat. It came to pass in the following manner. Shivaji's grandson Shahu had been captured with his mother by Zulfiqar Khan when he took Raigad in 1689. He lived in Aurangzib's moving camp for full seventeen years till 1707, when he was released on the advice of Zulfiqar Khan with the intention of creating dissentions amongst the Marathas. He had been befriended by Aurangzib and his daughter in his captivity, as a result of which Shahu imbibed a life-long sense of personal gratitude towards the Mughal imperial house. He could never entertain the idea of completely destroying the Mughal empire. On the other hand, he now and then gave a helping hand to the Mughals. As the orphan son of Shivaji's eldest son who had suffered death terribly at the hands of Aurangzib, and himself a long sufferer in captivity through all sorts of insults, privations and slavery, the Marathas naturally felt a sympathy for Shahu when he returned. But the army and the civil officers all divided into two opposing factions, creating a permanent schism in the Maratha polity, which is historically found perpetuated in the establishment of Kolhapur as a separate state.

Shahu triumphed over his aunt Tarabai, because he was the legitimate heir for whom common people felt a sympathy born of his miseries as well as on account of the shrewish behaviour of his overbearing aunt, who turned all her officers into enmity, one after the other. Shahu returned as a nominee of the Mughals, and as such received the support of all Muslim officers as well as all those who sided with the Mughals for personal gain. All opportunists and new candidates, who had nothing to hope from the party of Tarabai, naturally supported Shahu. Ambitious and unscrupulous men found a new opening for their talents in this fratricidal war. But his supporters overlooked one important constitutional point in their enthusiasm for the good new king. He had returned with the Mughal badge of slavery round his neck. The lands bestowed on him by the Mughal emperor are styled Zamindari lands.

His so-called kingdom can at most be styled an autonomous feudatory principality in the language of constitutions. And what was worse, he had accepted this status not as a policy to tide over the times, but in all sincerity which he meant to keep. His gentleman's attitude sealed the fate of the Maratha State.

Most of the men who had gone over to Shahu's side had gone with selfish motives of personal aggrandisement. They hoped to remain strong and almost free to do what they liked under a weak master such as Shahu was, on account of his precarious position between two mill-stones. The man who helped Shahu most in building up his party and stabilising his rule automatically became his Prime Minister or Peshwa. This was Balaji Vishwanath, comparatively a new man from Konkan and a careerist bent on utilising all opportunities to strengthen himself and his master, without regard to the distant effects of his steps on the Maratha polity. Shahu did not know Shivaji's ideals and ideas, ways and means, because he had spent his boyhood and youth in the Mughal camp. Balaji would not know, because that would not have furthered him in his rise. Shahu wanted a new class of persons to keep his poise in the face of overbearing, old officials. Balaji, coming from an outside caste, looked down upon by the entrenched ministers (Deccan Brahmins), wanted a needy master who would go out of the groove to do the needful. Besides, Balaji was endowed with all the personal qualities necessary for imposing oneself on persons of various denominations and motives. Being an outsider, he could pose as a third (disinterested) party in all tussles and quarrels, and would be accepted as such by others also. His position, in course of time, became unassailable.

Balaji's opportunism is seen in his support to the Sayyid brothers, the king-makers. He invited their help for crushing Damaji Thorat in his internal rebellion against Shahu's rule, while he accompanied them to Delhi in order to facilitate their intrigues against the lawful emperor. In return he received fresh orders under the seals of puppet emperors, bestowing the Maratha kingdom on Shahu, and the release of Shahu's mother from captivity at Delhi. Thus Shahu's collapsing rule was propped up with Mughal support! In addition, Shahu accepted the duty of serving the Mughal State with fifteen thousand troops, which were to be placed at the disposal of the Mughal viceroy in the Deccan to buttress his administration, one-fourth revenue (Chauth) of the south being his wages for the same. Shahu was thus not only to be a creature of the Mughals, but was to guarantee the continuation of their rule in the Deccan!

This was really cutting the roots of the Maratha State envisaged by Shivaji and reared carefully by his successors. Shivaji had envisaged the gradual withering away of the tree of Islam in India—though not necessarily through the agency of the Marathas—and planned his Maratha State for aiding the attainment of that end. The Marathas were expected to be the spearhead of the charge against Islam no doubt, but other Hindus were also expected to act their part in the grand achievement. The end was not a Maratha empire spreading all over India, but the complete freedom of all Hindus. If other provinces in India gained their freedom by their own exertions, so far so good. But the Marathas would not sit idle if there was no stir amongst them. They would do the work themselves, irrespective of the cost.

Aurangzib wanted to enrol the valiant Marathas as his loyal servants, like the Rajputs in the north. To avoid that fate they waged a continuous war and went through untold sufferings for two generations. And now Shahu became a Mughal servant without a struggle! He never struck his own coins, but only those of the Mughal emperors. His generals and ministers spread all over India, but only as Mughal grandees or governors. Even all the Marathas never became his subjects—and why should they be when they knew Shahu to have been a Mughal subject like themselves, albeit styled Chhatrapati? All who felt dissatisfied with the Maratha kingdom crossed over the border and got themselves employed under the Mughal viceroy of the Deccan on better terms than Shahu could hope to offer. This support was utilized by the cunning viceroy to stop the payment of Chauth in the first instance, and later for buttressing his own independent rule in defiance of Delhi. Shahu's ministers and generals had to fight for their very existence many a time when the viceroy (Nizam) had grown strong with outside support, or the Marathas had become weak by internal dissensions. This struggle was carried on intermittently for full three quarters of a century, and though the Marathas triumphed on most occasions, the Nizam's rule came to be stabilized in the Deccan. But the fundamental cause of this consummation was the primary mistake committed by the Prime Minister of Shahu in accepting the Mughal service on behalf of his guileless master, which was later on continued by his successors in office. Even Justice M. G. Ranade has misconstrued this point in his *Rise of the Maratha Power,* because the material before him was scanty. Others have fallen into the same error, because they have blindly accepted Ranade as their guide. Because the Peshwas throughout their career tried to act as agents of the Mughal emperors, others more clever played the same game and outwitted the Marathas by securing the orders of the puppet emperors set up by themselves.

The second short-sighted step taken by Balaji Vishwanath has also been similarly misconstructed by Ranade and others. In the worst days of the Maratha kingdom during 1690-1700, when king Rajaram had gone to the Madras coast and ruled from Gingee (Jinji), the Maratha ministers as a temporary policy offered fabulous rewards in land and money to the wavering Marathas, so that they might not go over to Aurangzib Many of these grants "under duress" were afterwards resumed by Tarabai, whose ministers would have again reverted to Shivaji's far-sighted policy of awarding no spoils or jagirs, but paying in cash from the central treasury. Shahu's return as a Mughal protege and the outbidding of his clever but short-sighted Peshwa put a premium on disloyalty to Tarabai the *de facto* ruler, and thus weakened the very basis of Shivaji's modern state. Ramachandrapant Amatya who knew at first hand Shivaji's state-craft, has put down for posterity Shivaji's ideas and ideals in his unique "Rajaniti." Balaji's policy of awarding a share in the conquered lands to ministers and generals created semi-independent barons who ultimately overshadowed the central government after Panipat. Balaji's precaution—lauded as a unique invention—against these barons growing strong and uncontrollable by the central authority, viz., not to bestow contiguous lands on one person, but to award the same in various parts of the country, led to such internecine rivalries, quarrels, wars, peculation etc., that the administration became weak and inefficient everywhere, as was found to his cost by Sadashivrao Bhau in his Panipat campaign. Historians know the part played by conservative tradition in the growth of England. Shivaji had laid down the foundation of a modern state and its healthy tradition was still in an embryonic state. It was a new thing understood by but few, and was almost stifled during the calamitous days of Mughal invasion. Still it was known to men like Ramachandrapant Amatya clinging to the *de facto* rulership. But the new Peshwa of Shahu knew little of that tradition and cared less. His adoption of the line of least resistance in the interest of his master began a new chapter in Maratha history, but it also submerged Shivaji's independent, modern and progressive state.

Balaji's two sons Bajirao and Chimaji were exceptionally clever and valiant. They continued the line laid down by their father and grew strong, almost oberbearing, for their weak, stay-at-home, master. Ostensibly the first ministers of state, they overshadowed Shahu in Indian politics. They chalked out their own policy (in defiance of Shahu's wishes on some occasions), led their own expeditions, defeated and set aside other ministers, in short, began an almost independent central government at Poona in opposition to Shahu's puppet court at Satara. Unfortunately they were short-lived and could not complete their work in their life-time. But when they died in 1740, they had created an independent military force under their unitary command, one lakh of Maratha horsemen ready to be led anywhere in India, a force which made history during the next generation under their sons and successors in office.

The third Peshwa Balaji Bajirao alias Nanasaheb, his brother Raghunathrao alias Raghoba Dada, and their cousin, Chimaji's son Sadashivrao Bhau, were the three men who made Indian history what it was during 1740-1761. Their hands were tied to a certain extent till Shahu's death in 1749. But the next dozen years found a free field for their talents as well as propensities. Nanasaheb was more cunning than valiant and he did everything to concentrate power in his hands. He overshadowed and put down his rivals in the Maratha State with the help of his father's independent retainers, Shinde and Holkar, who in course of time went out of the hands of their master. The old king's retainers were either completely eclipsed or found independent spheres for their valour far away from Poona. Raghoba led expeditions to Gujarat, Rajputana, Delhi and the Panjab. Being more valiant than cunning, he mismanaged the Maratha affairs in northern India. Sadashivrao Bhau had to manœuvre for power with his cousin, the Peshwa, for a full dozen years, before he found his way. Thenceforth, he managed the civil side in the state and had his say in military matters also, especially in the finance side of expeditions. By 1758, he had come to occupy the foremost place in the counsels of the Maratha empire—such as it was.

Ranoji Shinde who was the right hand man of the Peshwa Bajirao in all his dealings, was followed by equally valiant and loyal, though somewhat headstrong and independent-minded sons. Malharrao Holkar the left hand man was, though equally brave and in addition cunning, quite a different type of man. The reader will know more of him in the course of the narrative further on.

The rivalry and difference of opinion on questions of policy between Shindes and Holkar shaped the Maratha history in north India in the way it did. Nanasaheb tried to keep his supremacy by balancing these two pillars of the State. This had a disastrous effect on Maratha politics. The Peshwa should have directed one of them in a different direction. Their machinations in the same field benefited the enemies of the Marathas. The local officers of the Peshwa, like the Hingne brothers and Antaji Manakeshwar in Delhi, Govindpant Bundele and Naro Shankar in central India, had to take orders from these two noblemen in matters civil or military. They also took sides in their rivalries and, in general, in northern Indian politics, as lesser grandees in the same field. Antaji Manakeshwar, the chief of the guards kept for the personal protection of the Emperor, acted against the selfish interests of the Hingnes, the Maratha ambassadors at the Delhi Court. They were suspended by the Peshwa for some time and Antaji Manakeshwar called back to the Deccan. All these men had rented mahals from the state as a side-business, a thing which should have been forbidden by the Peshwa. The state suffered by their personal interest in the state lands. Gangadhar Chandrachud the Diwan of Holkar, and Ramaji Anant Dabholkar the Diwan of the Shindes, also had their individual share in these bickerings, rivalries, back-door machinations against each other. The Peshwa's officers in Poona like Sakharam Bapu, Mahadoba Purandare, Baba Fadnis, and others, were acting hand in glove with one of the parties in their appeals to the central authority. Unless this background is kept in mind, the trend of Maratha politics will not be understood. The genealogy of the Peshwa and Shinde families given elsewhere should also be remembered by the reader for a proper understanding of the narrative.

Another factor which influenced individual actions in all fields was the under-current of caste-consciousness. The Peshwa and his relatives employed in higher posts were Konkan Chitpavan Brahmins, in general rivalry with the local Deshasth Brahmins of the Deccan plateau. All civil ministers of Shivaji and his immediate successors belonged to the latter class, now ousted from their position by the new-comers from the sea-coast. They naturally felt the loss of their importance in the state. The Karhada and Saraswat Brahmins, both in a minority, tried to find independent scope for their abilities under different noblemen, besides the Peshwa. The Marathas, who composed the bulk of the army and belonged to the puppet king's caste, bore a silent resentment against the clerical usurpers of their supreme authority in the state, and this had had its effect on politics, too. Not all men, perhaps not even the majority, were affected by this virus, but its imperceptible effect seems undeniable. The rule of the Brahmin Peshwas had carried the clock of social reform in Maharashtra backwards, when compared with the seventeenth century. Malharrao Holkar's advice to Janakoji and Dattaji Shinde on this count, as presented in the Panipat Chronicle (Bhau Bakhar in Marathi) may or may not be true, or it may be even taken as invented by the writer to suit his construction, but the existence of such social undercurrent cannot be doubted. Its existence does not seem to have affected the Panipat campaign in any vital spot, however.

The third battle of Panipat was fought between the Marathas led by Sadashivrao Bhau and the foreign Afghans with their Indian allies led by Ahmad Shah Abdali. Bhau had been called by the Mughal Emperor Alamgir II before his murder. He was acting as Regent of the Mughal empire at the dead emperor's behest. The Marathas were fighting with Abdali, the foreign interferer in Indian politics, and not Abdali the champion of Islam. This point has not been emphasised by the historians uptil now, because they have misconstrued it. Bhau (and the Peshwa also) had invited Shuja-ud-daulah of Oudh, the Nizam brothers in the Deccan, Kamal-ud-din Khan Babi from Gujarat and even the Indian Ruhelas and Afghans, to join their forces with him. His main support in the campaign was Ibrahim Khan Gardi with his trained infantry corps. The Peshwa's half-brother Samsher Bahadur was a Muslim, who died of wounds received at Panipat. Many departments of the Maratha army, especially the artillery, were manned almost exclusively by the Muslims. On the other hand, no Hindu potentate from northern India fought as an ally of the Marathas. They were all, in their minds, siding with Abdali, and had taken part in calling him to India to punish the Marathas. It is unhistorical, therefore, to call the battle of Panipat a Hindu-Muslim fight, though Najib had screwed down Abdali on the religious count, for selfish ends. Verily religion is the last resort of scoundrels!

Temperamentally, the Marathas are incapable of bigotry, fanaticism, extremes. They take to a thing as a duty for the time being and leave it when found unnecessary. They had taken up arms for the defence of their gods and homes in the seventeenth century. They wielded arms in the eighteenth for keeping India free from foreign rule. But in the nineteenth they had so far forsaken their military life that they were classed by Lord Roberts with the Bengalees and Madrasees as one of the non-martial races of India. In 1930, the Bombay Presidency supplied only seven thousand men out of a lakh and fifty-eight thousand of Indian soldiers, and all the seven thousand were not Marathas. This transformation shows that the Marathas were not warlike or bred to the profession of arms in the same sense as the Afghans or the Turks. They were peasant civilians turned into soldiers for a cause.

* * *

Having depicted the historical background so far, it is but meet that I should pass on to the previous writings in the field I am about to enter.

It is instructive to study the gradual change of opinion on the Panipat affair. During the nineteenth century Kashiraj and Duff practically held the field. When Rajwade wrote his thundering detailed introduction in 1898 on the basis of new letters, in Marathi, he practically carried the public with him as if caught in a flood. Nobody stopped to inquire whether his analysis was correct, nor did any one point out the obvious defects in his editing of the letters. Ten years later, a level-headed professor of history (H. G. Limaye), writing a special essay on the European-modelled Indian armies and their relations with the Indian States in the eighteenth century, changed the trend of opinion by half. While still charging Govindpant Bundele and Malharrao

Holkar for their major share in the defeat, he also pointed out Bhau's personal defects and shortcomings as a commander-in-chief.' Rao Bahadur Sardesai, writing in 1922, summarises the various opinions without offering any new suggestion of his own. An analysis of his writing will bring forth the self-contradictory statements due to his defective method of copying all and synthesising none. Mr. D. V. Apte tackling the problem after him, first pointed out the obvious factual defects in Rajwade's arguments. The confusion of directions in Kashiraj's account of Panipat, Rajwade's misapprehension in taking Baghpat as situated on the right bank of the Jamuna, vitiating his whole strategical argument and similar other flaws were ably discussed by him. But even Apte failed to analyse the whole material and point out Rajwade's manipulation of the same. Prof. S. N. Sen's chapter on Panipat in his *Military System of the Marathas (1928)*, is the best short account in English, which omits nothing of the essentials. With the publication of the Peshwa Daftar, however, during 1930-33, a new chapter opened in the Panipat criticism. As soon as the second volume styled *Panipat Prakarana* was published in 1930, S. V. Athalye an old collaborator with Rajwade and a deep student of Maratha history, published a review of the same in the *Kesari* weekly (4th April 1931). He pointed out the incorrect dating of the documents published, and focussed the light of the letters on the events leading to the Panipat campaign. He absolved Holkar and Antaji Manakeshwar from the blame and made Bhau and the Peshwa mainly responsible for the disaster. Another young enthusiastic recruit for Maratha history, the late Mr. R. V. Nadkarni, began a series of articles on the Panipat affair in *Vividhajnana Vistara* and first pointed out on the strength of the new material certain obvious defects in Sardesai's *Panipat Prakarana.* His original contribution to the discussion consists of the constitutional aspect of the Maratha activities in the north in general, and with the Delhi Court in particular. The charge against Govindpant he thought now as more than proved, with an emphasis. But he was unacquainted with the whole Maratha system and not an expert in research matters. He has taken Agra as situated on the northern bank of the Jamuna and confused Saranjam with Kamavis! Govindpant was a Kamavisdar or Mamlatdar of various revenue taluks, but he had never received any specific Saranjam or Jagir conferred for maintaining an army as a military captain. Not understanding the difference between the two, Nadkarni's downright condemnation of Govindpant is based on a false premise. Besides, he wrote only on the basis of SPD 2 and before the publication of Nos. 21 and 27, supplying further information about the Panipat campaign. Sir Jadunath Sarkar, completely re-writing the whole episode in 1934, has still missed certain documents then available to him, and in general has taken a very unsympathetic view of the Maratha affairs. His factual errors, incorrect criticism, and non-comprehension of the whole affair in proper perspective have been pointed out and criticised in detail by us. Incidentally, the performance of this renowned historian proves our contention that history must be written by one of the nationals.

Mr. K. V. Purandare, editor of the documents collected from the Sardar Purandare family which was throughout the whole period on very intimate terms with the Peshwa family, has also, in his editorial preface to the first volume, offered criticism on the Panipat affair. His main contribution, based on the documents published by him, is to point out the promise of the Peshwa to go to Bhau's help by the month of Magha or February 1761. If Bhau was biding his time till the arrival of the Peshwa, the cause of his waiting is made clear thereby. He also points out the fact that Nanasaheb had no suspicion of Holkar's saving of his skin by running away from the battlefield. The Peshwa attached, after Panipat, not only the districts held as Jagir by Malharrao, but also those held by Shinde and Pawar who had fallen in battle, proving that the attachment was not on account of disobedience at Panipat but for some other reason, possibly financial. But as Purandare wrote his introduction in 1929 before the publication of the Peshwa Daftar, his criticism has to be modified in the light of those papers.

* * *

I should say something now about the nature of the work to be done and the difficulty of doing it in the proper manner. For this, I cannot begin better than by quoting from the letters of the Duke of Wellington about the battle of Waterloo, for comparison.

"The people of England may be entitled to a detailed and accurate account of the battle of Waterloo, and I have no objection to their having it, but I do object to their being misinformed and misled.... I am really disgusted with and ashamed of all that I have seen written of the battle of Waterloo.... And there is not one which contains a true representation or even an idea of the transaction and this is because the writers have referred to stories picked up from peasants, private soldiers, individual officers, etc. instead of to the official sources and reports.... It is very difficult for me to judge of the particular position of each body of troops under my command at any particular hour.... Surely the details of the battle might be left to the original official reports. Historians and commentators were not necessary.... There is one event noted in the world—the battle of Waterloo—and you will not find any two people agree as to the exact hour when it commenced.... I am accustomed to read so many conflicting descriptions of the battle that I would soon begin to believe I was not there myself."

Writing to Sir Walter Scott who wished to write authoritatively on the battle of Waterloo, only two months after the event, the Duke, expressing himself in the same tone, further said, "The object which you propose to yourself is very difficult of attainment, and, if really attained, is not a little invidious. The history of a battle is not unlike the history of a ball. Some individuals may recollect all the little events of which the great result is the battle won or lost: but no individual can recollect the order in which, or the exact moment at which, they occurred, which makes all the difference as to their value or importance. Then the faults or the misbehaviour of some gave occasion for the distinction of others, and perhaps were the cause of material losses; and, you cannot write a true history of a battle without including the faults and misbehaviour of part, at least, of those engaged. Believe me that every man you see in a military uniform is not a hero; and that many instances of individual heroism must be passed over unrelated; it is better for the general interests to leave those parts of the story untold, than to tell the whole truth. . . . I regret much that I have not been able to prevail upon you to relinquish your plan. You may depend upon it you will never make it a satisfactory work. I will get you the list of the French army, generals, etc. Just to show you how little reliance can be placed even on what are supposed the best accounts of a battle, I mention that there are some circumstances mentioned in General ——'s account which did not occur as he relates them. He was not on the field during the whole battle, particularly not during the latter part of it. The battle began, I believe, at eleven. It is impossible to say when each important occurrence took place, nor in what order. . . . These are answers to all your queries: but remember, I recommend you to leave the battle of Waterloo as it is."

With the words of these quotations ringing in his ears, how dare an Indian writer take up the well-worn theme of the battle of Panipat and hope to succeed in the attempt? Waterloo was fought between two most advanced nations represented by such extraordinary men as Napoleon and the Duke of Wellington. Everything about it was going on in the most civilized and up-to-date manner. There was no dearth of official despatches, reports, explanations, plans, memoirs, affirmations and contradictions. And still we have the comments of the chief actor in the field on the victorious side as quoted above. How much more unsatisfactory the state of affairs must be when dealing with Panipat—a battle fought between two parties, one of which was backward and the other barbarous! One party could not write an official report of the battle because it simply ceased to exist; the other would not write about it because it thought it superfluous. As for private writings, survivors from the defeated and annihilated party could write only apologetically and sometimes with a guilty conscience; the members of the victorious party wrote with exaggeration and bombast, sometimes without any regard for truth, knowing that nothing succeeds like success. The result is that the historian has to depend on later-gathered partial reports, individual memoirs, and chronicles written with a purpose, none having a complete vision of the whole affair. Even then the material available is very scanty, leaving many lacunæ in the connected story. One has to do without maps, plans, official orders, chits from the generals in their hand-writing, before the end of the battle, as well as later confirmations or denials. Such is the basis for Panipat.

But an historic event on which hung the fate of a nation, the destiny of a continent and the future trend of world affairs for centuries, cannot, and ought not to, go unrelated. And it will be granted that the story can best be related by one of the nationals; preferably by one belonging to the losing side. For thus only can the whole truth about the event come out or find expression. With this idea, I have ventured to take up the theme and write the following pages.

THE PESHWA FAMILY

- 1 Balaji Vishwanath = Radhabai (1713-1720)
  - 2 Bajirao (1720-40)
    - 3 Balaji alias Nanasaheb = Gopikabai (1740-61)
      - Vishwasrao (killed at Panipat)
      - 4 Madhavrao
      - 5 Narayanrao
    - Raghunathrao alias Raghoba Dada
  - Chimaji Apa
    - Sadashivrao Bhau (killed at Panipat) = Parvātibai

SHINDE GENEALOGY

- 1 Ranoji (died 1745)
  - 2 Jayapa (1745-55) (assassinated)
    - 3 Janakoji (1755-61) (slaughtered in captivity)
  - Dattaji (killed 1760 at Buradi)
  - Tukoji (killed at Panipat)
  - Mahadji (wounded and made lame for life)

CONTENTS

SYNOPSIS OF CONTENTS

Chapter IV.

Chapter V.

CHAPTER VII.

CHAPTER I

THE MARATHAS IN THE PANJAB AND BEYOND

THE historic document printed at the very beginning of Rajwade's first volume of original letters marks a turning point in Maratha history. Unfortunately the document is only a copy in Perso-Marathi of the original contract between the Emperor of Delhi and the Peshwa represented by Malharrao Holkar and Jayapa Shinde. The date of the document can now be fixed with certainty. It is May 1752.[1] Ahmad Shah Abdali, the new king of Afghanistan and the successor to Nadir Shah's eastern dominions, then loomed large on the Indian horizon. He had been beaten off in his first attempt of 1748. But he was not a man to be discouraged by one failure. He again invaded the Panjab in 1749 and secured a promise of tribute from its governor. Not receiving the tribute, he invaded for the third time in 1752 and laid siege to Lahore. But Mir Mannu,[2] the Mughal Subahdar of the province, was a clever man, not devoid of valour. He did not shrink from having a trial of strength with Abdali. Lahore fell, however, at the end of March and Mir Mannu consented to act in future as Abdali's agent. Ahmad Shah, the Mughal Emperor, allowed his governor to pay 50 lakhs of rupees[3] to Abdali, being the surplus revenue of the province after defraying all expenditure. The Emperor's consent had been given through the mediation of his favourite, Khoja Jawed, who acted as a sort of unofficial rival to the Wazir in all his dealings. The Emperor had been obliged to accede to the spoliation of his dominions as he could not help Mir Mannu in time. Khoja Jawed had alienated the Mughal grandees so effectually during the last four years, that none was ready to take upon himself the duty of defending the Empire against the Afghans. Wazir Safdar Jang had just then completely overpowered the Ruhelas with the help of Shinde and Holkar. The Wazir had returned to Oudh and the Marathas were on the point of going to the Deccan, when the Emperor's peremptory call obliged the Wazir to go to Delhi with the Marathas so as to bring pressure on Abdali. Before he could come, however, the timid Khoja and the terrified Emperor had acceded to transfer the revenues of the north-western subahs to Abdali, who took it to be a permanent arrangement. When the Marathas with their victorious army came to Delhi, the Khoja thought of counteracting the wrong step that he had taken under pressure. He, in conjunction with the Wazir, prevailed upon the Emperor to enter into a contract with the Marathas by which they would take upon themselves the duty of defending the Empire against its internal and external foes. It is not correct to say that the Wazir was the sole originator of this arrangement as wrongly read by most historians (e.g. *Fall. 1, p. 306*). The flaw in the interpretation has arisen on account of not minutely studying the document. The Peshwa had consented to remain loyal to and was to take orders from

1 *Shinde* 3.203-4.
2 His title was Muin-ul-mulk.
3 *SPD* 21.53.

the Emperor and the Khoja in preference to the Wazir. It is important to note this fact because on the basis of it the Peshwa's ambassador at the Delhi Court and the military guard under Antaji Manakeshwar had to take the side of the Emperor and fight for him against the Wazir in 1753, when Safdar Jang rebelled against his master, though by that time Khoja Jawed had been assassinated. The Marathas were to receive the Chauth of the north-western provinces already usurped by the Afghans. These included the Mughal Subahs of Sind, Multan, and Lahore, as well as the districts of Hissar, Sambal, Moradabad and Budaun, then under the control of the Ruhelas and other refractory nobles. The claim to one-fourth of the revenues of these lands could be made good only by conquest, of which there was only a remote possibility. To induce the Marathas to accept this hazardous adventure, something more tangible was necessary. Therefore the other two refractory Subahs of Ajmer and Agra in the possession of the Rajput and Jat chiefs were given to the Peshwa. Previous to this, the Emperor had tried to make good his claim to these lands by sending Mir Bakhshi Salabat Khan in 1749, but he had to return disappointed after spending more than two years in those regions without collecting any substantial amount of tributes. After ruining this great nobleman, Khoja Jawed had bestowed the Subahs on Ghazi-ud-din Khan, the eldest son of the Great Nizam-ul-mulk, and Intizam-ud-daulah, the eldest son of the late Wazir Qamar-ud-din Khan. These two noblemen, though heads of the Turani party after their fathers' deaths, were militarily of no consequence. When it was found in the crisis of Abdali's invasion that none of them was useful to the State, the Khoja had to make a compromise with the rival Wazir and bestow the Subahs on the Peshwa, while entering into a contract with him, as related above.

The transfer of the Subahs was facilitated because the dispossessed Ghazi-ud-din had another move in his mind, to make good his claim to the Viceroyalty of the Deccan as the eldest son of the Great Nizam. The Wazir Safdar Jang wanted to get his son, the boy Shuja-ud-daulah, nominated to the post, but the Peshwa had to set up a rival to Salabat Jang, a son of the Nizam, for which purpose Shuja was not useful, as the grandees of the Deccan, especially the Maratha Sardars of the Nizam, would not side with a person who bore no relationship with him. The Khoja had in fact created a counterpoise to the Irani Shia party of the Wazir by buying the Maratha support to the Turani Ghazi-ud-din and the Emperor. The Muslim party had gained a great point in bestowing the Subahs of Ajmer and Agra on the Hindu Marathas, as against the overbearing and refractory Rajputs. Thus they had set the Hindus against each other and made a common, solid, Hindu front against the Muslims impossible. The far-reaching effects of this fundamental move were seen in the next decade (1752-61). The refractory Rajputs came closer to the Muslim party and fought with the Marathas incessantly. Panipat was an outcome of it.

The Peshwa's desire to get complete control of the Deccan by setting up a weak pro-Maratha son of the Nizam as Viceroy, was foiled by the usual Muslim tactics of assassinating the person and calling in foreign help as that of the French. Bussy dominated the Deccan politics during this decade, and all the efforts of the Peshwa were directed towards checkmating his moves and machinations. He had to take the false step of joining with the English as a result of it. Thus Indian politics came to be dominated by the moves and interests of the foreigners instead of by the sons of the soil, whether Hindu or Muslim. The Afghans, the English and the French decided the fate and shaped the future of India during this crucial epoch.

The Wazir Safdar Jang clandestinely got Khoja Jawed murdered in August 1752, with a view to bring the Emperor completely under his thumb. But his aim of governing the whole Empire with the Maratha aid was not to be fulfilled. Ghazi-ud-din Firuz Jang, the Viceroy-designate of the Deccan, was also murdered by his step-mother in Aurangabad in October 1752, leading to a collapse of the Peshwa's arrangement as noted above. Salabat Jang had to be acknowledged as the *de facto* Viceroy, and the French influence became fully established at the Nizam's Court. Another unexpected outcome of this untoward happening was the emergence of a new character on the political stage of Delhi. This was Ghazi-ud-din the younger, a son to the murdered man. By playing upon the good feelings of Safdar Jang, this boy of fifteen got himself appointed as the Mir Bakhshi of the Empire. Soon after, he became the leader of the conspiracy against his benefactor, and in this he secured the help of the Marathas in the name of the Emperor on the basis of the agreement mentioned above. By making war on the Wazir and his allies the Jats, under the walls of Delhi, he succeeded in driving away Safdar Jang to his governorship of Oudh and Allahabad by the end of 1753. But in doing this he also created a future rival to himself, the wily Najib Khan Ruhela. With the help of the Ruhela contingent under Najib, and Malharrao Holkar with his master, the Peshwa's brother, Raghoba (Ragunathrao), Ghazi-ud-din went through another revolution at Delhi in June 1754. He deposed the Emperor Ahmad Shah, after first getting himself nominated as the Wazir in place of his cousin Intizam-ud-daulah! Alamgir II was crowned the new Emperor.

Safdar Jang's downfall had been hastened because the Irani Shia party of which he was the head was proclaimed as pro-Hindu by the Turani Sunni party of Mughal grandees. The popular opinion in Delhi held the Empire as well-nigh handed over to the Marathas. A plausible colour is given to this opinion by certain unverified clauses of the agreement of 1752, noted in the beginning. Besides the provinces actually mentioned in that agreement, it is mentioned in contemporary private letters that the Chauth of all the twenty-two provinces[4] of the Mughal Empire had also been granted to the Marathas, together with the administration of the holy cities of Benares, Brindavan and Mathura. Antaji Manakeshwar is found confirming this information a year later in his despatch[5] to the Peshwa. But these important clauses are not found in the document published by Rajwade. Perhaps it was a personal understanding with the Wazir and an administrative concession or favour. What-

[4] *Shinde* 3.203-4.

[5] *SPD* 21.53.

ever the case, it worked against the interests of Safdar Jang as well as his allies, the Marathas.

Having once supported the Emperor against their former ally, the Wazir, the Marathas should have consistently supported him thereafter. Instead they joined the upstart and unscrupulous new Wazir in deposing the Emperor and placing a new man on the throne. This method of changing their policy and allies to suit the interests of the intriguers at the Delhi Court ultimately cost the Marathas very dearly. They successively alienated the Rajputs, the Jats, the Oudh Wazir, as well as the Ruhelas, leaving not even one constant and staunch supporter of their cause. This looseness further increased on account of the conflicting self-interests of the various Maratha commanders and statesmen. All this has to be borne in mind when we come to judge the Maratha vicissitudes in north India, and its final culmination in the disaster of Panipat.

After the fourth invasion of Ahmad Shah Abdali, which came like an avalanche on the Delhi monarchy in 1757, the Empire was as good as broken. The Marathas came on the scene when the whole region from Agra northward had been looted to the last pie by Abdali. Even Ghazi-ud-din, their own nominee, had become disgusted with the Maratha behaviour. So he accepted the arrangement of Abdali, who appointed Najib as his military agent in the Delhi affairs. Following the advice of Abdali, he had started with two young Delhi princes to establish the Mughal rule in the lost dominions of Oudh and Allahabad. Just when he was about to attack Shuja-ud-daulah who had succeeded Safdar Jang, the Marathas entered the field, dispersed the Wazir's army, and again established their own supremacy at Delhi by ousting Najib. It seems that after this new revolution, they entered into a new treaty with Ghazi-ud-din. In place of the right to Chauth (one-fourth), they fixed their share at half of all the revenues that they might gather from the erstwhile Mughal dominions. Of course, there was no possibility of their getting anything without the application of force, which meant war on all fronts of Delhi. With a view to prevent Abdali from ever entering India, they now thought of establishing the Mughal rule in the lost region of the five rivers and beyond.

Ahmad Shah Abdali, while returning to his own country with immense loot in May 1757, left his son, the boy Taimur Shah, at Lahore as his Viceroy, with Jahan Khan, his best general, as his guardian. Besides the Afghan party of Abdali, there were two other claimants to the land of the five rivers. One was the Mughal party headed by Mughlani Begum, the ambitious, self-willed and profligate widow of Mir Mannu; the other was the democratic party of the persecuted Sikhs. Mughlani Begum had at first tried to rule with the help of her favourites; but in 1756 Ghazi-ud-din brought her under his control. He married her daughter, Umda Begum, and made Adina Beg Khan, who had already made himself powerful by raising a vast army to include the Sikhs, his deputy. Later on, when Ghazi-ud-din found out his mother-in-law's real character, he got her kidnapped by one of his assistants and brought her back to Delhi. He thereby also secured for himself her vast fortune. The Wazir's deputy ruled at Lahore for six months but was soon ousted by Abdali's nominee.

At the end of the year 1756, Ahmad Shah himself followed, as mentioned above, and returned after leaving Taimur to rule the Panjab. It seems that Jahan Khan was only a blunt soldier and not a diplomat such as one needed to be in the disturbed conditions of the Panjab of those times. Adina Beg Khan, who had been baulked in his ambition to be the chief administrator by the Afghan intrusion, now came out of his hiding in the hills. With the help of his Sikh allies, he carried on a guerrilla war-fare and made Abdali's rule a precarious one in that area. Another complication arose on account of Mughlani Begum who had joined Abdali against her son-in-law, Ghazi-ud-din, with a view to rule the Panjab herself. She had acted as Abdali's spy and agent in digging out the buried wealth of the Delhi nobles. Ahmad Shah was immensely pleased with her and carried her back to Lahore with him on his return. He had promised the Jalandar Doab containing the best land in the Panjab with Jammu and Kashmir to the north of it as her jagir. This arrangement could not succeed for military reasons. Ahmad Shah revoked it and thus Mughlani Begum became a pauper, because she was too proud to receive a small pension instead. Her jagir was in the occupation of Adina Beg, and probably she began to intrigue with him against the Afghan deputy. The matters came to the point of Jahan Khan beating the Begum with his own hand and confining her. The military power of Adina Beg was strong enough to baffle the Afghan ruler, and therefore Jahan Khan thought it best to leave Adina Beg in his post of the revenue collector for a payment of thirty-two lakhs. While Adina Beg wisely remained within his bounds, the Sikhs, perhaps with his connivance, scourged throughout the province expelling Afghan collectors. The Marathas who were at this time driving out Abdali's outposts in the Jamuna valley naturally supported this movement against Abdali and opened correspondence with Adina Beg. When the Marathas had completed their work in the Doab, news came that the Sikhs had defeated two Afghan generals, followed by a complete massacre and loot. Abdali's rule in his own country was also challenged by some local parties and the Shah of Iran. Finally, Adina Beg, who had the ambition to become the sole administrator in the Panjab, called in the help of the Marathas. They had already chalked out a policy of blocking Abdali at the Indus for fulfilling their responsibility of defending the Empire against both internal and external foes. At the beginning of 1758 they seriously devoted their attention to the problem and planned the campaign in consulation with the Wazir Ghazi-ud-din.

A clear idea of the extent of the Mughal Empire is necessary for us to understand this campaign. What has been called the Panjab in the British regime was not a Mughal province. The area between the water-sheds of the Satlaj and the Jamuna had been bifurcated by the Mughals. The southern and the eastern parts of that area were included in the metropolitan province of Delhi. The northern part of the land of the five rivers proper from Attock to Sarhind was included in the Subah of Lahore. The south-western Panjab, with districts beyond the Indus adjoining to it, formed the Multan province. The modern Sind was called Thattha province, and Kashmir was also a separate province. Beyond the Indus, Kabul and Kandahar formed two separate provinces, out of which Kandahar was lost by Aurangzib in 1652, and Kabul was annexed by Nadir Shah in 1738. But all along, the idea of these two provinces forming part of the Mughal's Indian Empire continued to exist. All these provinces had separate Governors and Diwans in the best days of the Mughal Empire. As gradual decay set in, sometimes more than one province was placed under the charge of one person, and occasionally the whole area came to be controlled by a single strong hand. During the anarchical times which followed Nadir Shah's invasion, Sind with portions of Multan as well as Kabul and Kandahar completely passed out of Indian hands. Only the Panjab proper continued to be a debatable land for some time.

We have briefly noted the condition after Mir Mannu's death in 1753. The Marathas cast the last die in the tragic drama with the slogan of the complete integrity of the Indian Empire as built up by the Mughals with their ancient boundaries. Unfortunately the Indian political world was not sufficiently intellectually or morally advanced to grasp this fundamental idea and fight for it. The Marathas had risen higher in transcending the bounds of race, language, religion and sect. They took their stand on the basis of India for the Indians to be governed and defended by themselves without foreign aid or interference.[6]

Malharrao Holkar accompanied Raghoba in this famous campaign, while Sakharam Bapu was the Diwan and chief diplomatic adviser. The

---

[6] I. S.—*Aitihasik Sphuta Lekh* 4.11.

Translation of Raghoba's letter, dated 4th May, 1758, from Lahore, received on 18th June, 1758, by the Peshwa (Lele archives)....

"...We have already brought Lahore, Multan, Kashmir and other subahs on this side of Attock under our rule for the most part, and places which have not come under our rule we shall soon bring under us. Ahmad Khan Abdali's son Taimur Sultan and Jahan Khan have been pursued by our troops, and their troops completely looted. Both of them have now reached Peshawar with a few broken troops. Ahmad Khan had invaded Ispahan with his troops. But Jabar Shah (?), the Padshah of Iran, came out to meet him and looted some troops of Abdali. So Ahmad has returned to Kandahar with some 12-14 thousand troops. Irani troops have come at their rear pursuing them. Jabarast Khan, Mukarab Khan and other sardars and zamindars of those regions, who had joined Abdali under compulsion, are now rebelling against his rule. They have written supplicatory letters to me and are ready to enrol under us, so as to chastise Abdali. Thus, all have risen against Ahmad Khan, who has lost control over the regions. Even if Abdali goes to Herat, he cannot hold on. In short, Abdali cannot get any more support from that side, and so his power must wane. On that side, the Padshah of Iran has driven him into a corner. On this side, we should do the same so as to establish our rule beyond Attock. Your Honour had sent Abdul Rahim Khan, Ahmad Khan's nephew and the (legal) heir to the dominion of the Abdalis who had gone to Poona to seek your support, to us. We have decided to establish him at some small place on this side of Attock to serve as his base, and to appoint him to the subah of Kabul and Peshawar beyond. I am sending him with Abdul Samad Khan whom we have captured at Sarhind with his Abdali troops, together with additional Irani and Mughal troops, to support him. I hope that they will begin the work of bringing those regions under control and with the (divine) support of your Highness' auspicious valour, defeat Ahmad Khan once for all, so as to begin our rule there. Myself and Malharba have received letters in his own handwriting from the Padshah of Iran, inviting us to Kandahar soon, so as to completely overpower Ahmad and fix the boundary (between Iran and Hindustan) at Attock (the Indus). But we are appointing Abdul Rahim, sent by Your Honour, to the subah of Kabul, and are helping him with troops and necessaries. *Kabul and Kandahar—these two subahs were in the possession of India from the times of Akbar to those of Alamgir. Why should (How can?) we hand these over to the ruler of Vilayat (Iran)? Therefore we are giving those subahs to Abdul Rahim here.* He (the Padshah of Iran) also must not be caring very much for these (rocky, unproductive, recalcitrant) provinces, he will rule over (his) Iran. We have decided to establish our rule upto Kandahar (as in times of yore) and to dispatch sweetly-worded replies to the letters from Iran. Envoys from the rulers of Lati (Sind), Jammu and Kashmir have arrived here (to settle the government of those regions)...."

TO FACE PAGE 6

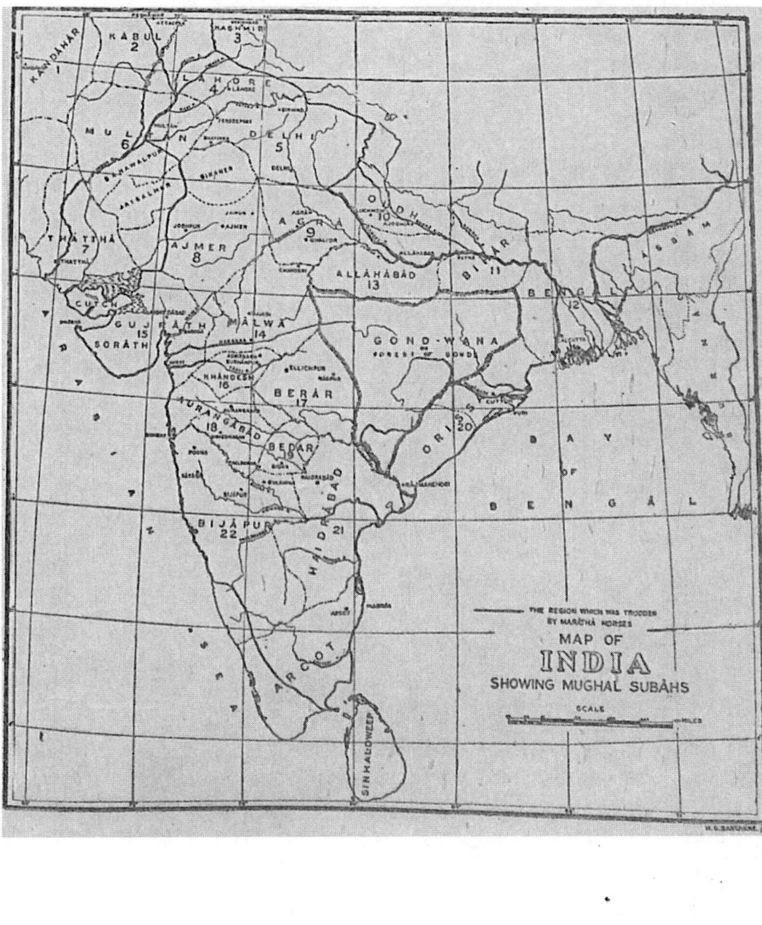

Maratha army first approached Sarhind which was governed by Abdus Samad Khan, a valiant general of Abdali. He was at this time on a punitive expedition against Alasingh Jat, the founder of the Patiala State. Hearing that the Marathas were advancing, he settled accounts with Alasingh, quickly returned to Sarhind and made preparations for defending it. The Maratha troops were not more than fifty-thousand in number, though rumour had swelled it to two lakhs. In the first week of March 1758, they began the siege of Sarhind which does not seem to have continued long. Abdus Samad Khan tried to escape, but was captured along with Jang Baz Khan and other Afghans. The Marathas and the Sikhs thoroughly looted Sarhind and afterwards destroyed it. Hearing of the fall of Sarhind, Jahan Khan, who had advanced from Lahore to help Abdus Samad, returned precipitately. The Maratha forces advanced further, Adina Beg Khan leading them on the way. Seeing them rapidly advancing with confidence, Jahan Khan and his ward, the boy Taimur, lost heart, as they had not more than twenty-five thousand troops with them to defend themselves. The valiant captain Manaji Paygude led the vanguard of the Marathas with ten thousand horse along with one thousand Mughals under Khwajah Mirza. On the 20th April, 1758, the Marathas entered Lahore. Prince Taimur and Jahan Khan had already evacuated it on the day previous, and carried all their property beyond the Ravi. The Marathas, after taking charge of the fort, quickly crossed the river and pursued the Afghans upto the river Chinab. Only the Durrani troops of Taimur escaped hurriedly with Jahan Khan at their head. All his other troops, Turkish, Afghan and Indian, were over-powered by the Marathas, who took vast spoils in their camp. The Marathas would have pursued Jahan Khan still further, but fortunately for him the river was deep and unfordable and all the boats necessary for crossing the river had been taken to the other side by Taimur Sultan.[7]

Raghoba stayed in Lahore only for a month and then prepared to return to the Deccan at the express orders of the Peshwa, leaving the administration of the whole province in the hands of Adina Beg who agreed to pay seventy-five lakhs a year to the Marathas. An equal revenue was to go to the Wazir at Delhi as his half share in the bargain. The Maratha corps engaged in this famous campaign were those of Manaji Paygude, Gangadhar Bajirao Retharekar, Gopalrao Ganesh Barve, Rayaji Sakhdev, Renako Anaji and Bapuji Trimbak, besides the Holkar's contingent. Hari Raghunath Bhide, a fast friend and supporter of Raghoba, had also accompanied them. Why Raghoba was not allowed to continue in the Panjab is difficult to say. In his only available letter (Note 6) he writes that he was returning because the Peshwa had recalled him.

As a matter of fact the five years from 1757 to 1761 were the most critical years in Indian history. The Marathas who aspired to take into their hands the political control of the whole continent, had to keep their attention on the problems arising in all corners of India. The Peshwa had recalled his brother from Lahore probably because he thought the Deccan politics were more important, and wished to end the French influence at the court of the

[7] *SPD* 27.218, 220; *Shinde* 3.93, 94.

Nizam by fomenting an internal revolution there, through the agency of the minister Shah Nawaz Khan. The Peshwa was in the very thick of the conspiracy just at this juncture, but Bussy proved more than a match for the Peshwa in this move. He took the fort of Daulatabad from the hands of Shah Nawaz Khan's retainer, in April 1758. Nizam Ali, the younger brother of the Nizam Salabat Jang, was slowly and cautiously feeling his way and coming forward under his brother's cover. He caused the murders of Haidar Jang the chief native assistant of Bussy, Shah Nawaz Khan and his son, thus ending the French as well as the Maratha influence at the Nizam's Court at one stroke. Anticipating these developments, the Peshwa seems to have called back his brother to be at his elbow in any crisis likely to arise from there.

But as things then stood, this meant the weakening of the Maratha strength in the Panjab just when it was most needed. Raghoba and Malharrao had acted wisely in choosing a proper time for pushing forward upto Lahore, just when Abdali's troops there had been reduced to a small force. But once having pushed so far, it was necessary to build there an impregnable line across Abdali's path. Instead, they chose the wrong path—which has often been repeated by the Marathas in their history—of returning home. They had already made over the management of the conquered parts to Adina Beg and left only a small force to aid him in any eventualities. Their whole plan miscarried as later developments showed. Raghoba and Malharrao returned at the end of May 1758. They were conscious that the Maratha troops left behind were inadequate. While returning, they ordered certain other Maratha brigades to proceed to the Panjab to canton there. Malharrao despatched Tukoji Holkar and Khandoji Kadam; Raghoba ordered Vitthal Shivdev to repair there. Janakoji Shinde, after his meeting with Raghoba in Rajputana on his way back, sent the old and experienced Sabaji Shinde to take over the whole charge of the Maratha affairs in the Panjab as a deputy governor. Of these, Vitthal Shivdev[8] seems to have continued there only up to October, together with his colleague Satvoji Jadhav. Sabaji reached Lahore some time after.

But in the interval Adina Beg died on the 16th September, 1758.[9] He was the only experienced and influential man in the Panjab not altogether ill-disposed towards the Marathas. After his death began again the vicious scramble for power in that region. Khwajah Mirza tried to assume the governorship at Lahore and renew his broken career. With the help of Tukoji and Khandoji he beat back an invasion of some Afghans and Gakkhars in concert. This was before Sabaji's arrival and his taking over the charge of the Panjab. Tukoji and Khandoji pushed on beyond the Jehelum[10] and the Indus in pursuit of the Afghans and thus carried the Maratha standards beyond Attock. This was sometime in October 1758, before the severe winter in those regions began. Sabaji followed them after a short interval and joined them in Peshawar.[11]

8 *SPD* 21.146.

9 *SPD* 2.96.

10 *BISM* (Persian Mss.) No. 696.

11 Ibid. No. 699.

This forward march of the Marathas was probably to place Abdul Rahim Khan, a nephew of Ahmad Shah Abdali and a claimant, on the Afghan throne. This Khan, though his name is not mentioned anywhere else, had proceeded to Poona to seek the Peshwa's help in re-instating him in Afghanistan. The Marathas seem to have taken him with them to Peshawar and tried to establish him there. They continued in Peshawar during the whole of that winter and returned to Lahore in March 1759, due probably to the Afghan pressure. The internal politics of the province deteriorated still further in the interval. The Maratha generals, left in the various parts of the province to help the local collectors and maintain peace, began to take sides amongst the rival factions for power in that province. Siding with Khwajah Mirza's enemies they ousted him from Lahore, whence he fled with his Sikh allies to the hills of Jammu. Bapuji Trimbak who had been placed at Multan to help the local governor, seems to have been entangled between the local parties of the Afghans and the Mughals in that region. Khwajah Mirza tried to take shelter in the Jammu state, but Ranjit Dev, who was ruling there, asked him to clear out by threatening him with dire consequences if he persisted in his attempt to continue there.[12] He seems to have become a champion of Hinduism at the instance of the Marathas, and openly declared his intention of brooking no impediment from the Muslims in his province. The Mirza, therefore, returned to Sialkot and made a common cause with his erstwhile enemies, the wild Gakkhars. In the meantime Abdus Samad Khan, who had been captured at Sarhind by Raghoba and afterwards sent back to Kabul to help Abdul Rahim Khan in his attempt to establish himself in those regions, again returned to India in the wake of the returning Maratha troops. He tried to create trouble for the Marathas by joining the opposite parties. He made common cause with Khwajah Mirza, and tried to make the Maratha hold impossible in the regions beyond the Ravi. Next he suddenly swooped down on Multan, held the city at ransom, and established his deputy there in opposition to Muhammad Ali Khan, who was governing there with the help of Bapuji Trimbak. Under the leadership of Muhammad Ali Khan, the people of Multan rose against the barbarous Afghan rule, drove that deputy out of the city, and looted his army. This happened in March 1759.

Abdali had by this time freed himself from his western engagements with the Shah of Iran and the affairs of Khorasan which had occupied him for two years. He sent Jahan Khan to re-establish his rule in the Peshawar region. His pressure and the failure of Abdul Rahim Khan's cause obliged the Marathas to recross the Indus and come back to their base at Lahore. After his return, Sabaji joined his forces with others and, thus reinforced, was able to beat back an invasion of Jahan Khan at the end of August 1759. The Afghan general lost his son in the attempt and many of his troops were killed or wounded. He himself was also wounded and had to retreat across the Indus. The summer of 1759 was the decisive time for the Marathas to make good their hold on the Panjab if they wished to keep it. But Dattaji and Janakoji Shinde who had gone up to the banks of the Satlaj in April that year re-

12 Ibid.

turned to Delhi after appointing Sadik Beg, a deputy of Adina Beg, as the chief revenue collector in the regions around Sarhind. There was an idea of appointing Naro Shankar[13] in place of Sabaji Shinde, but it never materialized. After camping at Bahlulpur and Machhiwada on the south bank of the Satlaj for a month or so, the Shindes returned with Naro Shankar. Their return this time was also due, like the return of Raghoba in the previous year, to the Peshwa's advice-*cum*-orders. The Peshwa was overburdened with debts. He was writing letter after letter to Dattaji Shinde to take up some new venture which would fill the Peshwa's treasury and add a new province to the Maratha dominions. Lahore, Allahabad, Benares, Patna and lastly Bengal were to be taken over, one after the other. This meant dealing with Najib Khan, Shuja-ud-daulah, Ghazi-ud-din, the Prince Ali Gauhar and last but not least, the English. Sitting at ease in his cosy citadel in Poona and ruminating over the thoughts of conquest over the whole of India was all right as a chamber pastime, but the Peshwa never seems to have realized the actual difficulties in that path. That a man of Ahmad Shah's type would take the ousting of his son from the Panjab lying down was obviously impossible; still, the Peshwa insisted on the Shindes returning to Delhi instead of proceeding to Attock and holding that line against all attacks.

The Marathas remained in the Panjab only for a brief period, from April 1758 to October 1759. They were, constitutionally, acting as agents of the Mughal Emperor and were normally trying to make use of the local machinery of government in carrying on the administration and collecting the revenues. They had to dismiss the Afghan nominees, no doubt, but in their place they generally appointed the Mughals. Whether the Marathas had acted wisely in taking upon themselves such a hazardous adventure as trying to conquer the Panjab and hold it out against such an exceptional man as Abdali must be judged by the result, which is history. A thoughtful historian will always consider that it was a wrong step for the Peshwas to cross the Narmada without first taking possession of the south up to Rameshvaram. After having crossed that river, they should have at least stopped at the Chambal and first secured the overwhelmingly Hindu provinces of Allahabad and Oudh which were just adjoining to the north, instead of touching the hornet's nest at Delhi. The Peshwa thought of first grasping the reins of the central government at Delhi and thus getting legal control over the whole empire. That it was a wrong step, impossible of fulfilment on account of the selfish, unpatriotic and pusillanimous attitude of the ruling Muslims is proved at the bar of history and no amount of casuistry can take away the blame from the Marathas for the fundamental mistake of choosing the wrong path.

From the military point of view, it was no wise step for the Marathas to lengthen their line of communication by five hundred miles at one stretch. Already the distance of one thousand miles from Poona to Ambala was long enough for them to defend successfully. To step beyond Sarhind was almost a mad-man's behaviour. The climate of the regions, with its extremes of heat and cold, was not very propitious and was well-nigh beyond the endurance

13 *SPD* 2.100.

of the ill-clad and unadaptive Marathas. An average Maratha soldier of those days wished to return home after eight month's service and very few were willing to continue in foreign lands for more than two camping seasons. Their preparation, their equipment, their physical stamina, not to say home-sickness, would not possibly make their sojourn tolerable beyond that period. These were very real and basic difficulties and unless the Marathas became successful colonizers in distant lands their hope of ruling India was bound to fail. The Muslims spread their rule over the whole continent by this method of establishing self-sufficient colonies, however small, in the provinces they entered, one by one. And still they took centuries to spread over the whole continent. They were, moreover, proselytising and intermarrying with the various local people, thus always strengthening and increasing their outposts. The Marathas, on the other hand, had not shown any of these characteristic virtues nor were they endowed with progressive ideas, methods, or instruments,—in short a higher civilization like that of the British. How could they, under these circumstances, make themselves good as successful conquerors in foreign climes?

To hold this new stretch of five hundred miles from Ambala to Peshawar would have required a permanent garrison of one lakh of soldiers judiciously distributed at the various key-points. This stretch is itself geographically divisible into two almost equal parts; one from Ambala to the Chinab and the other from the Chinab to Peshawar. Up to the Chinab the land is a vast, sandy, level plain. One can scarcely see any hill on the horizon unless one goes north. Beyond the Chinab, hills begin on a small scale, and beyond the Jehelum, the region is mountainous, rocky and comparatively barren, the proportion of cultivable land becoming less and less. In the time of Akbar, the whole of this western tract was included in the three Mughal Subahs of Lahore, Multan (to include Sind), and Kabul which included both Kashmir and Kandahar in those days. Afterwards, Sind, or Thattha, Kashmir and Kandahar became separate governorships, due probably to their distance from the centre and the exigencies of military defence. Anybody wanting to rule over these territories would have required good cavalry with horses inured to hot and cold climates, camel corps carrying guns to run through the arid deserts, as well as good mountaineers to pass through dangerous and sometimes snow-clad regions. When Raghoba is found seriously discussing the sovereign rights of the Mughal government or the correct policy for their agents, the Marathas, in these regions, it is doubtful whether he had visualised all these prospects or calculated their cost. The Marathas also employed camels in carrying express despatches, kettle-drums as well as baggage; but they had never taken the trouble to create an efficient, fighting camel-corps, much less organise a mobile artillery of swivel-guns carried on these animals, like Abdali. In fact, Abdali's chief and most successful innovation seems to be this mobile artillery which was always handy when compared to guns carried on carts drawn by bullocks. In the camel-corps, both the gunner as well as the driver were seated on the same animal; there was absolutely no impediment to its movement. Bullock-drawn artillery, on the other hand, needed a pioneer force of sappers and miners to prepare a tolerably good road to carry these heavy guns, requiring in many cases as many as fifty bullocks to draw each gun. The chief adviser of Raghunathrao in this far-famed Panjab campaign was Sakharam Bapu. He seems to have developed a faculty for easily disposing of the twenty-two subahs of the Mughal Empire by his parlour calculations.[14] Raghunathrao also had developed a similar faculty from his early boyhood.[15] Thus there seems to have been some brain-wave set in motion at the court of Poona whereby all such problems of high imperial policy were quickly settled at one sitting on the basis of theoretical or oral information supplied by Munshis! When Raghunathrao went on his first expedition to Gujarat in 1753[16] (when he was only nineteen), he had already discussed from his base in Kathiawad the possibility of proceeding to Sind and Multan via Bhujnagar, i.e. Cutch.[17] Had he followed that idea and put it into an actual plan, he would have then and there realized the necessity of organizing an efficient camel-corps; for his route would have taken him through the great Indian desert, between Marwad and Sind. As it was, the project never materialized, and Raghunathrao returned to pursue his way to Kumbher of Surajmal Jat to break his head there. There seems to be something fundamentally wrong in the plans of conquest hatched in the hen-coop of Shanwarwada (the Peshwa's palace in Poona), for the Peshwa is found constantly ordering his generals to proceed on new conquests and then as suddenly recalling them or transferring them to different fields! Otherwise we cannot account for the miserable failure of that decade of incessant activity preceding Panipat.

Raghunathrao had left behind not more than ten thousand troops in the Panjab when returning. Afterwards, when Tukoji Holkar and Sabaji Shinde arrived, the total number was perhaps twenty thousand. This force, with its shortcomings, was quite inadequate to keep back Abdali and govern the Panjab against a number of rebellious adventurers with local support. Raghunathrao's idea of setting up a rival claimant in the Kabul area and getting the necessary work of stopping Abdali done through him, was good on paper; but a rival who would be able to make even a semblance of a stand against the overpowering personality of Ahmad Shah Abdali was difficult to find. The only feasible plan in the circumstances then existing was to stop at the river Jehelum and try to defend the line of Multan, Lahore and Jammu by making a common cause with the Rajputs and Sikhs in those regions. This meant a departure from the policy of governing the Mughal provinces through the old decrepit machinery of derelict officers, civil and military. Men like Ranjit Dev of Jammu and Alasingh Jat of Patiala would have been ready to join such a front with an ideological basis different from the ideology of the Mughal Empire. But there was no personality of Shivaji's type amongst the then existing Marathas. That was the real difficulty of the Maratha Empire if it was going to be built. Ahmad Shah Abdali, it should not be forgotten, was a Shivaji amongst his compatriots. He had put the name of Afghanistan on the map. Before his advent the Afghans were divided into various independent, warring and backward tribes, ready to accept service under any con-

14 Ibid. 2.84.
15 *Purandare* 1.158-9.
16 *SPD* 21.58.
17 Ibid. 21.58.

queror and work as his slaves. Ahmad Shah not only freed his own tribe from the clutches of a Persian ruler, but he freed the other Afghan clans also. Then he welded them into a nation. Instead of seeking fortune as individual adventurers in India and Persia, as they had done from the times of Mahmud of Ghazni, the Afghans now thought of uniting amongst themselves and setting out on conquering expeditions as a well-knit nation. To meet such a personality and such a new nation was no easy task. The Marathas should have produced such a personality, or failing that, a combination of individuals who could match it. Unfortunately this could not happen, and the result is recorded in the pages of history.

In October 1759, Jahan Khan returned with a bigger army. He formed, in fact, the advance guard of Abdali's army in its new campaign. The Maratha army in the Panjab, at this time, was not more than fifteen thousand strong. Of this, five thousand under Bapuji Trimbak were in Multan, five thousand under Tukoji garrisoned Lahore, while Sabaji had another five thousand moving from place to place. The only region of the Panjab which was comparatively well settled and yielding any direct revenue, as distinguished from tributes and ransoms, was the Sarhind—Jalandar area. This had been placed under Sadik Beg—wrongly copied as Sandip Beg in Marathi chronicles. He had consented of his own accord to pay five lakhs more than originally settled with Adina Beg. His Diwan Lakshmi Narayan had been won over to the Maratha side. The mutual relations between Tukoji Holkar and Sabaji Shinde in the Panjab were none too good. Sabaji treated Tukoji as a lower official and kept the whole purse and power in his own hands.[18] Tukoji at this time was a junior officer and only a servant of Malharrao Holkar and not, as is wrongly thought, one of his near relations, though he ultimately succeeded to the Holkar's jagir. Malharrao wrote to Tukoji to send Holkar's share in the revenues of the Panjab to Indore. Tukoji replied that Sabaji Patel had taken all the money and had allowed him only the daily wages for his troops. When Tukoji remonstrated, Sabaji showed him a letter from Janakoji Shinde ordering Tukoji to draw only wages while the rest of the account would be settled by Janakoji and Malharrao, the masters, amongst themselves. As Tukoji had no intention of impeding the government machinery and fighting a civil war, he followed Janakoji's instructions. According to Tukoji, without the help of Malharrao the Shindes would never succeed in the Panjab. Moreover, Sabaji would never take Tukoji into confidence and settle the Maratha policy in consultation with him. Otherwise, complains Tukoji, it was possible to establish peace in the Panjab, had Sabaji followed his advice. In his incomplete letters[19] (and only two such letters have unfortunately come into the hands of historians) he clearly says that the Marathas had collected revenues from Sarhind, the (Jalandar) Doab, Lahore, Multan and Attock.

From this description it is clear that the Marathas had spread up to the Indus and beyond, and not stopped at the Chinab as emphatically stated

18 *Chandrachuda* Daftar I.49; II.4. (To be read together.)
19 Ibid. I.49; II.4.

by Sir Jadunath[20] and copied on his authority by Dr. Hari Ram Gupta and others. That they had gone to Peshawar is also clear from the contemporary Persian Akhbars which clearly say that Tukoji had reached Peshawar in October 1758, and that Sahibji (Sabaji) Patel had started from Peshawar and reached Lahore in March 1759. It is no "ignorant boast" of the Marathas, therefore, "that the Maratha standards were carried up to the Indus at Attock," as in fact they had not only reached that crossing but had, ignoring the so-called bar for the Hindus not to cross it, actually reached Peshawar and lived there for about six months.[21] This was the zenith of Maratha expansion, and it is not a sin, we think, if the Marathas feel some natural pride in that event.

Raghunathrao had kept Adina Beg as the chief administrator in Lahore and the Jalandar area because it was through his invitation and support that the Marathas had entered the Panjab. He is reported to have promised to pay the Marathas in cash for their help at the rate of one lakh of rupees for every day of marching and half a lakh for every day of halt;[22] but it is doubtful whether the Marathas did receive even a portion of such payment. It is known, on the whole, that Raghunathrao's campaign of Lahore had been anything but profitable to the Peshwa's government. Raghunathrao had presented a deficit account of eighty lakhs to the Poona court and Sadashivrao Bhau had an occasion to reprimand him in that connection. Nor does it seem that Adina Beg ever paid the seventy-five lakhs a year as promised to the Marathas. No doubt, he died within four months of the event and during the interval he had to wage incessant war against the Sikhs for whom he had no particular love, though he had made use of them in his rebellion against the Afghan rule. In fact, though an able administrator, he had no scruples against changing sides and he may be called a time-server or an opportunist in politics. After his death, his widow and a boy-child succeeded to his office with Sadik Beg, who was already a foujdar of Sarhind, as her deputy. This seems to have weakened the administration and become detrimental to the Maratha cause. In short, the Peshwa's idea of making use of the machinery of the Mughal government with all its encumbrances proved fatal to the Maratha cause in the Panjab as it had proved in other parts of India as well.

After his return from the Panjab in May 1759, Dattaji Shinde thought of going to Bengal through the territory of Shuja-ud-daulah in order to exact Chauth from the new Nawab Mir Jafar set up by the English and pay off the Peshwa's debts. The Peshwa's letters to the Shindes in this connection do not show him in the best light. He had no scruples in choosing any side provided money could be had out of it. The Marathas seemed to be auctioning the Wazirship of Delhi to the highest bidder.[23] Malharrao was directly responsible for the 1754 revolution in Delhi with a new Emperor and a new Wazir. But later he was convinced that the Wazir was anything but a straightforward man. So he turned away from Ghazi-ud-din and naturally inclined towards Najib Khan

20 *Fall* 2.76.

21 *BISM* (Persian Mss.) Nos. 696, 699; *BISMQ* No. 93 (Marathas Beyond Attock).

22 Gupta, *Adina Beg Khan*, p. 33.

23 *Ait., Patrem Yadi* Nos. 166, 167, 171.

who was antagonistic to the Wazir. In the 1757-58 campaign Malharrao shielded Najib against the orders of Raghunathrao, who became sick at heart as a result. While returning home, Raghunathrao met Janakoji in Rajputana and advised him to beware of Najib Khan and punish him at all costs. Malharrao who met Janakoji a few days later counselled him the opposite course of making use of Najib Khan against Shuja-ud-daulah. Janakoji pleaded his inability to do so as Raghunathrao had ordered otherwise. Soon after, both Raghunathrao and Malharrao met Dattaji and advised him in like manner, each exactly opposite of the other. The *Bhau Bakhar* which purports to report these conversations, says that Dattaji took to heart Malharrao's advice of keeping Najib Khan alive in order to checkmate the absolute power of the Peshwa, which would become inimical to their personal interests, in case all enemies were completely suppressed once for all! This advice, if it was ever given by Malharrao or seriously entertained by Dattaji, was cutting at the very root of the Maratha State. But we have no belief in it. Dattaji was too loyal a person to listen to such advice, much less would he act according to it. It is likely, however, that he was impressed by Malharrao's argument in favour of befriending Najib and doing away with the Wazir. Before proceeding to the Panjab in January 1759 he had already taken the Wazir to task and, after his return, he tried to win him over for his intended campaign in Bengal. Ghazi-ud-din had personally never any idea of moving out of the capital and conquering the lost provinces with the help of the Marathas. He always preferred to see the Marathas do the needful, himself entering the field when it was a question of spoils or settlement. Even when helpless, he would never easily grant away under his sign-manual any of the imperial rights, though these had been already usurped by others! At this juncture he was neither willing to leave the capital and accompany Dattaji nor again ready to grant, by issuing imperial rescripts, what Dattaji wanted. So Dattaji was obliged to turn to Najib Khan and enter into an agreement with him. Najib Khan would help the Marathas in building a pontoon bridge over the Ganges and would accompany them with his troops to Bengal. This agreement seems to have been brought about through the medium of Govindpant Bundele who had discussed the problem with both Najib Khan and the Wazir at the behest of Shinde himself. Govindpant had come north up to Hapad opposite Delhi, conquering the tracts in the Doab, and there was every possibility of his coming into conflict with Najib Khan in Meerut. Antaji Manakeshwar had been given orders for money on these Mahals under the management of Najib Khan. If Govindpant had entered these Mahals and devastated them, Najib would have refused to pay Antaji, as ordered by the Peshwa. Dattaji, to oblige Antaji, issued orders forbidding Govindpant to enter Najib's parganas. Najib allowed Govindpant something by way of aid in grain and fodder. Afterwards Govindpant came over to Delhi and stayed there for a week. He was officially honoured by the Wazir and had an audience with the Emperor also.[24] Thence, on 30th April, 1759, he had gone northwards to see Dattaji who was returning from the Panjab and there settled the whole arrangement about Najib Khan. These transactions have been

24 *SPD* 2.100, 102.

given a prejudicial colour by the author of the *Bhau Bakhar,* so as to make it appear as a clandestine agreement between Govindpant and Najib to support the latter. When the Shindes entered the Doab, Najib Khan was brought to the Maratha camp to discuss terms with Dattaji. The author of the *Bakhar* says of this interview that Janakoji, Naro Shankar, Antaji Manakeshwar and other Sardars wanted to arrest Najib Khan this time; but Dattaji, through the advice of Govindpant, at once forbade them from entertaining such a treacherous thought. This was in conformity with the whole Maratha tradition as exemplified in history and in accord with their general feeling. Had the Marathas ever taken to what they themselves called "Moglai kava" or "Moglai maslat," meaning thereby the politics of treacherous arrests and murders, their whole history would have perhaps been written otherwise; though it is a moot point in history whether they would not have been more successful —barring the moral stigma—in their undertakings thereby.

Najib, however, got a new lease of life by his double dealings in this affair. Had he flatly refused to help the Marathas in building a bridge over the Ganges, they would have possibly found out some other means of gaining their ends. Dattaji had the intention of proceeding to Bengal post-haste before the monsoon had set in and the rivers flooded. He had planned to canton in Patna[25] and thence to bring pressure on Bengal during the monsoon. His plan was completely foiled by the delaying and promising tactics of Najib. When a month passed and the monsoon actually set in, he pleaded his inability to do the needful, and promised to build the bridge after the rains. Side by side he was hatching a conspiracy of driving away the Marathas from the north. It seems that Emperor Alamgir II was himself a party to this conspiracy, being fed up with the tyrannical Wazir. Malika Zamani, the Dowager Empress, was whole-heartedly behind the idea or, perhaps, she herself was the originator of it, as depicted in all the Marathi chronicles. Najib Khan is depicted as following her orders and wishes. Madhosingh of Jaipur and Bijesingh of Marwad were also whole-heartedly supporting Najib in his invitation to Abdali to come back to India and drive the Marathas south of the Narmada once for all. Najib was so clever in keeping the whole project secret that even Govindpant Bundele,[26] who was a near neighbour of his and always on the alert for news of any kind, was unaware of this internal correspondence carried on for two years between these parties, and even sending of special envoys to the court of Abdali at Kandahar. The Marathas came to know of this secret only when Abdali actually entered the Panjab and began to drive away the Maratha outposts in that province, in October 1759. This bespeaks of great looseness in the management of Maratha affairs. That they should have no information of projects for ousting them and should not have properly appraised the characters of the various persons engaged in activities against their rule, shows that their intelligence department had none of that efficiency that it had in the times of Shivaji and Rajaram in the previous century. This weakness was fatal to the Maratha Empire.

25 Ibid. 2.104.

26 Ibid. 40.126.

When, after waiting for two months, Dattaji realized the impasse in which he had been placed by Najib, he thought of punishing him. By this time, however, Najib had formed his impregnable lines behind natural impediments on the bank of the Ganges at Sukartal and from that secure position defied the might of the Shindes. From this place of refuge he built a causeway for himself across the Ganges and thus kept open his line of communication with the Ruhela regions beyond. From these he secured supplies and also military help. He engaged Dattaji in this manner for four months, till the latter was obliged to raise the siege in order to meet Abdali coming down from the Panjab in December, 1759.

Sabaji was governing the Panjab with some ten thousand troops, a force quite inadequate to hold the line against the Afghan tornado. Abdali had sent his general Jahan Khan in advance with fifteen thousand troops from Peshawar and himself followed by way of Shikarpur in Sind along the right bank of the Indus. They had first to deal with the Sikh rebels. The Sikhs defeated Jahan Khan's vanguard and killed two thousand of his troops. Seeing that he could not possibly hold his own, Sabaji precipitately fell back from Batala and returned by way of Ambala and Kunjpura to Dattaji's camp at Sukartal on the Ganges. This was in the beginning of November 1759. Only the corps of Bapuji Trimbak which had been stationed at Multan had no time to run away and hence was caught in the Doab. It had come up to Firozpur on the Satlaj, where it was overtaken by a party of the Afghans who cut it to pieces. Only five hundred out of a total of six thousand returned on foot, unclad and underfed, all their property including horses having been plundered by the Afghans. They came a month and a half later and met Dattaji near Thaneshwar where he had proceeded to meet Abdali, by breaking up his camp at Sukartal, in the last week of December 1759. The *Bhau Bakhar* vividly describes the horror felt by Dattaji Shinde and his troops when they saw their comrades returning in such a wretched condition. The enthusiasm for fighting with Abdali faded away and all thought it as an evil omen of forthcoming disaster. This was the beginning of the end of the Panjab episode in Maratha history. That episode had occupied only a brief period of one and a half years and carried the Maratha standards up to Peshawar, but the cost of this glory was out of all proportion to the gains, and ended with the great setback of Panipat a year later.

CHAPTER II

SUKARTAL, BURADI AND AFTER

BEFORE proceeding to Bahlulpur[1] on the Satlaj to arrange for the government of the Panjab in February 1759, Dattaji had already forfeited the confidence of the Wazir Ghazi-ud-din by his policy of initiating things on his own authority without paying any attention to the Wazir's interests and susceptibilities. The Wazir complained that "even after giving its all, the Empire was not able to keep its prestige.[2] All who had taken part in the business had lost their all with nothing left to fall back upon." This was a true indictment. As the Wazir had found the Maratha power to be a broken reed in times of need, he had perforce to open negotiations with others and try to have something in his own power. Abdali, when he returned in 1757, had tried to establish a sort of balance of power at the Delhi court. He had restored the deposed Emperor to his place and therefore the Wazir was no more free to do away with him or to over-ride him when he liked.[3] Najib Khan had been appointed Mir Bakshi, thus placing the military power in his hands as a check on the Wazir. Ahmad Shah had also shown the wisdom of dismissing Intizam-ud-daulah (on whom he had at first bestowed the Wazirship) and restoring Ghazi-ud-din to his office. When the Marathas returned, they had to do away with Najib as the one real representative of Abdali's cause in India. But he was not arrested and put into prison as he ought to have been, if the Marathas wished to rule over Delhi. On the contrary, he was allowed to keep the districts under him, and to act as a collector for the Marathas! This meant that Najib had still left to him both the means and the freedom to create mischief. When Dattaji returned, he found a stalemate in the Delhi politics due to this position. While the Wazir had all the legal power of the Empire, of appointing and dismissing, of granting and resuming, centred in him, there was no sanction behind his decrees as the military power rested with Najib. Dattaji by his high-handedness alienated the Wazir, but did not, by any means, win over his rival for power, Najib. Dattaji discovered this fact when it was too late. As stated in the previous chapter, he confidently tried to make Najib join him in his cause through the mediation of Govindpant Bundele. But Najib completely foiled his project by procrastination. Dattaji, angered by this deceit and insult, at once besieged Najib with an overwhelming force. But even this overwhelming force was ineffective before the cunning and the ability of Najib.

There are certain natural impediments which it is impossible to overcome even with greater force. Najib's camp at Sukartal had the Ganges on three sides and on the fourth side the ground was so uneven that to approach Najib's camp with artillery or even with cavalry was well-nigh impossible, especially during the rains. The plains in the Gangetic Doab become so muddy

[1] *BISM* (Persian Mss.) No. 699
[2] *SPD* 27.170
[3] *Purandhare* 3.205

during the rains that a horse running at full speed would bury itself chest-deep in a few steps. The riverside land becomes boggy and too treacherous to be entered. Thick undergrowth of rushes and thorny bushes makes penetration by infantry also very difficult. While these were the difficulties which the Maratha army had to face, Najib's line of communications in the rear always remained open even during the rains, as due to a bend in the river, the force of the current there becomes the least troublesome. The trans-Gangetic region was peopled and controlled by his own kith and kin, the Ruhelas. There was never any difficulty in fetching grain and fodder, ammunition and other war necessaries. Added to these were, of course, the indomitable spirit, the singleness of purpose and personal bravery of his troops who were the best infantry trained on the European model in those days.

Dattaji was camping some two miles from Sukartal near the village Miranpur, which was the centre of the famous Sayyads. These Sayyads belonged to the Shia sect and hence hated the Sunni Ruhelas. Dattaji had built a temporary mud fort for his camp. Thence the Maratha troops would sally out and try to come into direct contact with the Ruhelas. But this had been made difficult for the Maratha cavalry, and it seems the Maratha footmen in the 18th century had none of the virtues of pluck and resourçefulness which were the most enviable and noticeable features of Shivaji's Mavlas. During a siege which lasted for more than four months, there were scarcely any actions as such. The *Bhau Bakhar* gives a vivid description of the conditions during these months. The exchange of artillery fire between the two armies was indecisive, because the shots from the Maratha side could not hit Najib's camp under any circumstances. At a lower angle the shot would fall into the surrounding ravines and at a higher angle the shot would go whistling across Najib's camp and fall into the Ganges. On the other hand, fire from Najib's camp was very effective and would daily kill a few who tried to approach. Dattaji had this time some forty thousand troops with him including the contingents of Govindpant, Antaji Manakeshwar's son Bahiropant and the local levies of the Sayyads. Najib had possibly not more than ten thousand troops, though it is quite impossible to be sure of the figures of those days. But though the troops actually staying in Najib's camp were comparatively few, beyond the Ganges the whole clan of the Ruhelas, some fifty thousand strong, was helping him in all possible ways. While the Maratha troops suffered from scarcity, Najib always had access to all the things he wanted. Besides, the climate of those muddy and boggy low lands was found unsuitable to the health of the Maratha troops and the animals of the southern breed. Whenever Dattaji tried to assault, he was repulsed at heavy cost. Two such offensive actions seem to have taken place during these months with more than a thousand casualties. Jivaji Shinde and his son Hanmantrao were killed in one of these actions.

As the siege was dragging on, Najib Khan's diplomacy was winning greater successes for him. Ahmad Shah had already started from Kandahar and was thinking of entering the Panjab from the southern side via Bhakkar and Multan. But he could not cross the Indus at any point and had to come north to Attock along the right bank of the river via Mithankot, Dera Ghazi Khan and Dera Ismail Khan. His general, Jahan Khan, entered the Panjab in October 1759 by way of Peshawar. Madhosingh of Jaipur, who was a party to the anti-Maratha conspiracy, made a firm stand against the troops of Malharrao Holkar who had been ordered by the Peshwa to go to Dattaji's help. Shuja-ud-daulah had been sounded by Najib, though their earlier relations were none of the best. Najib impressed on Shuja the gravity of the situation in which Shuja would find himself if the Marathas were ever able to cross the Ganges and enter Oudh. Feeling the impending danger, Shuja consented to help Najib in every way to hold the line of the Ganges.

When October came in, Dattaji devised a new strategy of squeezing out Najib. Getting the help of one Jeta Gujar who pointed out a ford higher up the Ganges, Govindpant Bundele with ten thousand troops crossed the river[4] at the back of Najib and attacked Jalalabad, the Ruhela fort, around which a town had also grown. There were no troops worth the name there, but at the call of Zabeta Khan, Najib's son, the Afghan clansmen all over Rohilkhand came to help him. They held the fort while the Maratha troops plundered and burnt their property and houses in the southern plain. Govindpant next turned due south to the bridge-head on the eastern bank of the Ganges, opposite Sukartal. The Marathas succeeded in cutting off the bridge-head and thus threatened Najib's line of communication by the bridge of boats. Hafiz Rahmat, the grand old man amongst the Ruhelas, advised Najib to come to terms with the Marathas, but Najib would not leave Sukartal under any circumstances and bided his time. His Ruhela troops were alarmed and began to waver, but Najib clenched his teeth and pulled on as best as he could, till he was relieved by the vanguard of the Oudh army sent by Shuja under Umraogir Gosawi. The rumours of Abdali's quick and near approach through the Panjab were also circulated by Najib to frighten the Marathas. As a matter of fact, Abdali was still far away. But the Maratha troops under Govindpant lost heart and precipitately returned without crossing swords with the Gosawi troops. The rumour of Abdali's coming to the Panjab and Janakoji's chit to return hastened Govindpant's sudden flight.[5] Thus the advantage which might have been gained by the Maratha side was lost by this sudden development. Though the troops returned in a hurry and as a result some were actually killed or drowned, Sir Jadunath's estimate that half of their number were drowned is very wide of the mark. This can be seen from Govindpant's letter to Sadashivrao Bhau.[6] Najib Khan was almost on the point of running away from Sukartal as most of his troops had left to defend their homes, but in all these affairs destiny ultimately is found going against the Marathas. Because Umraogir entered the scene just in time and rumours were circulated by Najib that Shuja was himself following with thirty-thousand troops, Janakoji thought it necessary to send a note to Govindpant to return at once. Similarly the early rumours of Abdali's march had their effect on

[4] RAJ. 1.140, 141, 142.
[5] Ibid. 1.143.
[6] *SPD* 40.126

Dattaji's removing his camp from Sukartal. Sabaji actually reached Dattaji's camp on 10th November, 1759, but the news of his coming back was circulated a month earlier so as to loosen Dattaji's grip over Sukartal. Abdali was still near Lahore and his troops had not penetrated up to Thaneshwar till the last week of December; but Ghazi-ud-din, who was chicken-hearted, was frightened when he caught certain news-carriers carrying letters to and from the Emperor Alamgir at Delhi. Therein the Emperor was found writing invitations to Shuja-ud-daulah on the one hand and Ahmad Shah Abdali on the other, and they were assuring him of their imminent arrival. Seeing the danger, the Wazir, who was quick in decision and had no qualms of conscience, got the Emperor and Intizam-ud-daulah (his rival for Wazirship) murdered on November 29, 1759, through Balabash Khan, his captain, and unceremoniously flung their corpses on the river-bank. Next, the Wazir's assistants produced a prince from the house of Taimur and crowned him as Emperor under the title of Shah Jahan III. This prince was a grandson of Kam Bakhsh,[7] the youngest son of Aurangzib, and was dragging his life out in the imperial prison. Thus the Wazir thought that he had taken precautions against Abdali's making use of the old Emperor and his possible Wazir. As a matter of fact, this event sent a thrill of horror through the Muslims of Hindusthan and the Wazir, who was already hated as a tool of the Marathas, lost what little respect was still felt for him. As the Marathas did not seem to have protested against this act, they were naturally held morally responsible for this butchery. It took away the sympathy for the Marathas and had a worse effect on Sadashivrao Bhau's campaign the following year.

Dattaji being thoroughly disappointed at the siege and at the negotiations for tribute and help from Shuja-ud-daulah, ultimately raised the siege on 15th December and divided his army into two parts. He placed the camp, the bazar and their inmates, together with his family, under the charge of Rupram Kothari and asked him to go back to Delhi with his Jat troops. He himself with his select troops proceeded to meet Abdali beyond the Jamuna so as to stop him from entering the Doab and joining Najib. He had perhaps twenty-five thousand chosen horsemen under him. He proceeded to Karnal by crossing the Jamuna south of Kunjpura at the Andhera Ghat on 18th December, 1759, and sent scouts to find out Abdali's movements. He learnt that Abdali's son, Taimur Shah, with forty thousand troops and all his Sardars had arrived north of Ambala and were camping at Laldu, Banora and Chhat[8] on Saturday, the 15th of December, and that Ahmad Shah was himself following. The first skirmish between the vanguards of the two armies took place on 20th December. Dattaji himself proceeded north with his chosen twenty-five thousand troops without any camp equipment, carrying only as much luggage as a soldier could carry on his horse. He had ordered Janakoji Shinde and the Wazir Ghazi-ud-din to remain at Karnal, some fifteen miles behind his advance line, with their parks of artillery, in order to check any surprise party of the Durrani troops proceeding south to attack the main camp and the bazar,

---

7 Ibid. 2.107.
8 Ibid 2.109.

from proceeding further south towards Delhi with Govindpant Bundele. Hearing that Dattaji was advancing with his unencumbered troops to cut him off before reaching the Jamuna, Abdali changed his intention of crossing the river by the easier crossing, south of Kunjpura, so as to proceed straight through Shamli and Muzaffarnagar to Sukartal. Instead, he kept close to the mountain side and arrived at Jagadhri on the 23rd. He himself with his select troops and a park of mobile artillery stopped to engage the advancing Dattaji, and ordered his camp with its heavy baggage to begin crossing at once. Dattaji advanced vigorously, but to his dismay found that he had been anticipated by the Durrani and thus was unable to cut off and loot his camp equipage. On the other hand, he had to face the sharp fire of Shutarnals which killed his troops *en masse*. Thus no effect could be produced on Abdali's army, while the loss on the Maratha side was considerable, amounting to some four thousand killed and wounded. There was no corresponding gain in obstructing Abdali's advance. On the night of that battle of 24th December, Abdali decamped with his whole camp crossing the river by the Budhia Ghat on his way to Saharanpur. Next morning, when Dattaji saw the number of killed and wounded, he must have felt deeply for his error of judgment in keeping his artillery behind. This was the first occasion on which the Marathas discovered the weakness of their traditional mode of warfare, which was found inadequate in dealing with the new mode based on artillery and musketry.

Dattaji now retreated to Delhi, arriving there about the 5th January, 1760. Thence he detached his camp and sent it back under the protection of Ruparam Kothari to the Jat territory. He himself was preparing to go to Meerut and attack Abdali and the Ruhelas combined. The Peshwa had long ago ordered Malharrao Holkar to leave Rajputana and proceed to Sukartal to help the Shindes. But his life-long habits of procrastination and perhaps his unwillingness to join his forces with those of the Shindes, especially in the work of completely crushing Najib against his will, delayed his march from Balwada which he was besieging then. As a matter of fact, Balwada was an insignificant fort under a captain of Jaipur. But it held out this time for some two months. This seems to be due to Madhosingh's policy of engaging the Maratha generals separately till the arrival of Ahmad Shah Abdali. As Najib Khan and Madhosingh of Jaipur were the two most important conspirators in the conspiracy of driving the Marathas south of the Narbada with the help of Abdali, it was but natural that Madhosingh should, in furtherance of their cause, try to pin down Malharrao to Rajputana so as to frustrate his plans of proceeding to help Dattaji. Anyway, Malharrao's conduct on this occasion had the effect of putting the whole brunt of meeting Abdali on the Shindes. Dattaji was trying now to postpone a trial of strength with the combined Durrani and Ruhela troops till the arrival of Malharrao. Malharrao in extenuation of his delaying conduct is found putting the plea that the Shindes[9] had cancelled their first call for help from Sukartal, when they found they had enough troops with them after the arrival of the Panjab troops under Sabaji and Tukoji. But after the first battle near the Budhia Ghat, Janakoji sent

[9] Ibid. 2.117.

an express call for help to Malharrao who started at once on the first of January, 1760. Had there been a man of Bajirao's type, he would have possibly covered the distance from Jaipur to Delhi just in time to join Dattaji. But Ahmad Shah probably knowing the speed of Malharrao's advance, decided to forestall him.

Ahmad Shah left Sukartal within a week and advanced by way of Meerut to Luni on the Jamuna. This place is about seven miles to the north-east of Delhi and opposite to it is the ferry of Jagatpur. Abdali was trying to find the least defended part on the opposite bank of the Jamuna so as to cross the river without giving any chance to the enemy to attack his force while crossing. It was impossible for him to cross near Delhi, because the fire from the Delhi fort could have been effectively used against him by the Wazir. The ghats just to the north of Delhi were guarded by Dattaji's scouts. Dattaji himself was camping in the vicinity of Majnu's hillock, two miles to the north of Delhi. He had so distributed his army as to meet any surprise crossing by the Durrani troops at any point. But the river was fordable at many points, and it was difficult to keep watch in a low land with the dense fog of January covering it. As Dattaji could have no intimation of Abdali's intentions, he had to depend on mere guess work. Three days passed in manœuvring for a crossing, and Abdali ultimately chose to cross opposite the village of Buradi, where the terrain was most uneven and difficult. This place is some seven miles to the north of Delhi. Dattaji had guarded the crossings to the south of this place well. In order to mislead the Marathas, Abdali sent small parties to each of the crossings and with the main army he went to Badarpur and tried to cross thence. He crossed over to Buradi because that was probably the least guarded part. The river there had separated into two streams with a sandy low island between. It was overgrown with thick rushes which attain in these parts a height of ten feet. If soldiers lie in ambush interspersed in these rushes, it would be impossible to see or locate them within a few yards. Till one actually arrives on the edge of the river, one cannot see it from any point in the vicinity. Nor can the crossing at this point be seen from any southern point on the bank, because the land there bulges out a little and shuts the view to the north. Though the Marathi chronicle indulges in vivid description, it is not known whether Dattaji had actually placed a force at this particular point. Perhaps he had not; and he seems to have been informed of the crossing when half the army of Abdali had already crossed. This was on the morning of 10th January, 1760.

Early that morning, Dattaji received news, one after the other, of his guards at various points on the river being simultaneously attacked by the crossing parties of Durrani and Ruhela soldiers and being very roughly handled by them. This was Abdali's ruse to send Dattaji on the wrong scent. But Dattaji would not move unguardedly and would not call in the help from his whole camp which was spread over a vast plain, each part being separated from the other by a considerable distance. In fact he had no mind to engage the enemy till the arrival of Malharrao Holkar for whom he was waiting and perhaps wanted to fall back on the city in case of need. His only intention was to keep the enemy at a distance from the city till Holkar's arrival so as not to be besieged within the city walls. But this was the very reason why the Durrani made haste and crossed over simultaneously at various points. It seems that none of the parties placed by Dattaji with a few thousand troops each could stand against the enemy's advance with fire from the light cannon placed on the elephants, who swam across in front. Practically the whole of the Shinde contingent was composed of horsemen used to sword and lance, unlike the Ruhelas who were footmen armed with muskets and rifles. The result was that in fights from a distance the Marathas were always at a disadvantage. When almost all the Maratha parties had been completely routed with heavy loss of life, Dattaji received news from Janrao Wable, a veteran captain of horse, that half the army of the enemy had crossed the river. Dattaji sent Bayaji Shinde to help Janrao in holding the ghat at Buradi, which is some three miles away from the village of that name. Receiving the news that Bayaji was worsted with his three thousand horse, and he himself killed by a bullet-shot, Dattaji ordered his whole contingent to follow him to the river-bank. He tried to go to the Buradi Ghat not from the west side but from the south-west along the village of Jagatpur. He crossed first an ordinary *nullah* and then the lake-like inner stream. When he entered the part overgrown with rushes, his cavalry could not keep any line or move in any close formation. The Ruhela infantry, which was lying in ambush in the rushes, opened fire from here, there and everywhere, and made it impossible for Dattaji to proceed. Janakoji who was accompanying Dattaji though forbidden, received a bullet-wound on the right upper arm. The news of this incident had the effect of still more demoralising the Maratha troops, and each tried to turn back to escape what seemed certain death. Dattaji was advised by those near him to order a retreat. But before anything could be done, he himself fell down with a bullet-wound in his ribs. The Afghans then rushed out and completed the rout of the Maratha army with a heavy massacre. The story of the wounded Dattaji being taunted and kicked by Mian Qutb Shah and his cutting off Dattaji's head after some talk, seems more dramatic than true and an invention of the author of the chronicle. We have no belief in it.

There was no regular battle at Buradi Ghat and the two armies were never drawn together in battle array, nor is the number of casualties known. Yashvantrao Jagdale, Bayaji Shinde and Maloji Shinde were the noted persons who lost their lives in this action. Govindpant Bundele does not seem to have taken any part in guarding the ghats as written in the chronicle, though he was not far away from the field of battle. Perhaps he was in the camp of Janakoji a few miles away from Delhi. On the Afghan side, Shuja-ud-daulah does not seem to have been present in Abdali's camp nor any of his troops like the Gosawi corps. Therefore, the story given in the *Bhau Bakhar* of Shuja begging for the head of Dattaji and Umraogir Gosawi buying it for two lakhs and afterwards attending to his full funeral rites must be treated as pure fiction written to console the Shinde family and recommend Ragho Ram Page and Rajaram Chobdar to their attention. The action was fought mainly between the Ruhelas of Najib and Qutb Shah, and Dattaji, though the Duranis followed soon after to turn it into a rout and pursue the Shinde contingent to a long distance. Purushottam Mahadev Hingne[10] who was present in the battle and received a bullet-wound on his thigh, writes that the action was a short and swift one, turning into a rout on account of the general's accidental death in the very first round and the leader receiving a bullet-wound himself. No battle could be fought because the place was unsuitable on account of the thick rushes, and because there was no intention either of offering one till the arrival of Malharrao Holkar. In fact, the main part of the Maratha army was at a distance from the river-bank and not ready for a fight. The division under Dattaji was not sufficient to meet the combined forces of Abdali and Najib with any hope of success. That is why Dattaji had asked Govindpant Bundele with his small brigade to continue with him all along and invited help from Surajmal Jat, who was the only ally left to the Marathas in Northern India. The Wazir's contingent was not more than five thousand strong this time, and was not very helpful or wholeheartedly with the Marathas.

The Durranis pursued Janakoji for twenty-five miles and then returned. Malharrao who had started on the 1st of January was still at a distance of some one hundred and fifty miles from Delhi! Janakoji followed in the direction of Rewadi towards which place his camp had been despatched with Ruparam Kothari and Ramaji Anant Dabholkar, the Shinde's Diwan. It was impossible for Janakoji to ride a horse with his aching wound which had become worse by the first day's headlong flight. As the whole baggage had been looted by the pursuers or left behind as heavy, there was no palanquin with carriers in the whole army. A char-pai (cot) was taken as a substitute and Janakoji was carried on it by the soldiers themselves acting as carriers, leaving their horses in the charge of others. After covering thirty miles in this manner, with great trouble Janakoji reached his camp with the remnants of his broken army after midnight that day. Bhagirathibai, who seems to be a second wife of Dattaji, was in advanced pregnancy and went with the retreating camp. As soon as Janakoji arrived in the camp, his wife Kashibai and Bhagirathibai came out of their tent to see what had happened. Coming to know of Dattaji's death and the defeat of his army, the whole camp was plunged into grief, and there was a great uproar and wailing. From the dramatic description of the *Bakhar*, Bhagirathibai who was not more than sixteen in age (having been married to Dattaji in March 1758) seems to have been a woman of exceptional self-composure and precociously wise. Instead of indulging in useless crying, she reprimanded others for not taking courage and acting as was necessary under the circumstances. She ordered a halt till the morning and stopped the march of the army so as to dress Janakoji's wounds and afford him rest after a run of twenty hours; but the camp which was terrified by what they had heard and afraid of being caught by the pursuing Durrani troops, started at once in the small hours of the morning in the direction of Rewadi. Disobeying her orders, the whole civil camp started, and as a consequence it became difficult for the leaders to continue the halt without the help of camp-followers. The officers in the Shinde contingent

10 Ibid. 2.114.

found it an extremely difficult problem to carry the heavy baggage, including stores of cloth, grain and fodder. They sought counsel with the two women who were now in place of their masters, and after a short consultation, took with them the most necessary and light equipment only, setting fire to the rest for fear of its falling into the hands of the enemy. They placed Janakoji in the lady's palanquin and began to search for horses for the use of the two women. Meanwhile, under the stress of panic, the camp-followers had caught all the available horses and run away with them. With difficulty two ponies were secured and the women started on them. Rupram Kothari, who was accompanying the party, suggested, in order to mislead the Durrani pursuers and to put them on the wrong scent, that the two women and Janakoji should separate themselves from the disorderly camp and go secretly to Kumbher. But Kashibai, for fear of falling into the Jat's hands should they turn traitors in this calamity, disapproved the plan and they continued with the broken camp and the army as best as they could. After four days of continuous trouble, the fore-runners of the army came into touch with the advance party of the Holkar's contingent and stopped there. On the 15th January, 1760, Malharrao came and joined the party to the north of Kot Putali. Then only the panic subsided and men found time to think of what had happened and to plan the future in accordance with it.

It seems from Janakoji's letter[11] to the Peshwa that the plight of the Shinde army was exaggerated by the *Bakhar* writer. The Shinde division though defeated, was not as helpless as the author of the chronicle would paint it to be. The action at the Buradi Ghat was fought on the 10th of January, and not on the 9th, as the day was Thursday.[12] Malharrao and his Diwan Gangadharpant Chandrachud were men of quite a different type from Janakoji Shinde and his Diwan Ramaji Anant Dabholkar. Cautiousness and far-sightedness were the chief virtues of Malharrao, and these fully coincided with the traditional habits and temper of the Marathas. Malharrao's whole policy was based on opportunism and not on any fixed principles. He would take no risk which would land him into a disaster. If the Marathas got something without much effort and little risk, that was sufficient and good. If they could not get the desired fruit and had to return without it, it was no dishonour to them, so thought Malharrao. And it was the guiding philosophy of his life. The Shinde family, on the other hand, was of a different temper. They were straightforward and would not mince matters in their dealings with friend or foe. They were more loyal servants trying to obey the Peshwa's commands as best as they could, and would shirk no risk in gaining their ends. The result is exemplified in the careers of the members of that illustrious family, which was mainly responsible for the Maratha activities in the north for three quarters of a century. Malharrao, on the contrary, would, in the greatest difficulties, first think of the safety of his life and property and then of everything else. With such a frame of mind, he was honest to himself but not necessarily to others with different principles, tempers and standards of conduct. This

11 Ibid. 21.182.

12 Ibid. 27.247

somewhat rough man with blunt manners looked out of place and bizarre in a mixed company of polished men with suave manners. At the same time there was always a substratum of truth in his mode of thinking, and others had to fall in line with it in times of difficulty. The present was such a time and Janakoji had to keep his family-dash in the background and follow Malharrao.

Malharrao sent back the families with the baggage and the bazar to their homes through the friendly territory of the Raja of Keravli to Gwalior under the guardianship of Govindpant Bundele. He started from Kot Putali on the 23rd February. Bhagirathibai gave birth to a posthumous son[13] of Dattaji that night, but he seems to have died soon after. Malharrao and Janakoji then started back towards Delhi with a view to check Abdali's progress and counteract his plans. The Marathas do not seem to have lost courage after the recent untoward happenings. They were still confident of being able to checkmate Abdali and the Ruhelas. Malharrao knew "that Najib Khan and Madhosingh were the chief wirepullers in inviting Ahmad Shah" and, contrary to the common belief, was ready now to reshuffle his former policy of befriending Najib and the Wazir, whom he himself had put on the pedestal. He had thoroughly understood that "Ghazi-ud-din was not acting in consonance with the dignity of his high office and was fickle to a degree. Even though weak himself, he would still indulge in vile machinations and back-door politics. He would do what he liked and on meeting others, humble himself to such an extent as to take away all wrath against his conduct and thus try to wipe out[14] the evil effects of his behaviour." The Peshwa, Nanasaheb, on the other hand,—and in this case acting on the information and the prejudices of Raghunathrao[15] —wished to stick up for a person up to the last, after once having taken his side, and would not change his position unless an open and sufficient cause obliged him to do so. He had instructed Dattaji to act accordingly, but Ghazi-ud-din would neither grant what the Marathas wanted nor issue imperial sanads bestowing Allahabad and Benares on the Marathas.[16] though Shuja-ud-daulah, his rival, would have been the loser. "You can conquer and take possession of the places you want as you are strong. Why do you want sanads for the same?" he would argue with the Marathas. Simultaneously he would write to Shuja-ud-daulah asking him never to grant or hand over these holy cities to the Marathas, but to prepare himself to defend them to the last. To which Shuja[17] would reply that he would do the needful. Thus the two rivals for the chancellorship of the Empire were simultaneously acting hand in glove with the Marathas and also trying to defend the Muslim dominions at all costs and by every subterfuge. Najib had already deceived, fooled and ruined Dattaji, and the Wazir was now following in his wake. But after his late assassinations, it was impossible for the Marathas to back him any more and they had to re-orient their policy.

---

13 RAJ. 1.162.

14 *SPD* 2.117.

15 *Ait. Patra. Yadi* 171

16 *SPD* 27.240.

17 Ibid. 27.240.

The Peshwa had, in his dire need of money, permitted[18] Dattaji to appoint Shuja to the office of the Wazir if he would grant the Maratha claims and pay down cash. Surajmal Jat was on good terms with Shuja as he was his friend's son and their interests also would not clash. On the one hand the Peshwa wanted these two allies to check-mate the Wazir in case he was not amenable to Maratha interests. On the other hand, he feared their combination as likely to prove too strong for the Maratha power and, therefore, he was willing to support Ghazi-ud-din at all costs, as there was no fear of his becoming powerful enough to defy the Marathas. Dattaji had, therefore, chosen the path of placating Najib while keeping the question of the Chancellorship pending. Now that that alternative had disappeared, Malharrao had definitely decided to do away with the double-dealing and ambitious Wazir and invest[19] Shuja with that office. Both Shuja and the Jat feared the Afghan union, as they were likely to be the next victims of that combination. Besides, Surajmal had the ambition of profiting and aggrandizing himself at the cost of the Ruhelas by spreading his power beyond the Jamuna and even the Ganges. Already the Jats had spread in the Doab and colonised certain parts of it. It was but natural, therefore, that they should rally round Surajmal as the "Lord of Braj." Just as Surajmal had made his power unassailable by building, strengthening and storing his forts of Deeg, Kumbher and Bharatpur, similarly he took the fortalice of Sabitgad, near Kol, re-named it Ramgad, and began to turn it into a second Kumbher. From this base he was trying to dominate the upper Doab and Rohilkhand beyond the Ganges. Malharrao had now established friendship[20] with the Jat Raja, forgetting the siege of Kumbher and his son's death. As it was in the interest of Surajmal to combat the Afghan power, he made common cause with the Marathas and helped them in this guerilla warfare.

From Kot Putali, Malharrao and Janakoji began their new plan of making sudden raids on the enemy's undefended depots and roving round the flanks so as to sieze every opportunity of spoliation. Ahmad Shah was now camping south of Delhi and thence despatching letters to the various chiefs asking them to pay him tribute and join their forces with his in his efforts to drive the Marathas[21] from northern India. But they knew his ways as well as his power and, therefore, chose to sit on the fence playing the game of procrastination, by neither acceding to nor refusing his demands, but merely pleading their inability to do anything. Ahmad Shah had to visit their territories personally in order to squeeze any money out of them. First he moved south and besieged Deeg near Mathura. He drove away the small parties of the Marathas hovering round him. He was not able to make any impression on Deeg and had to move in pursuit of the threatening Marathas. Malharrao, accompanied by Janakoji and Naro Shankar, was reported to be at Narnol,[22] whither Abdali moved next.

18 *Ait. Patren. Yadi* 167.

19 *SPD* 21.183.

20 Ibid. 2.121.

21 Ibid. 21.186.

22 Ibid. 21.186.

Leaving Deeg, Ahmad Shah proceeded south-west into the Jaipur territory plundering wherever he went. He ransomed the small local Rajas of Kadhake and Khobari (Kurke and Khohari?). He was thinking of proceeding against the non-committing Madhosingh to Jaipur. On the road he slaughtered the inhabitants of the resisting town of Mahwah[23] (twenty miles east of Bandikui), but spared the residents of Baswa[24] (ten miles north of Bandikui), as they offered ransom for their town. This was in the third week of February. There he received the news that the Marathas were looting the districts to the west of Delhi and had taken Rs. 10,000 as tribute from Kanaud.[25] Ahmad Shah, therefore, swerved north through Alwar territories,[26] leaving the direction of Jaipur. But before he could arrive near Delhi, Malharrao had formed another plan, depending upon Abdali's intended move against Jaipur which, had it been put into execution, would have engaged the Afghans there for at least a month or two. As Najib Khan and most of the other Ruhelas were accompanying Abdali on his march, Malharrao and his shrewd Diwan Gangoba Chandrachud thought of attacking the Ruhela lands in the Doab and beyond, in the absence of their proprietors. The Maratha army crossed the Jamuna to the south of Delhi on 20th February, 1760, and descended upon the rich town of Sikandrabad. There they halted and completely looted the town on the Holi Day i.e. 1st March, 1760. They should have moved from the place the next day and proceeded farther, but there they heard that Najib Khan's treasure of ten lakhs was coming into the Doab on its way to the Abdali camp. It had come up to the bank of the Ganges opposite to the town of Anup Shahar. Getting this clue, they sent pickets to see where the Ganges could be crossed. In the meanwhile, Ahmad Shah hearing this move of Holkar, suddenly changed his direction and ran to the south of Delhi. Thence he detached Jahan Khan and Najib Khan with 35,000 troops unencumbered with any artillery or camp equipage. Surajmal Jat who in this guerilla war was helping the Marathas, came to know of this sudden move of Abdali and sent information of the same to Gangoba Chandrachud to warn him in time. The Maratha army had, therefore, already divided itself.

The Shinde contingent under Janakoji as well as old Malharrao Holkar had fallen back towards Mathura and Agra. Rupram, the Jat envoy, accompanied them. But the rest of Holkar's troops who never had any acquaintance with the Durrani ways and no experience of battling against them, laughed at the idea of running away on mere news of the enemy, and taunted the Shinde's troops as being faint-hearted. Janakoji, therefore, separated from Holkar and started towards Mathura. Malharrao himself personally followed him and ordered Gangoba Tatya to check the Durrani advance. But his corps was surprised, caught unprepared and massacred with heavy slaughter

23 KHARE 1.21.

24 Ibid.

25 *SPD* 2.118.

26 Ibid. 21.186.

27 Ibid. 2.121.

by Jahan Khan. Gangoba, who was personally alert, was able to run away and save himself; but Anandrao Ram Yadav, Shetyaji Kharade and his son were killed in the running fight,[28] and the broken remnant of the frightened army crossed the Jamuna back into the Jat territory, wherever it could. The experiment of checkmating the Durrani forces by guerilla tactics thus ended in failure.

The Maratha forces, therefore, retreated to the borders of the Jaipur territory and encamped in the vicinity of Bayana. The Maratha tactics, however, had saved not only the Jats but also the Rajput princes. Abdali had to turn back from Jaipur because the Marathas had swept towards Delhi, and now his army had to be stationed in the Doab to ward off the Maratha raids against the Ruhelas. The Marathas now reached a complete understanding with Surajmal Jat and renewed their former agreements with him. Surajmal promised to follow the Maratha policy in all respects. His own territories in the Doab were now directly threatened and he concentrated his strength on the defence of Ramgad (the modern Aligarh), which, however, surrendered to Abdali's overwhelming forces within a month. As all the Ruhelas were not on good terms and in full accord with Najib, the Marathas now tried to divide them by entering into a separate arrangement with Hafiz Rahmat, the grand old man amongst the trans-Gangetic Ruhelas. He agreed to join his forces with the Marathas, send back Abdali after detaching him from Najib and not to help Najib in his fight against the Marathas. The Marathas agreed, on the other hand, not to invade the other Ruhelas but to content themselves with the cis-Gangetic territories. Abdali would have now left for Afghanistan, had not Najib induced him to remain in India for protecting him against the chafing wrath of the Marathas. His stay in India gave a new turn to the Maratha politics in the north.

---

28 Ibid. 2.121.

CHAPTER III

SADASHIVRAO'S APPOINTMENT FOR NORTHERN INDIA

WHEN the tidings of Dattaji's death reached the Peshwa's camp at Ahmadnagar in the south, none in the Deccan was prepared for such a bolt from the blue. All had full confidence in the military talents of Dattaji Shinde. They expected him at least to stem the tide of the Durrani invasion if not to defeat Abdali and drive him back. Besides, the Peshwa had ordered Malharrao Holkar to proceed to Dattaji's help and he was expected to be on the route towards the Panjab. This was in the middle of November 1759, after Sabaji's return to Sukartal. At that time, it was expected that the Nizam in the Deccan would be cowed down by ordinary manœuvring of troops and be prepared to part with the north-western portion of his dominions. It seems that the Nizam had consented to grant Ahmadnagar and Parenda forts together with the revenue of the surrounding territories amounting to ten lakhs, to the Peshwa.[1] But afterwards, due to the advice of his brothers, he tried to equivocate about the grant of Ahmadnagar which was not only a strong fort in the military sense, but was a place of prestige for the Muslims, being the old seat of the Nizamshahi Kingdom. The Peshwa was not in a mood at that time to tolerate any delaying tactics. His position at the hour was thought to be almost that of a dictator in India. Since the Maratha standards were carried beyond the Attock[2] in the previous year, the Peshwa's fame had spread not only throughout the length and breadth of India, but had travelled beyond the boundaries to Iran and Turan.[3] In the south his generals Balvantrao Mehendale, Gopalrao Patwardhan, Malhar Naik Raste and Visaji Krishna Biniwale had established the Maratha suzerainty south of the river Krishna.[4] In the north his brother Raghunnathrao and his generals Dattaji and Malharrao had created such awe that none in those parts was willing to cross swords with the Marathas. Even the chiefs not conquered by the Marathas were ready to send ambassadors and try to negotiate terms for their existence and continuance.[5] Shuja-ud-daulah had paid tribute[6] and the English in Bengal, though they had slyly usurped the power by a silent revolution without proclaiming themselves the masters, were still in need of the Peshwa's goodwill and forbearance towards them, and actually sent emissaries to the Poona Court to ward off Raghunathrao's proposed advance into Bengal.[7] The Peshwa had, it seems, actually assured Clive of his support, and Clive made political use of that assurance in imposing himself upon the Nawab Siraj-ud-daulah.[8] Similarly, the English advance through Orissa to Masulipatam and the occupation

---

1 RAJ. 1.154.
2 *BISM* (Persian Mss.) No. 696, dated 20-12-1758.
3 *Aitihasika Sphuta Lekh* 4.11.
4 *SPD* 28.200-02. 204, 210, 216, 217, 266
5 *BISM* (Persian Mss.) No. 699
6 *K. Patre Yadi* No. 166.
7 *JIHQ* 15.3.388.
8 Hill 2.387, 388, 400

of the French jagirs by Colonel Forde was made possible by Maratha forbearance and the Peshwa's pressure on the Nizam Salabat Jang, the grantor of these jagirs. Naturally the Peshwa was thinking himself as suzerain in all these parts of India occupied by the English, for both the Deccan and Bengal as well as Arcot were paying chauth to the Marathas and the English had still not remonstrated against or interfered with this right.

Bussy who had been recalled from the court of Hyderabad by Lally, had left for Pondicherry in July 1758. The result was that the fruit of his occupation of Daulatabad and of the assassination of Shah Nawaz Khan who was a protege of the Peshwa had been snatched away by others after his departure. Thus ended the French influence at the Nizam's Court. The Peshwa had succeeded in detaching Ibrahim Khan Gardi, pupil of Bussy, from the Nizam's service and engaging him himself.[9] Thus strengthened, the Peshwa sent his cousin Sadashivrao Bhau, with forty thousand troops to occupy Ahmadnagar as promised by the Nizam. He was saved the trouble of besieging that strong fort as Kavi Jang, its keeper, agreed to deliver it to the Marathas in consideration for a jagir with an annual revenue of Rs. fifty thousand.[10] Visaji Krishna took possession of it on 9th November, 1759. Thence Sadashivrao Bhau proceeded towards Beed and Dharur and commenced hostilities with the Nizam by fomenting and strengthening internal quarrels amongst the Nizam brothers. Basalat Jang separated himself from the Nizam and marched towards the south. The Maratha sardars of the Nizam, Nimbalkars and Khandagle, were sitting sulkily at home and not joining their forces with those of Nizam Ali, who had taken the lead after the departure of the French. Sadashivrao hoped for a quick decision in the campaign and after its successful termination intended to send Raghunathrao into the north to help Dattaji.

But Nizam Ali would not part with the territories demanded by the Peshwa without a trial of strength. Skirmishes began from the 20th January, 1760, and gradually the Maratha armies surrounded the Nizam and his brother. The Nizam wanted to reach the fort of Dharur and make a stand there, but the Marathas would not allow him to escape from Udgir and continuously followed close at his heels. By forming a hollow square, the Nizam marched out in the French fashion from Udgir and slowly moved towards Ausa, skirmishing all along the way. When the fort of Dharur remained some fifteen miles ahead, the Marathas held up his march by completely surrounding him on all sides and attacking him in the rear. In the battle of 3rd February, 1760, the Nizam was completely defeated and hemmed in, and therefore sued for peace. By the terms of the peace, the Nizam ceded to the Marathas practically the half of his remaining dominions. Nizam Ali, the chief instigator, was to go back to his jagir in Berar and the Nizam Salabat Jang was to remain in Hyderabad. His Maratha sardars[11] were to leave the Nizam's service. The foreign relations of the Nizam were to be guided by the

9 *Purandare* 1.382.
10 Ibid. 1.382.
11 Raj. 1.165.

Maratha policy, especially his dealings with the French.[12] Bijapur, Ahmadnagar, Burhanpur and Daulatabad, all four former capitals of the Muslim dominions, were surrendered together with the important forts of Asher and Mulher.[13] Sadashivrao Bhau had become the hero of the day. He writes that but for the new danger in the north, the whole of the south would have come under the rule of the Peshwa.

Unfortunately he reckoned without his host. Already the English had stolen a march politically, and now militarily also they loomed large on the horizon. Bussy had already been made a prisoner by them, and Haider Ali had so firmly set foot in Mysore as never to be ousted. While the Peshwa had just then taken possession of Underi and Kansa from the Sidi,[14] Janjira and Surat never became Maratha possessions. Even the Nizam brothers, though defeated with heavy loss and deprived of half their dominions, were only biding their time. They had given their consent to the treaty because they had to, but there was no intention in their mind of fulfilling the terms in the real spirit.[15] By the treaty they had merely played for time to reshuffle their matters, gain over their disaffected Maratha sardars to their side, seek help from the Pathans of Karnool, the Bedars of Surapur and also Murarrao Ghorpade. Their whole army had not been completely crushed and, in fact, they had sought peace at once to keep it intact. All these points had been placed before Bhau and he should have thought of them seriously. But the Peshwa thought more of recovering the prestige lost in north India as a result of the fall of Shinde. Consequently he ordered preparations to be made for despatching a strong force to the north to drive out Abdali.

Throughout the Udgir campaign, the Peshwa who had stopped at Ahmadnagar, and directed the movements from that place, now proceeded towards Paithan on his way to Patdur, southeast of Jalna, where he had summoned the Bhosle brothers from Nagpur to settle their quarrels. Sadashivrao Bhau himself proceeded north to that place, after crossing the Godavari, to meet him and thrash out the future policy through consultations with all. They met there in the first week of March 1760, and first celebrated their victory by playing the Rangapanchami festival with zest. Then began the discussions. All the three cousins were there, and it was the declared intention of the Peshwa and also of Bhau to send Raghunathrao to the north as originally arranged.

It should be remembered that up to that time the final route of Malharrao Holkar by Abdali at Sikandrabad, which took place in the first week of March, had not been reported to the Peshwa, as news travelled very slowly in those days. If the news had reached the Peshwa's camp at Padtur in time, that would have perhaps given a different turn to the whole affair. It seems that the discussions assumed the form of family bickerings in the Peshwa's family. Personal opinions, long cherished prejudices, partiality and selfish-

12 *SPD* 40.128.
13 Raj. 1.166.
14 Ibid. 1.157.
15 *SPD* 1.86.

ness had played their role in what should have been purely political discussions. The Peshwa had always shown his predilection towards his brother Raghunathrao, and had somehow formed a good opinion about his ability. Sadashivrao Bhau, for all his ability and wisdom, was still a cousin and therefore not on a par with Raghunathrao. He could have no legal share in the Peshwa's dominions and estates, and was only the first servant of the state. Gopikabai, the wife of the Peshwa, was supposed to be the chief instigator against the superior claims of Sadashivrao to high office due to his ability. When Raghunathrao was ordered[16] to take the command of the north, he put in a plea that he would not accept the responsibility[17] unless provided with ample funds. Sadashivrao Bhau who was a strict accountant and auditor-general held Raghunathrao responsible for the debts of the Panjab campaign and he strongly resented the charge. Raghunathrao had taken the past lesson to heart and, therefore, wished to absolve himself from the results of the forthcoming campaign.

After much recriminative discussion, the Peshwa ordered Bhau himself to shoulder the responsibility and lead the campaign.[18] The Peshwa was rather unwilling to spare such a consummate, able and all-round administrator as Bhau for a long time; but there was no help for it, as Bhau had been stung to the quick by a challenge from his cousin to prove his own valour and ability to add ample funds to the central treasury by going on the campaign himself. But Gopikabai feared the consequence of Bhau's going to the north, accompanied by his wife and with a big army. His prestige had already risen very high by the Udgir campaign. If he became equally successful in the north and were to establish a separate kingdom for himself, who was there to check him? It was necessary, therefore, to keep some constitutional check on his conduct and with this view Vishwasrao, the eldest son of the Peshwa, was placed at the head of the forces, with Bhau acting as his deputy. From the correspondence in the whole Panipat campaign, it is clear that Bhau was not free to settle anything on his own responsibility. Every time he referred the matter to and sought the previous sanction of the Peshwa. This was a false position in the then circumstances for a supreme authority like Bhau. It appears to have had a dilatory and derogatory effect on Bhau's conduct of affairs, making it impossible for him to free himself from the entanglement at Panipat later on, when need for a quick, decisive step arose. This point should constantly be borne in mind when reading the forthcoming account of Panipat.

While the suspicions and the prejudices of the Peshwa and his personal circle affected the Maratha policy throughout the Panipat campaign, Bhau's personal predilections also shaped it to a great extent. If Raghunathrao was always dependent on his assistants for shaping his policy, Bhau had a tendency towards the other extreme of acting on his own responsibility after abruptly cutting short the discussion on any subject and dictating the final thing him-

16 Ibid. 40.129.

17 KHARE 1.14. For the previous debts contracted by him the Peshwa had been obliged to impose a new debt-contribution on all his jagirdars. Vide *Satara* 2.292.

18 RAJ. 1.168.

self. The result was that he seemed, which he was actually not, proud or even haughty. This was a virtue as far as administrative efficiency—which depends upon quick and final decision—was concerned, but it cannot be said to be helpful when policy is to be shaped amongst equals. Over-riding opinions is always possible for a higher authority, but it is not always conducive to the best results, as ultimately the working out of the decisions devolves upon the subordinates. A commander-in-chief can scarcely act against the combined opinion and will of his generals.

Bhau selected his own assistants and corps from amongst the assemblage gathered in the Nizam's dominions. To begin with, his army was not more than twenty-five thousand strong, besides the infantry under Ibrahim Khan, which was nine thousand. Though Raghunathrao did not join, some of the corps subordinate to him were included in the army which accompanied Bhau to the north. The Maratha army was made up of the feudal divisions under the main sardars. These sardars employed subordinate corps under individual captains. The sardar was responsible for the conduct, training, equipment and payment of the corps employed by him. Certain revenue districts were assigned to him as jagirs for the expenditure thereof. Not all the noted captains in the Maratha army were sardars. Certain corps were directly employed by the Peshwa who paid them from the central treasury. There was no one fixed scale of payment, certain sardars being paid more favourably than others. The bigger sardars, like Shinde and Holkar, were treated more as partners in the state than as mere subordinates. They had specified percentages of the total revenues in certain regions permanently assigned to them as their inalienable share. It should be particularly noted that throughout the Panipat campaign, the payment of the whole army did not devolve on Sadashivrao Bhau. The divisions of Shinde and Holkar and also of a few other sardars were expected to be paid by the sardars themselves. Bhau was responsible for the payment of the Peshwa's own troops, called "Huzarat," and directly paid corps like those under Ibrahim Khan Gardi. The inconvenience felt by the non-receipt of revenues called in by Sadashivrao Bhau from men like Govindpant Bundele mainly affected the Peshwa's own divisions and not the divisions under Shinde and Holkar. The normal Maratha practice was for the moving army to subsist on its own earnings in the regions through which it passed. When the army was warring in a foreign territory, it would automatically subsist on tributes, ransoms and spoils, but when passing through its own dominions or the dominions of its allies, it had to buy everything it needed. In the Panipat campaign this was the condition in the main. Khandesh, Malwa, the Jat country, the Delhi region, were all non-belligerent territories. Besides, due to the continuance of almost constant war in the territories surrounding Delhi for almost a decade, the regions had become depopulated, non-agricultural and insecure. Unless there was good cash in one's pocket and one could keep the line of communication safe for caravans bringing supplies, it was impossible to go on for any length of time. There was no government commissariat department giving free rations or selling things at fixed prices in those days. The bazar which accompanied a moving army was chartered, guaranteed and given the necessary protection by the army commander no doubt, but the merchants were not responsible for the continuous supply as such, nor were the prices fixed. This was a constant source of difficulty for a moving army. There was no assurance of supply nor certainty about the cost, which led not only to slackness and even obstruction in the war effort, but to the bankruptcy of the soldiers and the authorities as well.

Sadashivrao Bhau's progress was very slow if he had the intention of joining Shinde and Holkar before the rains. These generals had been practically driven out of the Delhi area, and were then camping at a safe distance from the Durrani forces behind the Jat principality, using Surajmal as a middleman in their diplomatic negotiations.[19] Ahmad Shah Abdali had sent emissaries to both Madhosingh of Jaipur and Surajmal Jat, ordering them to unite their forces with his and send monies to aid him in his work of driving out the Marathas,[21] but both pleaded their inability to do anything in the matter and tried the game of procrastination and equivocation. Surajmal was the more cunning of the two. He would always call himself a mere zamindar, or even a tenant, and not a prince. He replied that he would pay the acknowledged Emperor the revenues due to him. If Ahmad Shah would himself assume that position and remain permanently in India, he would pay him as the legal sovereign. Till then he could not possibly do what he had been asked, especially as his territories had been ravaged by the movements of both the Maratha and the Durrani armies.[22] As the Indian summer advanced, Abdali encamped in the vicinity of Ramgad in the mid-Doab, exhausted by the three months' incessant running after the elusive Marathas of the Shinde-Holkar contingents. Each party now expected the other to renew the fight first, and would not start it themselves. This stalemate could have been broken only by the junction of the forces under Sadashivrao Bhau and the exhausted generals in the north.

Bhau started from Patdur on the 14th of March, 1760, but had only crossed the Narmada after a month, covering a distance of not more than two hundred miles. The delay was due to the preparation and joining in of the various corps with equipment for a long and distant campaign. Sadashivrao Bhau's Panipat campaign was, in fact, on the model of the Mughal Emperors and not like that of Shivaji or Bajirao I. The Maratha army had large tents, screens for women's apartments, and the various departments to look after the convenience of the leaders and the army. The chiefs rode on superb Arab or Central Asian chargers and wore gorgeous dresses of gold brocades. Their weapons and other equipment were also of the best type, and the brigades under Ibrahim Khan Gardi, trained after the French model, were the envy of Indian potentates of those times. The presence of these infantry corps with their cannon, regulated the whole movement of the army, and the daily marches would cover but a few miles. The heavy siege-guns which accompanied the army, together with the light field-artillery, slowed the rate of progress, as the long rows of bulls necessary to draw them would move but slowly over the rugged country and narrow passes in the Satpura and Vindhya

19 *SPD* 2.121.
21 Ibid. 21.186
22 Ibid.

TO FACE PAGE 36

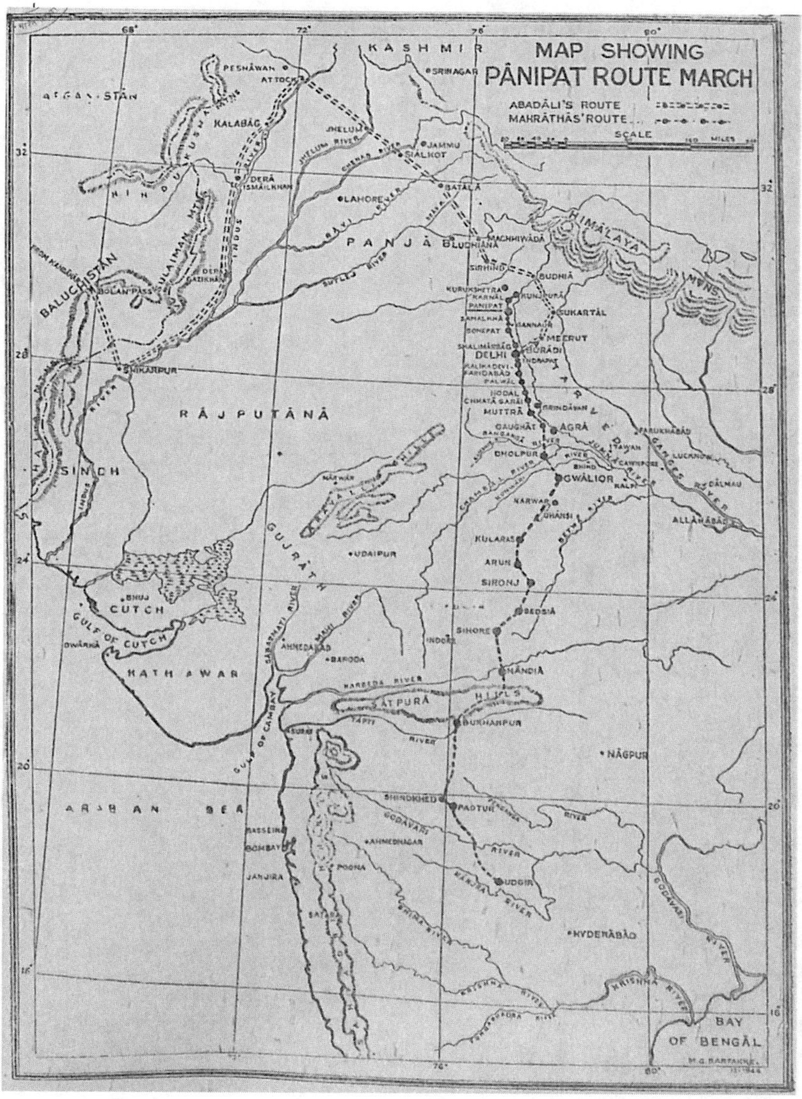

Foot-note:—Baghpat to the west of Meerut on the bank of the Jamuna and the village of Gauripur five miles to the north of Baghpat have been inadvertently omitted from this map. Ahmad Shah crossed the Jamuna at Gauripur and went to Sonepat.

ranges. The army crossed the Narmada by the usual Handia ford into Nemawar on the 16th of April,[23] and proceeded via Sihor and Bersia[24] to Sironj,[25] where there was a long halt for a week. Here the field-pieces left by Raghunathrao at Ujjain and Indore on his return from Lahore were brought out for use in the present campaign.

Bhau sent invitations to all the various chiefs in northern India, inviting them as allies to join their forces in the common cause of driving out the foreigner from the realm of Hindusthan.[26] Kamal-ud-din Khan Babi of Gujarat,[27] Madhosingh of Jaipur, Hindupat of Bundelkhand,[28] Shujah-ud-daulah of Oudh, as also the Rajas[29] of Bundi, Kota and other minor principalities, were appealed to, but none came to the Maratha help in this crisis. All sat on the fence, watching the movements and waiting for the final result of the contest between the two great powers. Knowing the weaknesses and the difficulties of the Marathas, they would not fail to take advantage of the same. Even the chieftains of Central India were not cowed down by the presence in their midst of this big army of Marathas! The Ahirs rose in rebellion at this time and tried to attack and loot the straggling parties of the Marathas and the convoys of supplies.[30] None would send the annual tributes unless troops were sent to exact the same from them. They knew well that the Maratha army under Bhau, moving in the grand old Mughal style, was in no position to delay its march by moving either to the right or to the left of the main road with their heavy encumbrances.[31] On the other hand the Marathas were exposed to all the dangers, difficulties and inconveniences to which the armies of Aurangzib had been exposed in former times.

Bhau was conscious of his difficulties, and the limitations of the Maratha army. He tried to do away with the defects and strengthen his position by various means like engaging new infantry and gunners from amongst the men of north India, by buying horses and pack animals to replace the losses suffered in the Udgir campaign. Many horsemen had lost their mounts in the fight with the Nizam Ali, and still more on the way through Malwa on account of the epidemic of a peculiar disease amongst the horses of the army on the march.[32] It is called "tamasha" in a Marathi letter, by which the animals became ill for some two days and then died. There was neither strength nor enthusiasm left amongst the soldiers on account of these troubles. To a Maratha horseman, losing his horse meant practically losing his whole capital, as he was no good fighter on foot; still Bhau would not alter his plan or mode and proceeded slowly, with no intention of attacking Abdali at once, but only feeling his way through diplomatic channels. There was news that Abdali had sent half of his camp-followers back to Afghanistan, and thus

23 *Aitihasik Tipane* 2.33.
24 Raj. 1.174.
25 Ibid. 1.180.
26 Raj. 1.174: *Shinde* 2.10.
27 *Aitihasik Tipane* 1.53.
28 *SPD* 29.41.
29 *Shinde* 2.10.
30 Raj. 1.180, 186.
31 Ibid. 1.186.
32 *Satara* 2.296.

lessened his expenditure. There was rumour of his personal return to Afghanistan[33] after appointing Shuja as the Wazir, Najib as Mir Bakshi and proclaiming the fugitive Prince Ali Gauhar as Emperor, thus doing away with the puppet Shah Jahan III, brought on the throne by the regicide Ghazi-ud-din. The Panjab would, of course, be surrendered to Abdali, who would be of help to the Delhi Emperor in times of difficulty. The Dowager Empress, Malika Zamani, had been specially deputed to induce Shuja by a personal interview, but she does not seem to have succeeded in her efforts. Shuja's mother was still alive and influenced the affairs of Oudh with prescience and wisdom. She knew that there was nothing common between the Sunni Afghans and the Irani Shias to which group her family belonged. The old officers of Safdar Jang's time knew the difficulties of the Delhi politics and feared to antagonise the Marathas, who surrounded the Oudh territory. Shuja was thinking of giving the slip to Abdali without directly saying "no" by proceeding towards Bihar to back up the Emperor Shah Alam II. But Najib Khan was supporting Abdali and directing all his affairs. He himself proceeded towards Oudh with Jahan Khan, the Durrani general. With a suavity equalled by his cunning, he impressed the Oudh Court by discussing threadbare the pros and cons of Oudh policy, and finally prevailed upon Shuja to put in his lot on the side of Abdali. Najib Khan personally stood surety against any possible harm to Shuja in the Afghan camp. The unsteadiness of Maratha policy in its dealings with Safdar Jang had now borne fruit. The Peshwa and his sardars had forsaken Safdar Jang in his need, and gone over to the side of his opponent, Ghazi-ud-din. The late Wazir had been left to die of a broken heart after his discomfiture before Delhi and his son Shuja had always to be on his guard lest the attention of the Marathas be directed against his dominions, which contained the chief holy places of the Hindus, namely, Benares, Allahabad and Ayodhya.

In his dealings with Shuja, Sadashivrao had put his chief confidence in Govindpant Bundele as he was a near neighbour, having known the ins and outs of the Oudh Court for a long time. This man had kept himself outwardly on good terms with Shuja and was credited with a sweet tongue, useful in prevailing upon an acquaintance. Sadashivrao Bhau had begun[34] to write to Govindpant from the Nizam's dominions long before the result of Udgir. When it was finally decided to send him to the north, he at once wrote to Govindpant to bring over Shuja to the Maratha side in the impending struggle against Abdali.[35] From his first letter of the 15th of March, 1760, up to the last disaster of Panipat, ten months later, Bhau is found putting too much faith in the goodness of Shuja. After coming to know his final decision to join Abdali in the first week of July, Bhau should have left the matter at that point and should have completely stopped his correspondence with Shuja. The only result of Bhau's importunities seems to have been to convince Abdali and Najib of the Maratha weakness. This conviction strengthened their resolution of fighting to the last. The Maratha diplomacy during

33 RAJ. 1.191, 222, 236, 246.
34 Ibid. 1.154.
35 Ibid. 1.167.

Balaji Bajirao's rule is always inexplicable, and it was much more so during the Panipat campaign.

Looking to the political condition then existing in India, and the strength of the Marathas, it was a first rate mistake to have left the south Indian tangle to take its own shape, and proceed to north India after Udgir, especially after knowing the complete defeat of the Shinde-Holkar forces. There were at least four fronts on which the Maratha attention was necessary then. The Abdali front in the north, the Haider Ali front in the south, the Nizam front in the Deccan and the English front—for such it was though the Peshwa was completely unaware of it—along the whole Indian coast. The Maratha power seemed to be at its zenith at the end of 1758,[36] but the fundamental weakness of their unplanned spreading became apparant soon. By the end of 1759 they were completely driven out of the Panjab and suffered a major defeat owing to the death of Dattaji soon after. In the south, Haider Ali who was strengthening himself silently, had slyly set aside the all-conquering Marathas, establishing himself finally in September 1759 by defeating Nanjraj[37] and imprisoning him with the puppet Mysore ruler. The English had established their power in Bengal equally firmly, and had, taking advantage of the Maratha support, occupied the best districts in the Nizam's dominion on the eastern sea-board by driving out the French. What Sadashivrao Bhau could conquer from the Nizam after his far-famed victory of Udgir, the British had taken away from the Nizam by merely marching a few thousand troops, under Colonel Forde,[38] from Bengal to the Northern Sarkars! The result of Bhau's going to the north at this juncture after the French defeat at Wandiwash in January 1760, was exemplified not only in the far reverberating defeat of Panipat on 14th January, 1761, but, simultaneously or quickly following on its heels, in the occupation of Pondicherry by the English on 16th January, 1761, and the defeat of the Emperor Shah Alam by Colonel Carnack in Bihar on 15th January, 1761, that is, a day after the Panipat disaster.[39] By these events, little noticed or thought of then, the future of India was decided, more than by the defeat at Panipat. Sadashivrao Bhau was fighting for the preservation of the Mughal Empire for the descendant of Taimur who actually became a prisoner and a tool in the hands of the English! Bhau thought that but for Abdali the whole south would have come into the possession of the Marathas![40] But by the defeat of the French in the south and the occupation of the Northern Sarkars, the English became powerful enough in the south to defy all others. The Peshwa had planned the capture of Janjira from the Sidi this year (1760), but by the covert action[41] of the English it never came to pass! Even the lands conquered from the Nizam at the beginning of 1760 had to be returned when he threatened Poona after Panipat. How can a historian account for these results but on the one supposition that

36 *BISM* (Persian Mss.) No. 696, dated 20-12-1758; No. 699, dated 15-4-1759.
37 Raj. 1.138.
38 *Cambridge History of India* 5.162.
39 *Fall* 2.542.
40 Raj. 1.166.
41 *SPD* 40.136.

the Peshwa had miscalculated the forces and had attempted a wrong solution of the problems?

From Sironj, Bhau proceeded towards Gwalior via Arun,[42] Malan,[43] Pohari and Kaledhar,[44] arriving there on the 30th of May, 1760. He took stock of the Maratha forces and tried to strengthen them in every possible way. But his efforts were wasted on men whom he wished to propitiate. The fault was not Sadashivrao's but of the times. By the middle of the 18th century, the dissolution of the Mughal Empire was practically complete and what an English historian has called "The Great Anarchy" began. This anarchy which lasted almost for a century, ended finally after the great mutiny of 1857. The various fragments of the Mughal Empire, great and small, powerful and weak, had entered into a general scramble for power and pelf, and none was thinking in terms of principles, nor was anyone in a mood to think of Indian unity. Only the Peshwa was thinking in terms of the whole of India ruled from one centre and following a common policy. But Sadashivrao Bhau's appeal fell on deaf ears and hence produced no result. All the previous sins of commission and omission by the three Peshwas raised their heads as ghosts from their graves. Everybody who had once been helped by the Marathas forgot all moral obligation to show gratitude or at least sympathy, while all who had any sense of having been badly treated sat on the fence in expectancy of the Marathas receiving a good drubbing at the hands of the Durrani king. The consciousness of having all the surrounding people against the Marathas must have had a demoralising influence on the Maratha army. Great battles are never won by despondent soldiers!

The Marathi Chronicles of Sadashivrao Bhau report that Bhau had sought the opinion of Malharrao Holkar and Janakoji Shinde, and they had advised Bhau not to come personally, but to send armies for their help on the strength of which they would defeat Abdali. Their opinion was based on the idea that the prestige of a nation is lowered when the chief himself is obliged to enter the arena of the battle, because it is thought as a sort of comment on the (in)capacity of his subordinates and if by chance or through ill-luck the chief is defeated, it becomes difficult for the army to hold out afterwards. On the other hand, the authors of the chronicles report the discussions in the privy council of Sadashivrao Bhau. Therein Bhau's supporters, like Balvantrao Mehendale, saw more than was obvious in the advice of Holkar and Shinde. "Because these sardars and mamlatdars in the north had up till then lived in perfect freedom without feeling the pressure of the chief's control, and feared that their misdeeds would be revealed in the presence of a strict man like Sadashivrao Bhau, they are advising Bhau not to advance any farther," they thought. When Bhau proceeded in spite of these remonstrances, the veteran Malharrao Holkar was reported to have let loose his tongue in wild rage at his advice being brushed aside with scant respect, and abused the advisers of Bhau. He wrote again that Bhau should at least stop at Gwalior and not cross the

42 RAJ. 1.186.
43 Ibid. 1.188.
44 KHARE 1.22.

Chambal, at which Bhau's councillors laughed again and said, "Shinde and Holkar, Antaji Manakeshvar, Govindpant Bundele, Vitthal Shivdeo and Naro Shankar who had acted as officers with full powers in these parts, are now ill at ease at our coming and can never feel happy at the event." We reproduce these lines not because we believe in their truth but because they show an undercurrent of thought diametrically opposite to that of Bhau's policy. There was a good substratum of truth in Holkar's advice. To proceed against Abdali with heavy camp equipage and the encumbrances of women and children with a paraphernalia of private servants on a lavish scale, was certainly a mistake. Delhi could never have been a secure base for the Marathas in the circumstances then existing. In all previous campaigns of the Marathas in the Delhi region, they had suffered from want of food and fodder, not to say money. The circumstances had grown even worse now, as Bhau experienced to his cost later on. There was no valid reason to believe that the circumstances would have been different in the present campaign. But Bhau felt confident of overcoming any difficulty and crossed the Chambal to Dholpur,[45] which in those times was not a Jat capital but a place of pilgrimage.

The Maratha army crossed the Chambal on 8th June, and encamped near the Muchakunda-tirth[46] near Dholpur. The whole army went through the ceremony of a holy bath and sojourned for a few days there. An eclipse of the sun on the 13th of June[47] added to the merit of the pilgrimage in this holy place. The delay caused by the performance of the rites of pilgrimage frustrated Bhau's original plan of crossing over the Jamuna before the rains near Agra into Govindpant Bundele's districts and attacking Abdali from that base. Agra was only some twenty-five miles distant from the Maratha camp between the Chambal and the Gambhira, alias Banaganga, river. But Bhau was unable to cross that small river and reach Agra for about a month more. The monsoon had set in somewhat early that year, and the small river was in spate. On his left hand was the Parvati, in front the Gambhira and at the back the Chambal. The region is extremely uneven. At every hundred yards there is a ravine, a continuous up and down. The land is sandy and the rivers and streams, though shallow, spread over for miles across the banks. It is difficult to set foot in the bed of the river and there is not enough water for boats to cross. In fact, no boats are available on those streams, for after a few days the water is completely drained away and only level sands, yellow and white in colour, are left to act as witnesses for the temporary floods. The whole camp must have suffered terribly because camping in those regions looked almost impossible.

Though Sadashivrao Bhau could not cross the insignificant river Gambhira, he was able to meet Shinde and Holkar and discuss with them the future problems and line of action, as both of them were encamping on the same side of the Gambhira in the vicinity of Keravli. The first to see Bhau was Gangoba Chandrachud, Holkar's Diwan, on 15th June.[48] Gangoba be-

45 RAJ. 1.199.
46 *Bhau Bakhar* p. 113.
47 13th of June was 30 Jyestha, Autobiography of Nana Phadnis, K. *Patre Yadi* 192.
48 RAJ. 1.203.

longed to that generation of the Marathas which grew up with Bajirao's conquests in Malwa. He was the confidential man of Malharrao and had perfect faith[49] in the wisdom of his master.

Malharrao Holkar seems to have purposely sent Gangoba to meet Bhau first and sound him in respect of his future policy and temper. Malharrao himself met Bhau along with Janakoji Shinde, a week later, on the 22nd of June.[50] No difference of opinion is reported at this meeting which seems to have ended amicably, thus belying the purposive colourful writing of the Marathi chronicles. At the end of the month, Surajmal Jat and the Wazir Ghazi-ud-din saw Sadashivrao Bhau and discussed the future line of action.[51] The plan at the beginning of July was still to cross over the Jamuna into the Doab by building a bridge of boats. But even this plan failed because of the rising waters of the Jumuna. In fact Bhau's slow march from the Deccan added four additional months of the monsoon to the Panipat campaign, and lowered the vitality and morale of the Maratha army thereby. From the tone of a letter written at this juncture, there does not seem to be any difference of opinion between Bhau and his sardars or Surajmal Jat.[52] The total strength of the Maratha army is given as seventy to eighty thousand while Abdali-Ruhela strength is reported as sixty thousand. The balance was to be decided by the joining in of Shuja-ud-daulah to either side. Shuja's army is reported as twenty thousand, with a very strong park of artillery. Besides, his army was one on permanent footing and therefore best trained, best equipped and altogether more efficient than that of the others. It was regularly well paid and therefore contented. Naro Shankar and Ramaji Anant Dabholkar,[53] Janakoji's Diwan, had been despatched as special ambassadors to Shuja as a last resort to induce him to come over to the Maratha side by offering him any terms he would choose to ask.[54] But he finally decided against the Marathas and proceeded to meet Abdali at Ramgad. Bhau at once changed his plan of crossing into the Doab and arrived at Gau Ghat to the north-east of Sikandara where the great Akbar lies buried. This place is some ten miles to the north-west of Agra on the bank of the Jamuna. There the Maratha army halted and bathed in the holy waters on the new-moon day of Ashadha, which fell on 12th July, 1760.[55] Thence Bhau proceeded to Mathura where he encamped on the 15th of July.[56] Thence he sent advanced troops to lay siege to Delhi, then commanded by Yakub Ali Khan, a cousin of the Durrani Wazir Shah Wali Khan.[57] He had only a small force, not more than two thousand strong. The rest of the camp with women in it went on performing the pilgrim's rites at Mathura and Brindavan. Nana Fadnis, who was accompanying Bhau with his wife and mother, indulged in the holy pilgrimage to his heart's content,

49 *SPD* 2.116.
50 Raj. 1.217; *SPD* 2.127.
51 *Purandare* 1.387.
52 Ibid.
53 Raj. 1.208.
54 *Purandare* 1.387.
55 *Bhau Kaifiyat* p. 9.
56 Raj. 1.217.
57 Ibid. 1.222, 223.

and rapturously describes it in his "Autobiography."[58] Bhau's wife Parvatibai, Mehendale's wife Lakshmibai, and some other women of high status had accompanied the army mainly with a view to perform the pilgrimages in the great safety of big camps fully provided with every necessity of life. The time of Maratha encampment at Mathura coincided with the Hindu intercalary month of Shravana, deemed the most holy especially near the scene of Krishna's childhood.

As discussed previously, Surajmal Jat and Ghazi-ud-din were of the same opinion as that of Malharrao Holkar in not proceeding to Delhi with the whole camp, but to keep the base of operations behind and to carry on the campaign against Abdali with unencumbered troops. But Bhau had decided, probably with the full concurrence of the Peshwa, to follow the new mode of warfare based on infantry tactics. He prepared to take Delhi and make it a base. Surajmal was not against the idea of occupying Delhi but he wanted it to be handed over to him as a keeper, and wished Ghazi-ud-din to be made a Wazir. After the assassination of Alamgir II, his son, the fugitive prince Ali Gauhar had crowned himself as Emperor in Bihar. He had naturally dismissed Ghazi-ud-din from the chancellorship and offered it to Shuja, for he could not allow his father's murderer to continue in the high office. Ghazi-ud-din had tried to strengthen his hands by the expedient of taking a young prince out of the imperial prison and crowning him Emperor with the title of Shah Jahan Sani and getting himself appointed as his Wazir. But his plan was miscarried by Dattaji's defeat and death in the preceding year, and he was now a fugitive at Surajmal's Court. Bhau had to act cautiously and take into account the general voice of the populace in the Mughal dominions. The Peshwa had not directly protested against Ghazi-ud-din's acts of foul murder and to that extent tried not to antagonise him as he had been a creation of the Marathas. But it was necessary to guard against Najib's propaganda and, therefore, Bhau could not approve of Surajmal's proposal to acknowledge Ghazi-ud-din as Wazir. Bhau also wanted to keep the office open in order to tempt Shuja to the Maratha side, if he could by any means be won over. Bhau, therefore, asked the Jat Raja and Ghazi-ud-din to accompany him to Delhi and help him in conquering and settling it. He sent Janakoji Shinde, Balvantrao Mehendale and Malharrao Holkar with eight thousand troops in advance on 21st July, 1760. This party reached Delhi on the 25th and at once took possession of the city without firing a shot. In the first surprise onslaught some fifty Marathas even succeeded in entering the inner citadel by scaling the walls, but instead of at once proceeding to the gates and trying to open them so as to make the whole army enter in, they foolishly engaged in loot and therefore gave time to Yakub Ali Khan, Abdali's keeper, to bring his forces to the scene and drive them out. Balvantrao's pride and impetuousness are illustrated in this event. He seems to have at once despatched a courier to Bhau who was following, with the main Maratha camp, to inform him of his victory, and Bhau rewarded the camel-rider for bringing in the good news. At the end of the day, however, Balvantrao had to retreat to his camp

---

58 Autobiography of Nana Phadnis, *Patre Yadi*, 192.

outside the city and place guns around the citadel. Bhau himself had advanced by this time from Mathura and was encamping at the famous serai at Chhatah. Now he advanced in haste via Hodal and Palwal and reached Delhi on 31st July. By this time the small party of Afghans under Yakub Ali Khan had been battered in the citadel and now with the coming of Ibrahim Khan's park of artillery, they found it impossible to continue the struggle and sued for peace. They were allowed to march out and go back to Abdali with their arms and baggage. Their number was only eight hundred.[59] The Marathas occupied the Red Fort on the 1st of August and celebrated their first victory amidst jubilations. Bhau himself seems to have sojourned there for a few days to arrange for the administration of the palace, city and the fort till he moved to Shalimar Gardens to the north-west of Delhi. He appointed Naro Shankar as the guardian of the palace and the city with six thousand troops made up of cavalry and infantry. Baloji Palhande was made the keeper of the fort.

Sadashivrao Bhau's camp at Delhi after the first fortnight was near the Shalimar Gardens watered by the famous Ali Mardan Khan canal. The place is still very charming, filled with the fragrance of the blossoms of the *lucat* trees during September and October. The water pavilions of the luxurious Mughal Emperors are still to be seen there with their mur paintings of birds and flowers, though in a dilapidated condition. Already three conquerors, namely, Nadir Shah, Ahmad Shah and Raghunathrao, had lived in them during two decades. Now Bhau had occasion to halt there.

Though from the military point of view the possession of Delhi was no great gain, it restored the prestige of the Maratha name. Ahmad Shah was, at this time, camping at Anupshahar on the Ganges but he was unable to send any succour to his nominee, Yakub Ali Khan.[60] Shuja-ud-daulah was actually encamping just on the opposite side of the Jamuna[61] but he was also helpless to do anything in the matter. Perhaps they knew that it was impossible to face Ibrahim Khan's artillery and therefore remained silent. In the popular mind, however, the Maratha prestige, lost and lowered by the previous year's events, was completely restored. Shuja, who had willingly joined Abdali, began to waver in his resolution.[62] He began to exert himself in the peace-move. The Indian allies of Ahmad Shah Abdali in this campaign had joined their forces with his as a lesser evil only. The trans-Gangetic Ruhelas under the leadership of the sagacious Hafiz Rahmat had no love lost for Najib Khan, whose faithlessness and unscrupulous dealings they would not approve. The lame Ahmad Khan Bangash was always shaky in his resolution, never being sure which side to choose. His situation was always precarious as his district of Farukkhabad was situated amidst the more powerful states of Oudh, the Ruhelas, the Marathas and the Jats. Though weak, Ahmad Khan was not unselfish either. He would side with the Marathas with a view to gain some

59 *Bhau Kaifiyat* p. 9. RAJ. 1.223.

60 ELLIOT. 8.147.

61 RAJ. 1.224.

62 Ibid. 1.191

portion of Shuja's dominions or the land of the Ruhelas. When not threatened by Shuja and when the Maratha armies were not in his neighbourhood, he would not shirk from invading and occupying the Maratha districts in the lower Doab.[63] He would never offend any party by his words and always tried to keep himself on speaking terms with all. Ahmad Khan had come to Abdali's camp but seeing that there was no work there for three months of the rains he and also the Ruhelas, except Najib, left for their homes with Abdali's permission.[64] From their homes they kept on writing to Bhau that they had joined Abdali under duress. Bhau seems to have misjudged their motives as they were always keeping up a correspondence with Bhau and promising to join him under certain conditions. It is difficult to say whether they actually feared the consequences of joining Abdali as against the Marathas or were merely fooling him this time so as to save their dominions from the armies of Govindpant Bundele and Gopalrao Ganesh Barve. But Bhau was trying his best to take advantage of the enforced delay and hoping to separate some of his allies from Abdali. Many Afghan sardars wrote to Bhau that they would detach themselves from Abdali as soon as they found an opportunity to do so. But Abdali kept a strict watch over them and never once allowed them to move away from his camp. Bhau even tried to detach some of the Afghan tribes who were accompanying Abdali with the hope of loot but were not directly employed by him, and were actually starving. Ahmad Shah's Durrani troops were at this time living on loot. Najib was supplying Abdali with 200 maunds of grain and 15,000 rupees cash every day for his aid. But this was sufficient for his personal slaves only. Bhau had ordered Govindpant to engage them if they came over to his side and to send them to Bhau's camp if necessary.[65] He had asked Govindpant to remain where he was and try to move in such a way as to make Shuja and the Ruhelas leave Abdali's camp for defending their threatened territories.[66] But the terror of Abdali's forces was such that it made any move on Govindpant's part well-nigh impossible. The Maratha officials in the Doab seem to have been completely demoralised by the experience of the past four years, and no one was ready to take any risk in the matter. This is clear from Sadashivrao Bhau's order to Govindpant in the middle of August to forbid any Maratha employed under him to send back his effects to the Deccan, as Bhau had come to know of such a move.[67] It meant that the Marathas living in those regions were not very sanguine about the outcome of the war and feared the worst. This explains the cause of the non-compliance of Sadashivrao Bhau's orders by Govindpant and Gopalrao Barve. They were unable to do anything vigorously or enthusiastically because the overwhelming majority of the Maratha employees had completely lost heart.

Notwithstanding such sombre atmosphere Sadashivrao Bhau was going on with his plans of meeting Abdali after the rains. Though the hope of solving the political problem of the governance of India without resort to arms was

63 Ibid. 1.236.
64 Ibid. 1.237.
65 Ibid. 1.257.
66 Ibid. 1.242.
67 Ibid. 1.228.

very remote, still peace parleys continued throughout. Najib Khan's proposal forwarded through Shuja was to hand over the regions beyond Sarhind to Abdali and hand over the Delhi affairs into his hands. Shuja wanted the Chancellorship as well as the command over the army of the Mughal Empire.[68] But Najib would never allow the military command to pass out of his hands. Bhau's idea was to fix the boundary at Attock, leaving Peshawar and Kabul to Abdali, while the imperial defence would be left as it was, meaning through the agency of the Marathas. But Bhau was not obstinate on any point. He knew that no one could have everything his own way. In diplomacy "give and take" is necessary and inevitable, and therefore he still hoped to find a *via media* out of the *impasse.*

The condition in the middle of September was as follows: There was no money left in the government treasury nor was any forthcoming from the revenue collectors like Govindpant Bundele. Bhau knew the economic condition of the region surrounding Delhi very well and understood the difficulties of recovering government dues in the then conditions of northern India. Besides the military trouble due to war with Abdali, nature also had some say in the affair. Hail storms and certain pests had that year destroyed the crops in many parts and there was a consequent deficit in revenue collection.[69] The dismissal of old collectors like Naro Shankar and his brother and recently of Mahadaji Govind Kakirde[70] appointed in his place, had adversely affected the Maratha revenues in Bundelkhand. Bhau also suspected the sincerity of the collectors who, he thought, were withholding payments with a view to take advantage of the difficulties of the government.[71] They would pay after the event instead of before it, as they were not sure of the result of the war and hoped to profit thereby. As the army was starving and not even a week's payment out of the month could be made to them, Bhau had recourse to the politically disastrous action of taking out the silver ceiling of the Diwan-i-khas, and minting it into money. He was able to secure only nine lakhs by this process and thereby feed his army for one month only. It seems this action was tom-tomed as insulting to the Mughal throne by the Muslim partisans of Najib, and it inflamed the Muslim population in the surrounding regions against the Marathas. As a matter of fact, the Wazir Ghazi-ud-din had already taken out a part of that very ceiling previously when he was in need of money, and Bhau was not the first vandal to touch it as made out by partisan historians.[72] But none seemed to have noticed the Wazir's act while all flared up against Bhau's behaviour. When the famous peacock-throne of Shah Jahan was taken away by Nadir Shah or when the whole palace and its inmates were completely stripped of their effects by Abdali, none seemed to have thought these as an insult to the Mughal throne then, possibly because the spoliators were devout Muslims.

68 *Purandare* 1.389.
69 *Shinde* 1.222; *Purandare* 1.386.
70 *Satara* 2.294; *Dabholkar Mss.* 152.
71 *SPD* 27.232.
72 Ibid. 27.257.

Bhau's difficulties were increased by the Peshwa's ignorance of northern Indian affairs. It was customary for the Maratha army to subsist on the land they marched through; but, after experience, the people of the regions through which they marched had become wiser than before, and left nothing on the spot to be carried away by the Marathas. Bhau had himself taken Raghunathrao to task for not being able to defray the expenditure of his campaign, and now he could not possibly ask for funds from the Deccan. The stress of circumstances, however, obliged even the proud Bhau to beg for funds. The Peshwa first ordered the revenue collectors in the north to pay half the revenues to Bhau. This order only facilitated equivocation by the delaying collectors. They would write to the Peshwa that Bhau had taken the whole revenue from them and write to Bhau that they had sent the whole money to the Deccan. Bhau, therefore, over-riding the Peshwa's orders, asked the collectors to send the whole amount to him only. Still no money was forthcoming from anybody. Bhau had received two lakhs from Govindpant and eighty thousand from Baburao Koner of Jhansi. This was all he was able to receive at Delhi. While Bhau was besieged at Panipat, Govindpant brought four lakhs and twenty thousand to Delhi at the beginning of December, only a quarter of which reached Bhau's camp in safety. Besides Govindpant, some other collectors like Gopal Keshav of Bhander (*SPD*, 29-12) also seem to have forwarded their collections to Delhi after Bhau's move to Kunjpura. The capture of Delhi had placed an additional burden on Bhau's depleted treasury because he had now to provide for the palace-expenditure which came to more than a lakh per month.

There is some ground for suspicion that Bhau's plans were being obstructed by certain forces in Poona, antagonistic to him. Gopikabai, the wife of the Peshwa, always feared, it seems, the complete usurpation of power by Bhau as he was already the sole administrator. The Peshwa was every day growing weaker and weaker both physically and morally. This fact also enhanced the lady's fears. She, as well as the Peshwa's advisers in Poona, especially the wily Sakharam Bapu, who it should be noted, was with the Peshwa in the Deccan and had not accompanied Vishwasrao to the north, as wrongly stated by Sir Jadunath,[73] seem to have been responsible for advising the Peshwa to withhold any more help to Bhau for fear of his increasing power. Sakharam Bapu was perhaps the cleverest brain in the Poona Court of those times. He was from very early days a sort of rival to Bhau in diplomatic matters. The Peshwa seems to have used Bapu as a tool to keep a balance of power at the Poona Court. Bhau's ways were open and straightforward. Bapu's conduct was exactly the reverse. The two could not go together with these contrary dispositions. Sakharam Bapu had, therefore, always sided with the party opposite to Bhau. He accompanied Raghunathrao in his north Indian campaigns as his chief adviser and administrator. Though Raghunathrao as the master cannot be absolved from the blame, the chief responsibility for the financial mismanagement of his campaigns should be properly placed on Sakharam Bapu's shoulders. Being conscious of his share in the guilt,

73 *Fall* 2.240 (foot-note)

Bapu naturally must have come to loggerheads with Bhau when the final accounts of the campaigns came to be settled.

Peculation was quite rampant in those days in official circles and the Maratha state was no exception to the rule. Profiteering at the cost of government was thought to be no sin and was a normal part of a wise man's living. While some of the generals and diplomats and administrators waxed fat, the state languished for want of money. The Peshwa's government perhaps suffered more than the other governments through this mischief, because the ruder Maratha generals were more grabbing and the selfish and brainy Brahmin accountants and collectors were clever at figures. To spite Bhau now, Bapu must have taken full advantage of his difficulties in tutoring the Peshwa against him. Bhau's advisers and assistants in this campaign were also rivals of Bapu at the Poona Court. Trimbak Sadashiv alias Nana Purandare and Balvantrao Mehendale were not well disposed towards him; Nana Purandare was on almost inimical terms with Bapu.[74] In short, Sakharam Bapu belonged to the party of critics of Sadashivrao's policy. One is, therefore, led to believe in the truth of that one line commentary copied and reproduced in Khare I,[75] which also explains to some extent the attitude of the Peshwa towards the Delhi campaign of Sadashivrao Bhau as reported by Naro Gangadhar from the Peshwa's camp in the Deccan.[76]

Sadashivrao Bhau, writing from Delhi in the middle of September 1760 to his intimate friend, Dhondo Malhar Purandare, states that there is no difference of opinion between him and the two sardars Shinde and Holkar. It means that the dramatic episode of Surajmal described in detail in the *Bakhar* is all imaginary and an after-thought. Honest difference of opinion about the policy to be followed against Abdali might be there, but the cause of his abruptly leaving Delhi without taking leave of Bhau must be his disappointment. Bhau would not place the city in the charge of the Jat, but appointed Naro Shankar as the guardian of the city and the palace, instead. Surajmal was, no doubt, very shrewd and cautious. His advice to keep the main camp with its heavy encumbrances back in the Gwalior region was sound. But he was personally very selfish and always tried to secure his ends under the cloak of humbleness. This time he wished to follow the same path and set himself up as a regent in Delhi with the help of the Marathas. His past behaviour towards the Marathas was neither very honest nor consistent. After Raghunathrao's campaign against him in 1754, he occupied the lands in the Doab surrounding Kol-Ramgad during their absence from the north in 1755.[77] In 1756 he would not risk his troops against Abdali by joining Antaji Manakeshwar, though he took full advantage of Antaji's cover to guard his dominions and save his forts. When Raghunathrao again returned to the north, he still kept himself studiously aloof and saved his skin. Meanwhile he had reaped the harvest out of Maratha weakness due to Jayapa's assassination. He suddenly descended upon the strong imperial hill-fort of Alwar which guarded

74 *Purandare* 3.82.
75 KHARE 1.25.
76 *SPD* 2.133.
77 *Hingne* 1.159.

the route from Delhi to Jaipur, and occupied it without much trouble. When Dattaji returned in 1758 with a strong force he again assumed humbleness and tried to make a common cause with him in the spoliation of the Mughal empire. He had kept on good terms with the Shinde family since the time he was saved by Jayapa Shinde against Malharrao's fury at Kumbher, and thus shielded himself against Malharrao's exactions. But he respected neither friend nor foe when it was a question of aggrandizing himself at the cost of others. For the present he had made common cause with Shinde and Holkar, fully knowing that they would not be troublesome to him after their late defeats at the hands of Abdali. On the other hand they were useful to him in meeting the calls of Sadashivrao Bhau on his resources. Now finding himself unable to fulfil his life's ambition of governing Delhi, he silently walked away from Bhau's camp with a show of anger at Bhau's policy. Bhau certainly felt the loss of his help at this crucial time and tried to recall him. Mahipatrao Chitnis, Gangoba Chandrachud and Ramaji Anant were sent after him to bring him back.[78] This proves that Bhau had no intention of insulting him as is made to appear in the *Bhau Bakhar*. Nor was he remiss in trying to win him over with assurances. But it looks as if the Jat Raja was thoroughly selfish and left the Maratha camp, ostensibly on account of a difference in outlook on matters of policy, but really to save himself from Bhau's demands and importunities due to the starving condition of his men and animals. Throughout the Panipat campaign, Bhau was never once suspicious of the Jat's attitude towards the Marathas, but always hoped for good behaviour from him. Though he had openly consented not to help[79] Bhau in his diplomatic talks with Najib and Shuja as Abdali's emissaries, with a view to excuse himself from paying tribute to the Afghan monarch, Surajmal did not do anything antagonistic to the Maratha interests, but on the other hand considerably helped them by allowing provisions and money to pass through his territory unmolested.[80] There seems to have been talk of Surajmal's son, Jawahirmal, coming to Bhau's help with the Jat forces at the beginning of October. When Prince Javan Bakht was proclaimed on 10th October and the seals of his father were brought into use, the Jat Raja became finally reconciled to the Maratha side.[79] All these facts refute the criticism of Bhau's behaviour in his dealings with Surajmal Jat. His humane behaviour and the monetary help he afforded to the Maratha fugitives after Panipat completely belies the story so dramatically related in the chronicle.

As related above, the peace parleys were dragging on all along, but without sincerity on either side. Ahmad Shah had changed his camp of thatched huts at Anupshahar on the Ganges at the beginning of August.[81] This was first a countermove to Bhau's occupation of Delhi, and was also due to the unhealthiness of the place. Thousands of his horses and camels succumbed to the heavy monsoon in the low-lying Gangetic valley.[82] His first thought was

78 *SPD* 27.258.
79 Parasnis *Persian Akhbars Mss.*
80 Raj. 1.259.
81 Ibid. 1.226-7, 246.
82 *SPD* 2.131; Raj. 6.404.

to move north to the strong fort of Sukartal and remain there. At the beginning of October, he was reported to have left his camp at Sambharam Serai and moved to Ahmad Ganj.[79] But soon after he came to Shahadra, opposite to Delhi on the bank of the Jamuna, and encamped there with Shuja and Najib. A distant cannonade was also sometimes indulged in by both the armies from the two banks of the river. It could not be very effective from a distance of more than a mile with the artillery of those times. Besides, none of the parties was willing to waste its ammunition for merely terrifying without military effect. Internal trouble was also brewing amongst Abdali's allies. Shuja and Najib were strange bed-fellows whom only destiny had brought together. Najib had promised that no demands for money would be made on Shuja if he joined Abdali's camp. This hope was belied, for the hungry and grabbing Afghans tried to make encroachments on him, knowing full well that he was rich. This led to a quarrel between Shuja and the Durranis. Shuja felt himself deceived by the false promise of Najib and was almost in a repentant mood.[83] The Abdali troops, on the other hand, were reluctant to continue their stay in India amidst misery and destitution, with little hope of earning anything in the future.

Bhau had sent one Bhavanishankar as a Vakil to Shuja across the Jamuna, and Shuja also sent his Vakil to Bhau in return.[84] It seems from Kashiraj's account that he also accompanied Raja Devidatta, Shuja's envoy. But there is no corroboration of the same in Marathi correspondence, a fact which makes one suspicious about the truth of his narrative. As Bhau was not satisfied with Raja Devidatta, he sent him back with Bhavanishankar. This Bhavanishankar is scarcely mentioned anywhere in the Marathi narrative as a person of importance. Kashiraj says he was a native of Aurangabad and belonged to his caste. As the Brahmins of Aurangabad had taken to Persian studies, they were in great demand at the courts of various north Indian potentates who had any dealings with the Marathas. Knowing both Persian and Marathi, they were able to correspond and interpret between the Maratha and other courts, and settled in various capitals. The Hingne family was also engaged by the Peshwa for the same qualifications. Bhavanishankar first came in contact with the Peshwa in his dealings with Shah Nawaz Khan at the Nizam's court, and seems to have spread his influence over Bhau also.[85] As Nana Fadnis in his "Autobiography" adversely comments on Bhavanishankar's influence over Bhau and expresses himself in disapproving terms about his conduct, it may be taken as a general opinion of the Maratha camp about the man. Bhau over-rode the opinions of intimates like Balvantrao Mehendale and Nana Purandare and completely put his faith in Bhavanishankar's advice, which was also the main cause of Bhau's decision to follow Ibrahim Khan Gardi's French-tutored mode of warfare. Perhaps, even in the successful Udgir campaign,[86] Bhau had followed Bhavanishankar's advice and the thundering success in it had established Bhavanishankar in Bhau's confidence. Whatever the fact, his conduct of peace-parleys at this juncture did not prove successful as Najib-ud-daulah threw every obstacle in the way. Mal-

83 RAJ. 1.236, 246.
84 *Satara* 2.297.

harrao and Surajmal were also keeping correspondence with Shuja and seeking his advice as to the future line of action. Shuja advised the Marathas to follow only the traditional mode of guerilla warfare, and to Surajmal he advised to return to his own country. To Bhau, Shuja professed friendship, while declining to leave Abdali's camp, and promised to help the Maratha cause by giving his best advice. From Kashiraj's account it seems Bhau had receded back a great deal on his original terms one by one. As a last resort, he was ready to surrender the Panjab upto Sarhind, but wanted Abdali no more to interfere in the Delhi affairs. But, as mentioned above, nothing came out of this boring of the mountain, not even a mouse. Both sides seem to have put their final faith in a decision by arms. From the beginning, Bhau was ready to allow Abdali to return to his own country if he so desired. But if he really had a mind to gain that end, it would have been better had he never crossed the Chambal. In that case Abdali would possibly have left India through sheer weariness. But with Bhau's big army advanced to Delhi, it was impossible for Abdali to retreat without offering a battle. From that point of view it would have been better for Sadashivrao Bhau to have turned his attention to Shuja's dominions and to have proceeded to Benares instead of Delhi. But unfortunately for the Marathas throughout their career, they had chosen the cockpit of Delhi as their fighting arena and ultimately lost their all in it.

Meanwhile the condition of the Maratha army deteriorated day by day. The bullocks of the artillery department died by hundreds and there were not enough left with strength to drag the guns.[87] Bhau had also ordered[88] both Govindpant and Gopalrao Barve to cross over the Ganges and threaten Shuja's and the Ruhela's territories. But Govindpant was unable to move, firstly, on account of the rains, and secondly, because the zamindars in the Doab and Bundelkhand had become defiant and treacherous, and there was no safety for the Maratha posts in those regions. Bhau had taken possession of all the main ghats between Agra and Kunjpura and blocked the crossings for the enemy. He had kept small patrols to guard the ferry-ghats and collected all the boats at Selimgad near Delhi. Though Bhau had now placed his main faith in the artillery of Ibrahim Khan,[89] still he could not recruit any Marathas for service in that department. He had to call the men from the enemy's territories to do such work.[90] Bhau seems to have called some European gunners from the eastern parts also. Many Portuguese, French, English and other European adventurers and renegades were at this time spread over India, ready to offer their services for good money. The war between the French and the English had detached a number of Frenchmen from Chandranagar and other places in Bengal. These were probably the persons Bhau was hoping to engage. But none of these projects materialized and only a certain number of Pathan followers of Ahmad Shah came over to the Maratha side, only to create confusion and disaster in the last fight.

85 Raj. 1.85.
86 *SPD* 25.279.
87 Raj. 1.231.
88 Ibid. 1.233, 237.
89 Ibid. 1.174.
90 Ibid. 1.176, 235.

CHAPTER IV

KUNJPURA

To UNDERSTAND Sadashivrao Bhau's campaign north of Delhi, it is necessary to acquaint oneself with the terrain on both sides of the river Jamuna. The whole of this area is one vast, continuous, sandy plain formed by the silt of the river. It is a gradually sloping plain from the north to the south, and just near the river-banks very slightly sloping towards the river. This plain is between seven and eight hundred feet above the sea-level on an average, with practically no hills worth the name. The rocky arm of the Aravalli Range, starting from Mount Abu north of Gujarat, extends just up to the north of Delhi city, and ends in the famous Ridge of Mutiny fame. This is the last rocky spot in the whole area. North of it one can see scarcely a stone anywhere. The very few elevated spots to be found in this even terrain look more like mounds than hills, being made up of sandy rubble, and one sometimes suspects these of being the handiwork rather of man than of nature. Where such elevated spots occur, they are sure to be occupied by towns if sufficiently large, or otherwise by a temple, a mosque, a Sadhubava or a Pir. Sonepat and Panipat, reputed to be dating from the Mahabharata War, along with Indrapat or the oldest Delhi, are situated on and alongside small hillocks, less than a hundred feet above the surrounding level plain. Both were walled towns with small citadels on the hill tops.

The main features to be noted for the history of the eighteenth century in this region were that the region was bounded by the river Jamuna on the east, and by the imperial Ali Mardan Khan Canal (Shah-nahar) on the west. The imperial road with the Kos minars or pillars at an interval of two-and-a-half English miles passed through the Doab formed by these natural and man-made aqueducts. The road ran parallel to the east of the canal at a distance of about five miles on an average, but it passed by the towns of Sonepat, Panipat and Karnal. The canal ended in the Delhi palace, after supplying the famous Shalimar gardens to the north-west of the city with ample water. It had been built to meet the needs of the imperial family in the main, but was probably utilized by others also to the extent possible after fulfilling the requirements of the palace.

The area along the canal and beyond was thickly wooded while that by the side of the river was boggy and marshy, overgrown with rushes and other water-plants for miles together. There are fords at a distance of about five miles on the river at present, but these were probably fewer in former days, when irrigation canals had not drained the river dry. There were ferries and bridges of boats, however, at convenient and necessary places. The river remained unfordable during the rainy season and sometime after. At some places where the river had divided itself into several channels with sandy banks and islands between, fording was easier and these places became the high roads of movement and commerce like those near Kunjpura and Budhia. Where the river-bank was steep and the water deep, crossing was very difficult, if not impossible.

Sadashivrao Bhau, after the first fortnight of August in Delhi, moved[1] his camp from Kalkadevi to the south of the city on the bank of the Jamuna to the west of the city near Seetaram's serai beyond the canal, and this camp seems to have extended upto the Shalimar gardens to the north-west, thus covering an area of more than three miles in length from north to south. Here he lived for almost seven weeks, till he began his northward march to Kunjpura in the first week of October. The Maratha army suffered great privations[2] in this camp. The food supply of Delhi was derived from the eastern Doab side in normal times. But this region was in the possession of Najib Khan and Abdali. Besides, the Jamuna was in flood making commercial intercourse difficult, if not impossible. Added to the food and fodder scarcity, there was the scarcity of money. No money was forthcoming from any source; neither from the revenue collectors of the Maratha lands in north India, nor from tribute, nor even from loans. Even men of position had to keep from starvation by selling their jewellery and other personal belongings.[3] The result was a great deterioration in the physical stamina of men and animals. It must have also told on the morale of the army, though in this case the cool courage and optimism of the commander-in-chief counteracted, to a great extent, the evil effects of the same.[4]

Placed in this quandary, Bhau had recourse to such things as taking out the silver ceiling of the Diwan-i-khas to coin money wherewith to pay a bare subsistence allowance to the troops as stated before.[5] But this was only a stop-gap. The nine lakhs of rupees derived from this vandalic source were just sufficient to feed the army for one month. During a period of three months, only two weekly payments to the soldiers had been made possible, so precarious was the situation. Nor was it possible, while the rains continued, to get out of this plight.

The future plans of Abdali were as yet inscrutable. The early setting in of the rains that year with the continuous high flood level of the Jamuna for four months had miscarried the earlier plans hatched by Sadashivrao Bhau to meet Abdali in a pitched battle. The waiting-time factor had gone against the Maratha anticipations. Shuja-ud-daulah's pusillanimous efforts to be on good terms with both the parties had at last resulted in his completely falling under the influence of the wily Najib. Even after going over to the side of Abdali, Shuja still continued his efforts for peace during the rainy season, but to no purpose. Nana Phadnis accuses him of chicanery, though the historian of Oudh vouchsafes his good intentions.[6] All the same, Bhau would not rely on such a broken reed and decided to open the campaign against Abdali by

---

1 RAJ. 6.404; *SPD* 27.258.
2 *SPD* 130, 131.
3 *Aitihasika Tippane* 1.14.
4 RAJ. 6.404.
5 *SPD* 27.257.
6 Ibid. 2.131: SRIVASTAVA. *Shuja*, 93.

first taking the offensive himself. His difficulties at Delhi obliged him to take this decision which was urged on him by all and sundry in the Maratha camp.

Before he could continue his march, Bhau thought it wise to make a political move to counteract the anti-Maratha propaganda of Najib and men of his ilk. He had already estranged Wazir Ghazi-ud-din and his supporter Surajmal Jat by his non-committal attitude towards their aspirations and designs. All his approaches to Shuja had proved futile. It became necessary for him now to give a demonstrable proof of his ultimate intentions. So, setting aside the boy Emperor, Shah Jahan III (elevated to that dignity by Ghazi-ud-din after the murder of Alamgir II in the previous year), Bhau proclaimed the wandering Prince Ali Gauhar as Emperor with the title of Shah Alam II. In his unavoidable absence, his son Prince Javan Bakht, residing at Delhi, was installed as Vali-Ahad or Crown Prince and Vicar of the absentee Emperor on 10th October 1760.[7] Mints struck new coins in the new Emperor's name, and his seals were also prepared and brought into use. The ceremonies and processions connected with these acts were seen through by Nana Purandare and Satvoji Jadhavrao, who had been specially deputed by Bhau for the purpose while encamped at Lalera, three miles to the south of Gannaur[8] while on his way to Kunjpura. The office of the Wazir is said to have been conferred on Shuja *in absentia,* but there is no mention of this fact in Marathi correspondence and hence seems improbable.

The details of this occurrence in Delhi throw a flood of light on Maratha manners in politics. The puppet Emperor, Shah Jahan, was politely asked to vacate his seat as his days were over. This was perhaps the first time in Mughal history when an emperor had been set aside without violence to his person. The Prince Javan Bakht was escorted to the Juma Masjid by Bapuji Hingne, the Maratha envoy, who sat with the prince on the elephant, while Satvoji stood behind with peacock feathers, a sign of royal insignia, in his hand. The ex-Empress Zinat Mahal, the grand-mother of the prince, was civilly asked to pay 25 lakhs from her privy purse for the expenses, but she paid only 5 lakhs. The Marathas never set their hands on the persons of the royal household to get money, like the Afghans of Abdali or the Persians of Nadir Shah. The grateful ex-Empress took it upon herself to inform Abdali of these proceedings and tried her best to bring about a settlement between him and the Marathas, by forwarding the Maratha draft treaty to him with her recommendations and consent. The good result of this action was seen in the satisfaction of Surajmal who was now convinced of the Maratha intentions and henceforward helped the Marathas, though he could not join them with his army. The Afghan rule in the Panjab was challenged by the rebellious Sikhs who wholeheartedly came over to the Maratha side. *They proclaimed Bhau Sahib as the coming ruler with a beat of drums, and devoutly prayed for his victory in Lahore. They beseeched their Guru Sahib to punish Abdali for his misdeeds.* Khwajah Mirza Khan, the son-in-law of Adina Beg, with the Maratha troops under Krishnaji Pawar stationed at Jammu, invaded Gujrat-

7 RAJ. 1.258-9: PARASNIS' *Persian Akhbars* (unpublished).
8 Ibid. 1.259.

Shahdaula and cleared the regions upto Attock. In the Jalandar Doab, the Sikhs firmly established themselves, driving out the Afghan posts. Alasingh, the founder of the Patiala State, promised to join Bhau with his troops. Thus, at the beginning of October 1760, Abdali's hold over the Panjab had been completely lost, but for a post here and there. Abdus Samad Khan found his position in Sarhind untenable and was reported to be coming down to Kunjpura on the Jamuna on his way to join Abdali in the Doab. *(Persian Akhbar-MS.)*

From the news available in the *Persian Akhbar* dated 15-10-1760, it seems as if Abdali also had become weary of waiting and was ready to solve the political tangle by negotiations. Up till then, Shah Abdullah Darvesh Pirzada had come as the envoy of Abdali. But now it was thought necessary that these roundabout ways should cease and the plenipotentiaries of the two sides, if not the chiefs themselves, should meet face to face to have a personal talk before taking the final plunge. It was suggested that the rendezvous should be near the Buradi Ghat, strongly guarded by Damaji Gaikawad; the chiefs should meet in midstream, each in his own boat, standing in juxtaposition. But this meeting never took place, however, as Bhau had to hurry up to Kunjpura so as to cut off Abdus Samad Khan.

The plan of marching to Kunjpura was maturing in the mind of Bhau for more than a month,[9] but the rainy season had delayed the project. The Deccan bullocks, connected with the artillery department, had suffered most from the rains. Many of them died, probably on account of the northern Indian climate being unsuitable to them. Bhau had sent an express letter to Govind Ballal for sending 500 bullocks, as early as 17th August, and had also called for 400 Pathans or northern Indian men capable of enrolment in the artillery on 27th August.[10] He took over all the ghats on the Jamuna and made arrangements for guarding the same. This had made Abdali powerless to do anything in the matter. Nothing remained for him but to wait till the subsidence of the river.

When Bhau started for Kunjpura in the first week of October, he had calculated that the water of the Jamuna would not subside for at least one month.[11] But his calculation seems to have been based on incorrect information. Two important persons of Bhau's office, writing three weeks before he wrote, calculate one month or even a fortnight as the period necessary for the river level to go down.[12] According to them, the water should have subsided by the middle of October, almost the time when Bhau wrote and started for Kunjpura. If we take the calculation of the two officers to be mere guess work and very rough, we cannot say the same thing of the written opinion of Balvantrao Mehendale, supposed to be the most intimate friend and adviser of Bhau during the Panipat campaign. Writing on 14th October he

9 Ibid. 1.237.
10 Ibid. 1.231, 237.
11 Ibid. 1.252.
12 *SPD* 2.130-31.

says, "Four to eight days are necessary for the river water to go down."[13] And Abdali actually crossed the river at Gauripur on 24th October.[14] It is impossible to account for this wide discrepancy in the information and calculation of the two most important personages in the Peshwa's army, the commander-in-chief and his first general. It is difficult to imagine that these two persons, living in the same camp or even as neighbours, should not have exchanged ideas and discussed the probabilities amongst themselves. But unfortunately for the Marathas, some such untoward thing seems to have happened. Bhau, basing his calculation on the idea that the river water would not go down before the second week of November, planned his campaign accordingly. His plan was to take Kunjpura, then proceed to Kurukshetra to perform the pilgrimage, seek allies amongst the Sikhs and the Jats of those regions[15] and then return in time to meet Abdali after refreshing his starved troops, horses, and other animals with the ample grain and fodder supplies of those fertile regions. This plan succeeded as far as the capture of Kunjpura was concerned, but failed in its second part: to obstruct Abdali while crossing the Jamuna.

The immediate cause which made Bhau hurry up to Kunjpura within a week was the news received from the Panjab as mentioned already. Abdus Samad Khan whom Abdali had kept back in the Panjab as the Faujdar of Sarhind, had come to Kunjpura with an army of ten thousand and more for carrying supplies to Abdali in the Doab. He was waiting there for the river to subside. It was necessary to defeat him before he could cross the Jamuna and strengthen Abdali's forces. Starting from his camp at Shalimar Bag, seven miles to the north of Delhi on 7th October, Bhau reached Lalera, three miles south of Gannaur on 8th October in the evening. He was at Panipat on the 14th and reached his destination on the evening of the 16th. Abdali who had full information of Bhau's movements, sent an army to aid his men at Kunjpura along the eastern bank of the Jamuna. But it had to stop opposite Kunjpura for want of transport. Viewing this additional peril, the Maratha army decided to storm the fort forthwith. Bhau sent for Ibrahim Khan Gardi who was lagging behind by one march. He came hurrying up on the night of the 16th and commenced the bombardment of the fort soon after his arrival, on the morning of the 17th.

The fort of Kunjpura lies seventy-eight miles to the north of Delhi, and is situated some two miles distant from the west bank of the Jamuna. It guarded one of the most frequented roads through the Doab to the Panjab. The river Jamuna to the south-east of Kunjpura, being divided into several channels, was easily fordable by men and animals. The important town of Karnal on the main imperial road lay only six miles to the west of it. The riverside of the fort was marshy and hence easily defensible. Nejabat Khan Ruhela was in possession of the fort and he had a few thousand footmen of his tribe with him to defend the fort. Abdus Samad Khan, Mian Qutb Shah and Momin Khan, the Ghilzai Sardar who had come from Sarhind, had with

13 *Ait. Tip.* 1.14.
14 RAJ. 1.260.
15 *SPD* 21.197.

them some seven thousand horse.[16] They were encamped outside the fort and tried to defend it to the utmost. But the musketry fire of the Gardis soon broke their resistance by fast withering away their ranks, and they tried to save themselves by entering the fort. Nejabat Khan was at first apprehensive of opening the fort gates to get them in, but had to yield to their entreaties and open the same. Taking advantage of this opportunity, the Marathas also followed behind them and forced themselves into the fort along with the Durranis. The Durrani horse and Ruhela footmen fought for some time but were ultimately overpowered by the Maratha arms and defeated with heavy slaughter. Four thousand Ghilzais were put to the sword[17] and the rest, taking grass in their mouths and uttering the words, "We are your cows,"[18] were allowed to go, after laying down their arms. The majority of the Ruhela footmen had been wounded together with Nejabat Khan, who died soon afterwards of his wounds. Momin Khan died in the battle from a bullet-shot. Abdus Samad Khan and Mian Qutb Shah were captured alive, beheaded after heaping insults on them and their heads paraded through the Maratha camp. Mian Qutb Shah was derided, cursed and insulted most, especially by Shinde's men, as he was responsible for the decapitation of Dattaji Shinde on the battlefield of Buradi, the previous year. Their bodies were exposed to be eaten up by vultures and jackals, no funeral rites being allowed them. The conversation between Qutb Shah and Bhau given in the *Bhau Bakhar* seems imaginary, as contemporary letters from Shinde's camp do not say a word hinting at such a thing. It has been fabricated to suit the dramatic tone of the whole of the *Bhau Bakhar*.

Bhau got some seven lakhs of rupees in cash, five thousand horses, camels and elephants, arms and the rest, as spoils. But the most opportune gain was of 10,000 *khandis* of wheat collected at this depot for the Abdali troops. Starvation in the Maratha army ended for the time being, as the troops were paid in kind instead of cash.[19] Horses and other animals also got fodder and grain. More important than this material gain was the revival of optimism in the Maratha army after a four months' period of doldrums, leading to a deterioration of morale. The prowess of the Gardi fire had been put to the test and proved up to the hilt.

Bhau spent a week at Kunjpura destroying the fortifications and arranging matters in the new light. He seems to have felt no apprehension of any impending danger as he ordered a march to Kurukshetra of at least a part of the army. While on his way to Kunjpura, Bhau's idea was to finish the work there in four days and then to cross the Jamuna by some upper ghat like that at Budhia, into Saharanpur. He had already seized practically all the boats on the Jamuna on which he could lay hands, and kept them together near the Selimgad fort on the bank of the Jamuna at Delhi with a view to making use of them in case of necessity. He had also kept pickets with small parties of soldiers to guard the main ghats over the Jamuna from

16 *Shinde* 3.234, 392; Raj 1.260, 265.
17 *Purandare* 1.391.
18 *Shinde* 3.234.
19 *SPD*. 21.197-8.

Agra to Kunjpura, a distance of nearly two hundred miles. Thus he had unwittingly lengthened his line of communication and taken a certain risk in proceeding to Kunjpura. Had he, after quickly finishing the job, crossed over the Jamuna into Saharanpur as intended, or, failing that, at once returned to Delhi, he would have been saved. But here his miscalculation about the fall in the level of the Jamuna waters proved wrong as we have already noted. The second factor which delayed the Maratha army was that after a long period of comparative starvation they had found themselves in a land of plenty, which the army was naturally reluctant to leave and return to barren Delhi. The third and the human factor which made Bhau delay his march was the encumbrance of a horde of women folk, family members and priests who had accompanied the army for performing distant and dangerous pilgrimages under its protection. Kurukshetra is less than thirty miles from Kunjpura and it was but natural that all the devout people in the army should wish to visit that holy place of the Mahabharata war where Lord Shri Krishna preached his philosophy of life to the hero Arjuna. But this natural desire resulted in an unforeseen calamity and thus proved a veritable Kurukshetra to the Marathas.

The Maratha army, after spending or rather wasting a week at Kunjpura, moved toward the holy place for one day, but before they could reach their destination, at the first halt for the night Bhau received the disquieting news of Abdali's beginning to cross the river, on 25th October.[20] He at once made up his mind and turned back toward Delhi with a view to intercepting Abdali before he crossed the river. But such a fully equipped army made up of three lakhs of people can move but slowly. All became disappointed and sullen as they missed by a hairbreadth the pilgrimage to Kurukshetra. They were still more scared by the news of Abdali's crossing the river and blocking their return. On the first day of their return march they halted near the ancient bridge at Karnal[21] for the night, the bridge over the famous canal of Firuz Shah Tughalaq and Ali Mardan Khan which flowed from the eastern to its western side. Because the editor of Bhau's *Kaifiyat* was unaware of the geography of these regions, he could not with confidence read the description in Modi script and the place of halt on the bridge. Though Bhau made a long march of fifteen miles for the day, the camp could not move as fast, so on the next day he could cover only eight miles, and on the third day came near Panipat. Here he heard the news that Abdali's army had completely crossed the river, bag and baggage, and was halting at Sonepat.

Bhau cautiously sent a party of five thousand men under Baji Hari Deshpande of Supa to meet and check the advance guard of Abdali and take a view of his camp and movement there. They were in the vicinity of Sonepat, resting unguardedly after a long march. Half of the party was composed of Shinde's men who had already known and experienced the scourge of the Durrani army. Their leader asked Baji Hari to be on his guard lest he should find himself surprised. But Baji Hari's inexperienced and unbeaten troops

20 *Raj.* 1.260.

21 *Bhau Kaifiyat* p. 12.

took the warning lightly and slept soundly on the plains, allowing their horses to roam in the green fields for grazing, and the unexpected attack came as forewarned. Shah Pasand Khan, one of Abdali's best captains of cavalry, suddenly pounced upon the sleeping party. Shinde's men had kept a picket on a tall tree watching for the danger. As soon as clouds of dust were seen at a distance the picket came down and cried aloud of the danger. Shinde's men who were on guard at once took to their horses and ran away.[22] Baji Hari's party found it impossible to get hold of their horses in the grazing field and it was some time before they could get them. In the meanwhile, men of Shah Pasand Khan came, seized as many horses of the Marathas as they could and cut down the horsemen. Very few were fortunate enough to escape and carrry back the news to Bhau. This event checked the further march southwards, and Bhau had to fall back on Panipat and begin encampment there.

We shall now turn to study Abdali's movements. He and his Indian allies were encamping on the opposite bank of the Jamuna near Delhi. Shuja-ud-daulah was the first to move to that place in the beginning of August and encamp to the south of the area near the grain mart of Patpatganj. The Ruhelas and Abdalis followed sometime later, probably at the end of the month. They encamped to Shuja's north, near Shahdhada. When Bhau came to Delhi at the beginning of August, he had encamped to the south of Delhi near the Kalkadevi Temple, just opposite to Shuja on the other bank. In September, Bhau moved his camp to the Shalimar gardens, seven miles to the north-west of Delhi amidst pleasant surroundings, and his army encamped to his south, to the west and north of the city. From these encampments the rival armies were eying each other inquisitively. They occasionally discharged their heavy long-range guns and threw some heavy cannon-balls into each other's camps just to create confusion and fear. But the river flowed roaringly between. None dare cross the river in the face of the other, though diplomats were individually going and coming and carrying on peace-talks. As Abdali had the fertile Doab at his back, and as the home lands of the Ruhelas were on the other side of the Ganges, his army was comparatively well supplied with the necessaries of life. To lighten the burden, he had allowed many of the Ruhela soldiers to return to their homes, asking them to keep themselves ready to return at the first call. The Maratha army, on the other hand, was living from hand to mouth. The whole of the surrounding area had been eaten up by the constant movements of the rival armies in the fields during the last seven years. The districts to the west of Delhi had been assigned as jagirs to the Baluch sardars of the Emperor. They were recalcitrant generally, and just then at loggerheads with the Marathas. Tukoji Holkar and Khandoji Kadam[22a] had been sent against them at the beginning of October. For getting the food stuffs from a distance the Marathas had to pay fancy prices to the Banjaras. Nana Phadnis, Bapuji Ballal Phadke,[22b] Balvantrao Mehendale and others, writing from Delhi during September and October, describe the woeful state of the Maratha army: "The horses have forgotten to chew the grain; the

---

22 *Bhau Bakhar* 0.126.
22a *Persian MS.*
22b *SPD* 2.130-1.

grain is selling at seven or eight seers a rupee. High-class people like us had to sell our gold and silver trinkets and live from the proceeds. The climate of Delhi has been found unsuitable to the Deccani oxen of the artillery department, and they are dying in hundreds." To escape from this dilemma, the Maratha army had moved to Kunjpura to feed themselves and their horses, with the consequence noted above.

When Bhau moved toward the north, Abdali also sent a party to accost him from the other side of the river; that party could not do anything to save their brethren on the other side and had to see with open eyes the fall of Kunjpura. They returned to Abdali who was chafing at the result. He at once issued orders to his army and his allies to be ready for the march. From Shahdhada he moved to Luni, thence he came to Baghpat, twenty miles north of Delhi, in search of a ford for crossing. But he searched in vain. He chided his Indian allies for not knowing the fords, but they pleaded their inability to find any. After two days' vain search, Ahmad Shah who was a devout Muslim, fasted in his agony and beseeched God to point out a ford and tried all the superstitious and religious methods of search. After getting an inspiration from that source he made his horsemen plunge into an unusual and less frequented part of the river and tried to cross. He succeeded in the trial, though a number of horsemen were carried away by the current before the exact line of crossing could be fixed by driving wooden stakes in the river on the two sides of the shallow passage and thus clearly lining the way. The place where he actually crossed is not given in histories, though all say that it was near Baghpat. A pontoon bridge used to be constructed at Baghpat in the fair season in those days as at present; but in the rainy season the place was not suitable for crossing as the river has a somewhat sharp fall here and consequently the stream turns into a torrent. Where the river divides itself into several streams and spreads over a wider area, it becomes easily fordable. Such a place Ahmad Shah seems to have found five miles to the north of old Baghpat near the village of Gauripur. This place is mentioned in the Bhau's ballad we have copied down from the bard of Siwa.[23] Because Ahmad Shah crossed at this place, he could come straight to Sonepat through Kheora and could elude the Maratha pickets placed at well-known crossings such as Baghpat.

Ahmad Shah could dare attempt this because he was experienced in crossing the rivers and knew all the intricacies connected with such crossings. The Marathas seem to have never taken to such daring. Big rivers seem to have blocked their way throughout their military career. They could never cross the Ganges without the help of local allies. A Najib-ud-daulah could always laugh at Dattaji and keep him waiting at the ford. Ahmad Shah, because he could take such a risk with confidence, was able to entrap the Maratha army under Sadashivrao Bhau. Bhau, on the other hand, could never perform such a feat, and hence had perforce to entrench himself at Panipat.

Ahmad Shah must have begun his crossing on the 24th October, as Bhau had received the news the next day at his first halt on the way to Kuru-

23 *BDCRI* 4.3. stanza 33.

kshetra. Abdali took three days to cross the river with all his army, cannon, elephants and other camp equipage. The place where he crossed was a little out of the way where there was no proper ghat for landing. The army had to cross the various streams and shallows over a distance of half a mile. Sometimes the horses would swim, at others they would wade through sands in knee-deep water. On the other side was the silt deposited by monsoon floods. Horses and men found themselves bogged in the soft mud. It was difficult, almost impossible, to take a step without sinking still deeper. This difficulty they overcame by cutting down the various water plants and rushes growing on the river-bank, and spreading them deep over the passage all along the route. When these had sunk into the mud, a thatchy road was naturally built over it by the trampling of thousands of horses and men. Had there been a daring and resourceful guard of a few thousand troops with a few guns of precision, a crossing would never have been possible. After safely reaching the other bank, Ahmad Shah at once sent a small party to drive away all the Maratha pickets on the western bank, and seize any boats they could find bound fast at the ghats. They seem to have succeeded in collecting some, which were used in ferrying the baggage on the second day. Ahmad Shah himself crossed after half the army was on the other side. There were a few casualties, no doubt, in the tumult and hurry of crossing. But at last the whole army was safe on the other bank and began their march to Sonepat, which they reached on the 27th October.

Next day they moved to Gannaur where Ahmad Shah halted for three[24] days. Baji Hari's attempt to scout must have happened during this interval. The number of casualties in this attempt is not correctly reported anywhere, though Kashiraj gives the figure at two thousand, and the place where they crossed swords as near the serai of Samalkha. Bhau fell back as a result of it and encamped at Panipat. Ahmad Shah advanced to Samalkha on 31st October, and to Pasina the next day. A distance of some three miles was left between the advanced posts of the two armies. The two armies came face to face at last after four months of eying each other on the opposite banks of the swollen Jamuna. It was seven months since Bhau had started to meet Abdali, and here he was at last.

But for a final decision by arms, two and a half months had still to pass. From the first of November 1760 to 14th January, 1761 the two sides in the struggle for power put their faith in strategy and manœuvring, living in entrenched camps.

---

24 Raj. 1.261

CHAPTER V

PANIPAT

To JUDGE from the letters which were sent out in the first fortnight[1] from the Maratha camp at Panipat and even for a month after, the Maratha army and its commander[2] seem to be quite confident of victory. This seems strange when we remember the hardships which the Maratha army had to bear since it started for the north, seven months earlier. Not that they had no proper understanding of the strength of Abdali's army; but the spectacular victory at Kunjpura and freedom from want of grain and fodder which followed seem to have worked out a change in the despondent mood on the Maratha side. They had seen with their eyes the strength and use of Ibrahim Khan's splendid corps which, as Kashiraj says, "in the twinkle of an eye smashed the defences of Kunjpura fort and entered it in no time." Intimate friends of Bhau, like Nana Purandare and Krishna Joshi Sangmeshvarkar, are not only confident but over-jubilant with expectancy of (what they judged as) Abdali's sure defeat. It is true that full stomachs are prone to create enthusiasm and confidence; still it is strange to think that these intimates of Bhau who should have known better, were writing in the vein they have done. Even Bhau is found writing in the same tone for a month more. Only during the last fortnight the crisis seems to have developed though even then Janakoji Shinde[3] —writing no doubt to the revenue collector—does not betray any sign of hopelessness when giving out the news at Panipat. This is in sharp contrast with the writing of Kashiraj and the whole tone of it. The Marathi chronicles, though they do not enumerate the events in a similar tone, are found criticizing Bhau for his attitude during the entire struggle. It is difficult to believe that all the writers on the Maratha side were ignorant, not to understand the real situation and the strategy of such a consumate general as Abdali, and still that is the impression created while reading Kashiraj and even historians like Sir Jadunath. Now we know by complete analysis of the whole material that, because the chroniclers wrote after the event, and because they wanted to shift and fix the responsibility of the disaster on those who had not survived it, they have assumed a sliding attitude so as dramatically to break on the rock of final disaster. But we think this methodology wrong in history, and for that reason have not accepted chronicles as history where psychology plays a part.

In the first fortnight, before Abdali could build up his line of communication to bring in the supplies from the Doab and beyond, his army was definitely in a weak position, and comparatively the Maratha army was in a better position. Why Bhau did not try to decide the conflict by a bold attack at that favourable juncture, we cannot say. He seems to have put his faith in quite a different strategy—that of tiring out Abdali and his allies and making them fall on his well-fortified, almost impregnable lines. In this strategy

1 *SPD* 21.197; 27; RAJ. 1.261, 62, 64, 65; *Purandare* 391.
2 *SPD* 2.134.
3 *Shinde* 1.222.

TO FACE PAGE 62

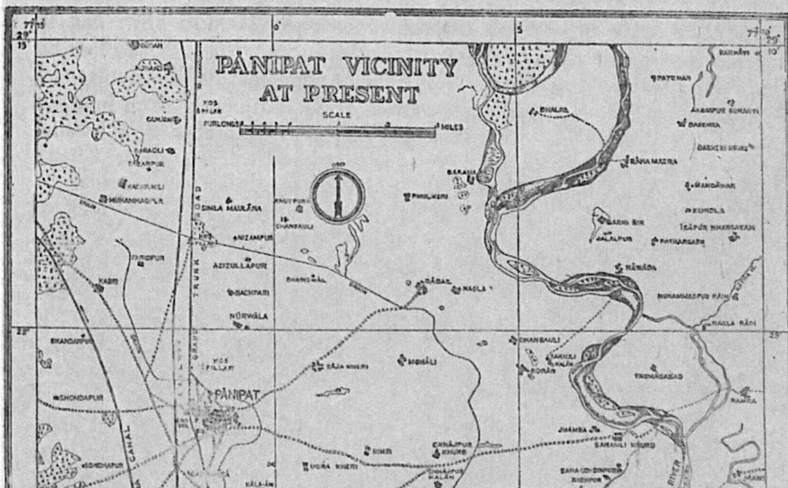

Bhau was depending upon the activities of Govindpant Bundele and Naro Shankar. Had they succeeded in cutting off Abdali's supplies and making him move from his camp, Abdali would have had only two alternatives before him, either to run away to his home without offering a battle, or attacking the Marathas in their strong positions. We do not think that it would have been difficult for him and his allies to disperse to their homes, as suggested by Krishna Joshi in his letter,[4] though ostensibly his road to Afghanistan was blocked by the Maratha camp at the very onset. But Govindpant was scarcely a fit man to carry out the orders of Bhau, because primarily he was not a soldier but a civilian. The military circumstances in the regions surrounding his area have also to be taken into account. Not only were the Rajput zamindars, with their strong fortalices, disaffected towards the rule of the Marathas internally, but externally also the Ruhela chiefs and Shuja's nominee, Veni Bahadur, were vigilant and bent on taking advantage of the difficulties of the Marathas. Shuja had taken only a small part of his army to the battlefield, leaving the main portion under Veni Bahadur[5] to defend his dominions in his absence. Shuja himself had only willynilly gone to Abdali under strong pressure for avoiding the invasion of his own territories by Abdali and his Ruhela allies, and never took any important part in the whole campaign or in the final battle. By his behaviour he was insuring his safety between two powerful rivals. When Bhau blames Govindpant for not devastating Shuja's dominions so as to exert a pressure on him to return to his dominions for defence, he seems to be unaware of the fact that there was sufficient army on the spot to defend it. Govindpant's leaving his dominions meant exposing them to an invasion by Veni Bahadur, as was found to his cost by Gopalrao Govind Barve[6] in his attempt.[7] But sometimes it is necessary to take the risk of completely exposing one's dominions in order to gain a necessary military advantage. Only a man like Frederick the Great of Prussia or a Madhavrao Peshwa could dare it and reap the harvest. It was too much to expect such an action from Govindpant, and when he tried to perform it for escaping the charge of disobedience, he had to pay for the attempt with his life and complete defeat.

This exposition should convince the reader that Bhau's strategy was based on precarious means, and he was misguided in depending on a man of Govindpant's calibre. There were other means of gaining his end, but Bhau never seems to have tried these. In the last resort, why Bhau should have waited up to the breaking point of the 14th of January, completely passes our understanding. Bhau knew of Govindpant's death on 23rd December, and we can find no excuse for Bhau to defer the attack for three weeks, thus weakening still further the Maratha side during this long interval by starvation, exposure and disease. The only suggestion that might explain Bhau's delay is the idea of his waiting for the coming of Nanasaheb from the Deccan so as to catch Abdali between two grind-stones. This suggestion finds no conclusive evidence in documents. The Peshwa seems to have been informd by his son,

4 Raj. 1.265.

5 A. L. Shrivastava, op cit., pp. 94, 111.

6 Ibid. 111.

7 See the section on The Trans-Ganges raids further on

Vishwasrao, and some other men about the gravity of the Maratha situation at Panipat, and if the Peshwa had correctly judged the situation, he should certainly have gone immediately to succour his cousin. From the correspondence it seems that the Peshwa had not received any communication from Bhau for more than a month, which means that Abdali was successfully intercepting all couriers. On the other hand, when the Peshwa's suspicions about the real state of the army in the north had reached their climax and silent dread had taken their place, he is found writing to Bhau in an almost repentent tone for not having done his duty, or, as previously promised, succoured Bhau. From this letter, the Peshwa seems to have promised to send a contingent from the Deccan so as to reach Panipat in February 1761.[8] If Bhau was hoping to carry on till this promised contingent reached its destination, by being able somehow to get supplies, then a different turn would have been given to the whole narration of the campaign. Apart from the truth of such a promise, it looks impossible from the military point of view that the promised help could have reached Bhau in time. If Bhau had been able to get supplies *ad infinitum,* there was no particular point why he should be wanting support from the south. If supplies were not forthcoming, the coming of the support would not have helped the matters in any way, at least not in time. Only such an illustrious captain of cavalry as Bajirao could possibly have reached Panipat in time to be of any help. But there was no such man available at Poona, at least not of such great calibre, to lead this express expedition. All these considerations, which historians can discuss at leisure now, should have been better understood by Bhau. He should have made up his mind, at least after Govindpant's death, to offer battle—whatever the result—then and there, without waiting till the last day, as he actually did. This waiting seems to have considerably changed the prospect of giving the slip to the enemy, fortune favouring, and marching past Abdali to Delhi, after losing only a part of the army instead of the whole. For, on the 30th of December, 1760, Abdali changed his camp for the last time, and leaving his river-side position, took post directly across the imperial road to Delhi so as completely to block the Maratha movement to the south.

We shall now proceed to describe the strategical position in the area surrounding Panipat. This city is situated on the slopes of a small hillock, less than a hundred feet in height above the surrounding plain. In ancient times, the river Jamuna is reputed to have passed along the eastern edge of the hill, but now it is some eight miles away to the east. The river changes its course now and then, and we cannot be very sure what its actual course was in 1760. From our observations, it seems to have been a mile to the west of its present course in some places. The river does not flow in one stream always, but now and then divides into a number of channels when it comes into a comparatively plain country. Nowhere is the edge along the bank more than thirty feet high. In most places it is less than twenty, and the average is somewhere near ten. There are large areas along the banks on both sides where there is scarcely any edge visible, the flood-water spreading far and wide into the interior where it

8 *Purandare* 1.395; *Bhau Kaifiyat* p. 20.

TO FACE PAGE 65

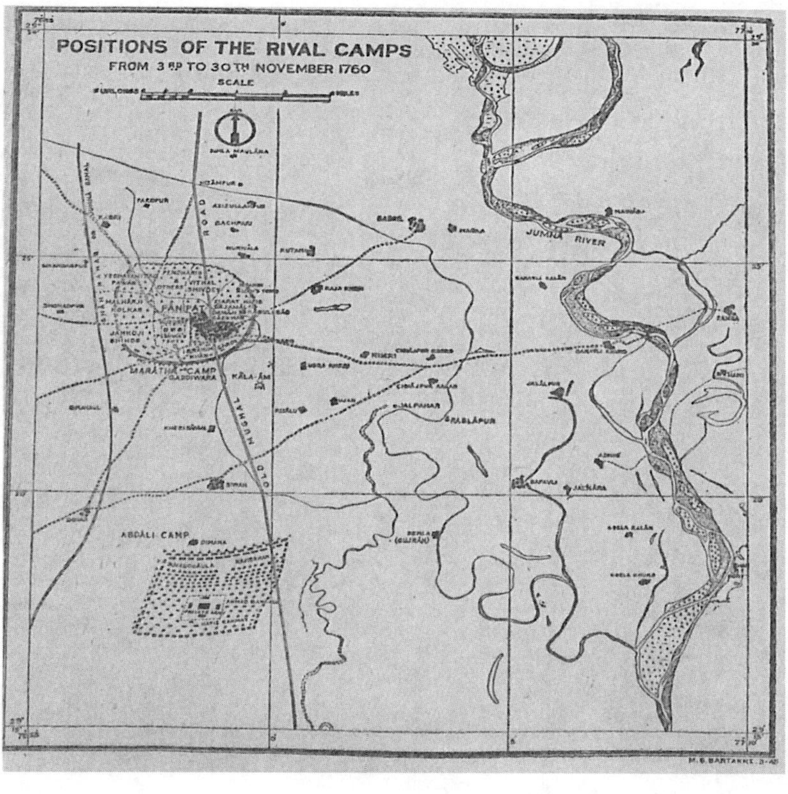

creates a marsh and a bog. To the south-east of Panipat such a condition prevails near the village of Goyenla. At such places, ferrying by boats is neither possible nor necessary during the fair season, and people ford the river through knee-deep to chest-deep water. Where the edges are sharp and the river-basin narrow—though nowhere would it be less than half a mile in breadth—the waters generally collect in one deep stream which has then to be crossed by boat. This situation must ever be borne in mind when visualising Abdali's movements and changing camps. The Maratha army had chosen for its camp the site to the north-west and south-west of Panipat. The imperial road passed directly through the town of Panipat, and the Maratha army had completely taken possession of it on the northern side. Though there is no mention of the canal in any original letter on Panipat, we believe that the famous Ali Mardan Khan Canal was still[9] flowing along or at a short distance to the west of the Maratha camp, thus at once supplying a part of the camp with water, and also acting as a fosse to the Maratha camp on that side. The Maratha camp seems to have spread over a long distance to the north of Panipat, if we are to believe in the traditional description supplied by the ballad singer of Siwa. It provides the information that the 700 elephants of Bhau were kept at Gharonda, which is ten miles to the north of Panipat. Incidentally, it means that there was a sufficient water-supply for these elephants in the vicinity, suggesting that the place must be along a tank or canal.[10] We have come to this conclusion from the fact that there was no complaint about the dearth of water, though there was a dearth of everything else. Abdali first came directly opposite to Panipat with a view to meeting the Marathas and deciding the contest at one stroke. But the Marathas, entrenching themselves strongly, foiled Abdali's plan of taking a quick decision by direct attack. From their secure base they were able to defy him in his camp and even to assume an offensive. Bhau marched out of his moat a little under the cover of his strongly placed guns, built temporary stands for his movable guns and from them opened fire on Abdali's camp.[11] The shots reaching Abdali's tents and killing his men and animals, obliged him to vacate it and pitch again at a distance of some five miles to the south-east along the river bank near the villages of Behrampur, Bapauli, Mirzapur and Goyenla.[12] In making this retrograde movement, Abdali seems to have cared for the supply of water which was perhaps completely stopped by the Marathas using up the canal water higher up above Panipat, as well as for the easy communication with the Doab by merely fording the river, so as to need no boats to fetch his supplies. The Marathas had hit upon a well protected site, no doubt, with the canal-marshes on the west side, the Panipat hill on the east side and a deep, broad, dry moat on the front and facing side. But once entrenched, they had no space to move one way or the other, while Abdali remained free to change his camp as it suited him. At first his line had spread along the Dahad, Siwa, Risalu villages, but in a few days he receded and settled down along the Dimana village. This first

9 See Appendix. "Was the Imperial Canal Flowing, etc." at the end of this chapter.
10 *BDCRI* 4.173.
11 *SPD* 2.134.
12 Raj. 3.224; *Bhau Kaifiyat* p. 14; *SPD* 2.134; *BDCRI* 4.179-81.

camp he changed between the 26th and the 30th of November as a result of Bhau's cannonading as stated above, when he retreated to the riverside, the centre of the battlefield between the two armies lying along the village of Chhajpur. The reputed wooden war-pillar[13] erected by the Marathas and found described in the *Bakhar* was somewhere on the plain of Chhajpur, and here the fight on the 7th of December took place, resulting in the death of Balvantrao Mehendale. For a month Abdali remained in the second camp till he moved to Pasina on 30th December, and his line spread across the imperial road to Dimana. The main site of the final battle was between Risalu and Nimbdi. This last move on the part of Abdali obliged Bhau to change his final plan of battle to suit the new disposition by Abdali.

During the first month, or almost for five weeks, the Maratha army was on the aggressive. Every day they came out with their field guns, supported by some sardar's contingent, to the front and tried to cut off anyone from the Afghan side who had come out of his camp for skirmishing, or was loitering on the plain. The Pendharis on the Maratha side wandered round Abdali's camp and carried away horses, camels and even elephants which had been let loose for grazing outside. Still nobody from Abdali's side would come out and try to protect their animals and men. The discipline in Abdali's camp was of the strictest type and he had issued orders to his army not to stir out of the camp and offer battle themselves. This seems to be due to the superiority of the long-range fire on the Maratha side. The big guns placed advantageously on the mud ramparts surrounding the Maratha camp were able to mow down anyone coming within their range for some two miles. The Marathas captured more than a thousand horses, four hundred camels and four elephants during the first three weeks.[14] The guns on the Afghan side were also not less effective though somewhat shorter in range, and their shots also could reach and kill men in the Maratha trenches. Krishna Joshi met his death from one such shot while he was sitting in his kitchen behind the trenches.[15] But Abdali had probably taken the decision of not attacking in order to economise his powder and shot, which he thought could be used more effectively in an open battle. On the 22nd November there was a lunar eclipse and the Maratha camp was rather inactive on account of this. No one had possibly come out of the camp that day as usual. Abdali's Wazir Shah Wali Khan had come out to watch the Marathas that day. Seeing no danger nearby, he ventured to go very near the Maratha lines in the course of his patrol. As he was waiting near a well, the Maratha troops on the opposite side saw him and came out suddenly to take advantage of his unprotected state. A desperate battle ensued and the Wazir had great difficulty in holding his ground. But the Afghans in the rear were also watchful and ran to his rescue. Shinde's men drove them all back to their lines and inflicted considerable loss on them. The Wazir lost four hundred of his troops and double that number were wounded.[16] The loss on the Maratha side was forty dead and one hundred and fifty

13 *Bhau Kaifiyat*, p. 15; *BDCRI* 4.179 verse 36.
14 *SPD* 21.197.
15 Ibid.
16 Jadunath Sircar, op. cit., 2.302; *Aitihasika Patra Vyavahar* p. 97.

wounded.[17] The Marathas were able to capture more than a hundred horses and but for the nightfall the result would have been still more decisive, as men from that part of the Abdali camp which was attacked by the Marathas had begun to run away from their posts. There was again a similar skirmish after a few days, with no decisive result. The tone of the rank and file in the Maratha army, as well as of the commander-in-chief himself, is found to be all optimistic for over a month, and there is no ground for taking Kashiraj as a correct reporter for this period. Not only are Kashiraj's forebodings incorrect, but the tone also of his narrative is vitiated by his personal predilections.

As Abdali had to retreat from his first position to the riverside, it is proved thereby that the Marathas were in the ascendant till then. Kashiraj describes with awe all the actions of Abdali. He praises his arrangement to guard his camp and to watch the other side day and night. As no such vivid description is forthcoming from the Maratha side, a wrong impression is created in the mind of the reader, and he thinks that there was no such system followed by the Marathas. This is absolutely wrong. Just as parties of thousands were appointed to guard the camp on the Afghan side, similarly the Marathas were also mounting guard and patrolling around their camp at night. Kashiraj says that the Afghan monarch was in the habit of going round not only his own camp and that of his allies, but he also took a round about the entire Maratha camp from a distance, and every day returned by noon after having ridden fifty *kos* in person with a small escort. This seems a gross exaggeration of Kashiraj. We do not think that the Maratha watchmen and patrols were so slack as not to see even once the Afghan monarch going round their camp during a period of more than two months, and one can guess that it was impossible for the daily rounds of Ahmad Shah to go unseen, at whatever distance he might be encircling the Maratha camp. We also think that it was geographically not possible. The canal on the west side of the Maratha camp was a great impediment to such a movement, and on the east side also the land was not very favourable for such an excursion. The river on the north-east side coming very near and the bogs and the zils, which exist to this day, do not make such a supposition look feasible. Only during the last fortnight, when the Maratha army had become quite despondent and taken to heart the lesson of cold massacre, the Afghan monarch might have indulged in his rounds, though at great risk even then to himself. Kashiraj was perhaps remembering this last period when he wrote nineteen years after, and made it applicable to the whole period of two and a half months.

A fortnight after the Wazir's discomfiture, a major engagement took place between the two armies. As we have noted above, Abdali had moved to the riverside by then. As the Afghan camp had now gone far beyond the range of Maratha fire and in a somewhat difficult terrain, and as the Afghans would not come out of their own accord to offer a battle, it became a teasing problem for the Marathas to pass the days in futile inactivity. The Marathas, therefore, hit upon a plan to call them out. At some distance from

17 *Bhau Kaifiyat*, p. 21.

the Maratha camp, and to the south-east of it, they began to clear the jungle so as to make easy approach possible.[18] They cut down the thick bushes of short palasa *(dhak)* trees and prepared a somewhat level battle-field and planted a pillar there. The site of this new battle-field seems to have been, from the description in the ballad,[19] at Chhajpur, beyond which a big *nullah* separated it from the Afghan camp. They began to drag out their movable cannon to this place and, standing behind them, to challenge the other side to come out and dare battle. Cut to the quick by these challenges, the Ruhelas one day came out and began an engagement by firing from a distance. The Marathas advanced a little but by this time it was about sunset. Seeing that the Marathas would take some time to reach back to their camp, Najib's brother came out to deliver a flank attack as the Maratha army turned its face in the direction of their camp. At this unexpected attack the Marathas had to leave their guns and run pell-mell, which again drew the Ruhelas farther on, close on their heels. They almost reached the edge of the Maratha camp when soldiers from the camp came out, finding their comrades in danger. The Ruhela cavalry fled away, taking advantage of the pitch darkness of that new-moon night, but their infantry was closed in from all sides. They fought with their usual bravery and created havoc in the Maratha camp by their marksmanship. They were well-nigh defeated, with great slaughter of fifteen hundred Ruhelas, and pursued upto a distance. But in the midst of this victory, Balvantrao Mehendale received a bullet-shot and came down from his horse. Seeing that he was a sardar of some consequence, the Afghans tried to cut off his head so as to carry it as a trophy back to their camp; but some Maratha horsemen, noticing it, turned back to snatch it away just when it was being cut. Khanderao Naik Nimbalkar was responsible for dragging back the corpse of Balvantrao Mehendale by the feet in the thick of that fight, though himself wounded. Both parties then returned to their camps. Though the Marathas were victorious, the death of Balvantrao had taken away the zest out of it from them. There was a great wailing in the Maratha camp on that night of the 7th December, 1760. Balvantrao's wife, Lakshimibai, was one of the few women who had accompanied their husbands to that famous battlefield. Her son, Krishnarao, alias Appa Balvant of later fame, a boy of fourteen or so, was also with them in the camp; still she at once took the decision of offering herself as a Sati on her husband's funeral pyre. No dissuasion by Bhau himself or by the mother of Nana Fadnis, who was Balvantrao's sister, was able to change her decision. She courageously made over her son to Bhau's care and faced immolation, making that incident the most dramatic in the whole Panipat campaign.

The seventh of December is taken as a turning point in the Panipat campaign. No doubt it deprived Bhau of a most intimate lieutenant. The biassed Maratha *Bakhars* and, following them, some Persian chronicles, have shown Balvantrao as the villain of the piece. The *Kaifiyat* merely depicts the difference of opinion between Bhau's advisers from the south, and the north

18 Ibid. 14.5.
19 *BDCRI* 4.179.

TO FACE PAGE 68

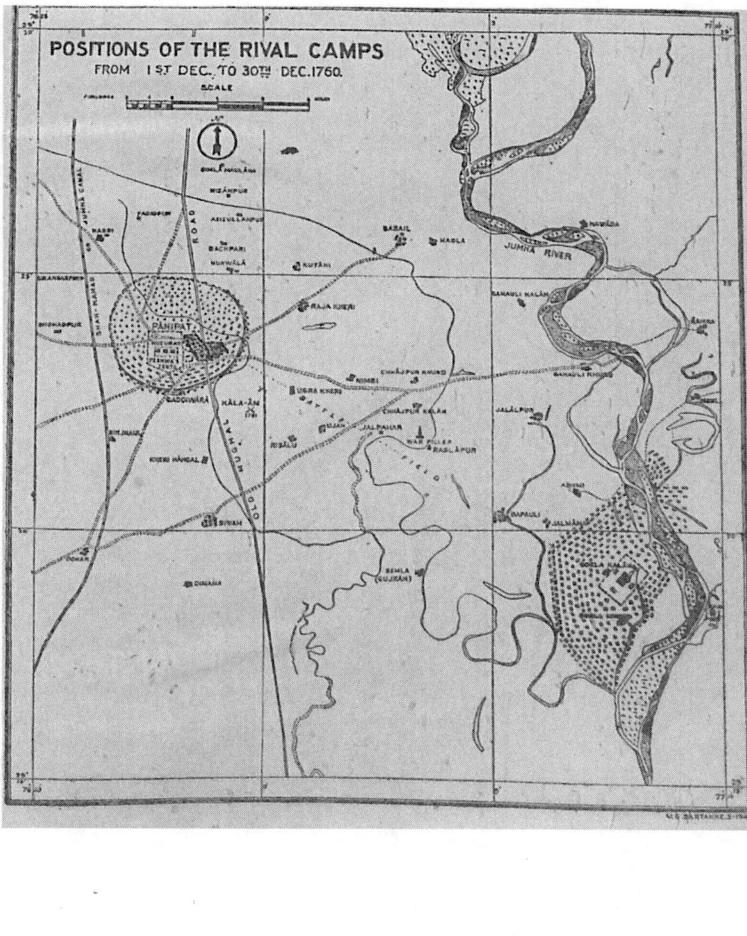

Indian party. But the *Bakhar* from the very beginning of the Panipat campaign makes Balvantrao the chief instigator in a dramatic manner, every time giving a twist to the political talk in the Maratha camp throughout the campaign. We think that the writer of the *Bakhar* was Chinto Krishna Fadnis of the Shinde contingent. The *Bakhar* tells us that it was Balvantrao who first fanned and fomented the family differences between the Peshwa, his wife and his brother Raghoba on the one hand, and Bhau and his supporters on the other. This resulted in changing the original plan of sending Raghoba with an army to the north to retrieve the disaster which had fallen upon the Marathas by the death of Dattaji, and the subsequent events. Balvantrao accompanied Bhau, and at every step—so it is depicted—made him take a contrary step to the advice of Malharrao and other responsible men. The truth seems to be that Balvantrao was rather sharp of tongue with a bad opinion about Malharrao and other Maratha officials, but could not have been the villain of the piece. There was probably a substratum of Brahmin-Maratha rivalry or feud also at the bottom. But, historically, it is incorrect to say that Bhau was following Balvantrao's advice on all occasions and had never any differences with him. Bhau was angry at Balvantrao's carelessness in his impetuous, though daring, first attack on Delhi. He was unaware of Balvantrao's information or guess about the going down of the Jamuna waters, or at least he did not base his calculations on it. Bhau's letter to Dhondoba Purandare from Delhi clearly says that both the sardars were in complete accord with him,[20] and Bhau was not averse to—in fact was rather favourable to—peace negotiations, with a give and take policy. As the letter is a private one, every word in it can be accepted as true, as not couched in diplomatic language. This knocks the bottom out of the impeachment of Balvantrao by various chroniclers.

Sir Jadunath, while he professes to reject[21] "much of Nana Fadnis' autobiography," still accepts one vital sentence from it[22] and makes Nana Fadnis say that "it was only night-fall that saved the Maratha army from destruction" on the 7th December. In truth, his sentence means that but for the night-fall the Marathas could have pursued the Ruhelas into their camp and completely destroyed them. This is quite clear from two lines in his two letters[23] in which he says that "this battle had turned out well" (and not as Sir Jadunath translates "we fought well"), but it stopped after an hour and a quarter after night-fall due to pitch darkness, and not after three hours of the night as Sir Jadunath states.[24] Such a partial understanding of the Maratha documents makes him take a gloomier view than is actually warranted by the original letters in the earlier part of the campaign, though it fits in well with the final disaster.

There are no letters from the Maratha camp during most of this period. The Peshwa did not receive any communication from the north for

20 *Purandare* 1.389.
21 *Fall* 2.368.
22 *Aitihasik Patra Yadi* 2.176.
23 RAJ. 1.376; *Satara* 2.300.
24 *Fall* 2.305.

over a month.[25] That most of the letters sent were intercepted by Abdali is clear from Nana Fadnis' letter[26] to Ramchandrapant Natu at Delhi, which shows that this work of stopping the Maratha correspondence had begun from the third week of November, though occasionally a messenger was lucky enough to elude Abdali's patrols. This should also have something to do with the Maratha distress, as the possibility of the outsiders knowing the real condition of the Maratha camp was lessened. But there is no mention of any distress in the Maratha camp in the above-mentioned letter of 12th December, from which it would not be wrong to conclude that Abdali had not upto that point succeeded in completely cutting off the Maratha supply from the north. On that side the Sikhs and the Jats were quite well-disposed towards the Marathas. Alasingh Jat, the founder of the Patiala State, living at that time at Manuk, seems to have been actually helping[27] the Marathas as he was grateful for being relieved from the exactions of the Afghan soldiers of fortune like the chief of Kunjpura and the infamous Mian Qutb Shah. The Sikhs were directly interested in the result of the contest and even after the disaster were the chief beneficiaries of it. Sir Jadunath's harping on the disaffected Jat villagers seems a figment of the brain. There is no ground for such a supposition, though the Marathas suffered before, during and after the war by the vindictiveness of the Muslim population, who were equally numerous in those regions and incomparably more powerful than the submerged Jats and Gujars. Bhau is still a hero in their ballad[28] and fire-side stories, for whom they have the liveliest admiration.

Within a fortnight of Balvantrao's death, Govindpant Bundele also met the same fate. Throughout the Panipat campaign, nay, even before starting for it, Bhau had demanded money of Govindpant.[29] The latter sent two lakhs in the first instance and now at the beginning of December he came to Delhi with four lakhs and twenty-thousand. This was all he could possibly bring, though it was not even a fourth of what Bhau demanded from the beginning.

Handing over the treasure to Naro Shankar, Govindpant sallied forth with his contingent and crossed over into the Doab. He began to cut off Abdali's supplies coming from the trans-Ganges districts and passing through the Meerut district to Abdali. Bhau had intimated to Govindpant that there were none now to oppose him in the Doab as the Ruhelas had been tied up to the camp of Abdali. So, leisurely and unguardedly, he continued his march, chastising the refractory local zamindars on the way. He seemed to have been collecting grain also for carrying it to Bhau's camp across an upper ghat on the Jamuna, to Panipat.

But news of Govindpant's depredations soon reached Abdali's camp. The Ruhelas became apprehensive of the safety of their homes. The regularity of the food convoy reaching Abdali's camp through these regions had

25 RAJ. 3.210.
26 *Satara* 2.300. Letter dated 12th December 1760.
27 *SPD* 27.262; *Purandare* 1.416.
28 *BDCRI* 4.
29 *SPD* 40.129

been taken away. Abdali, therefore, despatched a select force of some five thousand horsemen under impetuous Atai Khan, the Durrani Wazir's nephew, who had recently come from Afghanistan. A few thousand Ruhelas also joined him to show him the way and properly guide him in their home lands. Crossing the Jamuna at Baghpat and covering some fifty miles in a day and night, they suddenly alighted upon Govindpant as he was somewhere between Ghazi-ud-din-nagar (now Ghaziabad) and Meerut. It seems that one Jeta Gujar, a robber-chieftain in that area, had promised a ransom to Govindpant, and Govindpant was stopping to recover it. Jeta communicated the news to Abdali and he sent this force. It is also said that the Ruhelas had assumed different colours, seeing which Govindpant thought the army from a distance was that of Naro Shankar.[30] While Govindpant was preparing to take a bath and to dine in the afternoon after a day's hard work, he was overtaken by Atai Khan's cavalry. He suddenly snatched a horse and began to run with his army. In the hurry of flight twice he came down from his horse, as he was not properly seated on a saddle, but reseated again by others. But when he fell for the third time, none returned to save him, even his son who was accompanying the army having fled away to a distance. Govindpant's head was cut off and his whole camp looted. The Maratha loss was some four hundred.[31] The rest of the Maratha army with Govindpant's son Balaji after first having fled to the south, afterwards returned to Delhi. Atai Khan returned with the loot which contained a good quantity of grain, and Najib presented Govindpant's head to Ahmad Shah. He sent it to Bhau, announcing his triumph in the undertaking. The news had already reached Bhau by 23rd December,[32] though the head reached Bhau's hands two or three days later, from which it appears that the attack on Govindpant must have taken place on 20th December or so, and not on the 17th as assumed by Sir Jadunath.[33] Govindpant had atoned for all his past sins of commission and omission with his life, and, therefore, the gravamen of accusations against him is taken away. He might be called slovenly and not up to the mark in military matters; but none can say that he was disloyal.

After Govindpant's death, when the plan of cutting off Abdali's supplies and directing these to the Maratha camp had failed, the real difficulties of the Maratha camp began. The Maratha camp was short of not only food and fodder, but also of coined money necessary to make cash payments for any supplies brought to the camp from the Panjab. Bhau found it difficult to fetch money from Delhi where it had been deposited by Govindpant. The first batch of soldiers from Payagude's troops under the leadership of Krishnarao Ballal, carrying with them one lakh, ten thousand, started on 22nd December and seems to have reached the Maratha camp in safety.[34] But the second batch under Parashar Dadaji carrying one and a half lakhs with them, which started on 2nd January, 1761, was cut off by Abdali, as Abdali had shifted his camp for the last time on 30th December, and was now lying astride the imperial road

30 *Bhau Bakhar* 129.
31 RAJ. 1.376.
32 Ibid. 1.272.
33 *Fall* 2.311.
34 RAJ. 1.281.

from Delhi to Panipat.[35] The news of this shifting had not reached Delhi, and so the Maratha troops were passing along the road in the dead of night as usual. There were with him three hundred soldiers each carrying five hundred rupees. In the severe cold of January, with their bodies benumbed by night exposure, they unsuspectingly entered the Afghan camp five miles to the south of Panipat, thinking it to be the Maratha camp. They alighted from their horses and tried to warm themselves by the burning fire-sides. Some took out their pipes and began to smoke. As they had entered from the back of the Afghan camp without fear, none at first seems to have recognised or obstructed them, the Afghans taking them probably as a batch of their allies. But when the Marathas began to converse, the Afghans got the clue and raised a hue and cry. Only one escaped from the tussle and returned back to Delhi.[36] The rest were deprived of their cash and horses and put to the sword according to Kashiraj,[37] while the *Bhau Bakhar* and the *Kaifiyat* say that they reached the Maratha camp safely after the mishap.[38]

As more than five lakhs of people were living in that small area from Panipat to Samalkha for more than two months (in the two camps together), all the wood and fodder in the vicinity had disappeared and the whole area had become one vast barren plain. Some ten villages had left their sites and gone to live elsewhere. The citizens of Panipat had to remain confined in the small walled area, with no space left for movement. Their farms and gardens had disappeared from the scene. Naturally they had become hostile to the Marathas and being Muslims for the most part, seem to have acted treacherously from behind in giving news to Abdali and carrying on nefarious activities in collusion with the Afghans of Kunjpura and the surrounding area. The civil behaviour of the Marathas with such people has cost the Marathas very dearly in history.

In their two and a half months' beleaguerment at Panipat, the Marathas must have spent practically every pie they possessed for buying the victuals at ten-fold prices. The system adopted for fetching grain from a distance was to send an escort of some thousands to accompany the caravan from Karnal to Panipat, and while returning to see them back with their pack-bullocks to Karnal again. But after a time this source also dried up, either because there was no grain to sell, or more probably because the Afghans had recovered their posts like Kunjpura and Karnal in the north. Abdali was furnished, some time in the second week of December, with fresh troops from Afghanistan to the extent of eight thousand. Atai Khan was their leader. Before joining Abdali, he seems to have followed not the direct route to Panipat, but the safer route across the Jamuna by the Budhia or the Andhera Ghat north and south of Kunjpura. Before entering the Doab, he could not but have driven out the small Maratha out-posts at Karnal and Kunjpura with the help of his splendid troops. Dilir Khan, the only son of Nejabat Khan, left

35 *Shinde* 1.222.
36 RAJ. 1.281, 383.
37 *Battle of Panipat* 1926, p. 24.
38 *Bhau Bakhar* p. 132: *Kaifiyat* p. 21.

TO FACE PAGE 72

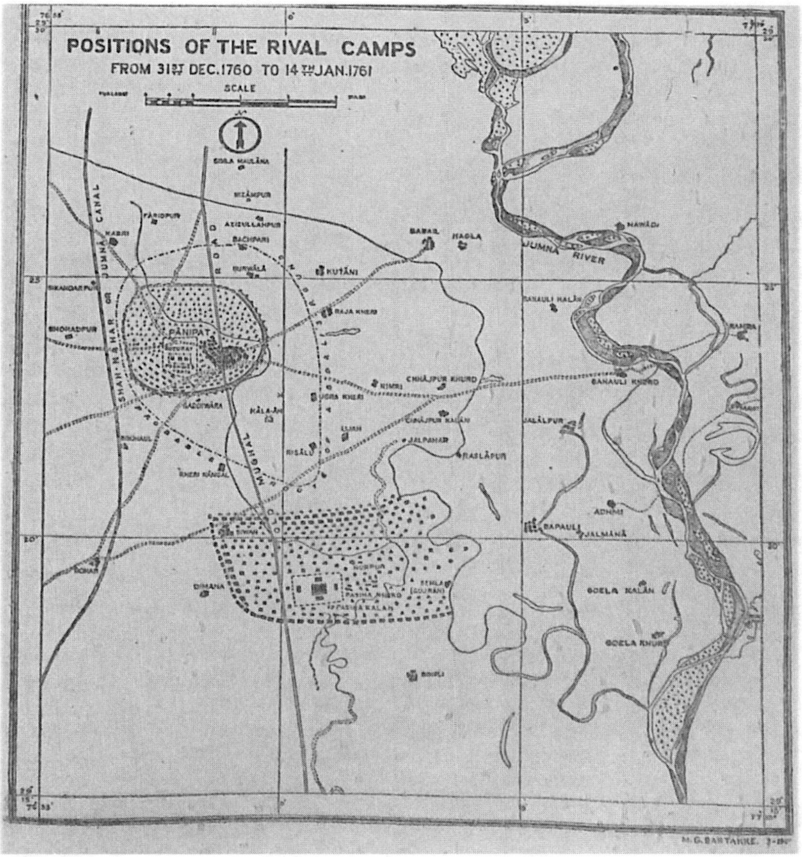

free, now recovered Kunjpura with Atai Khan's help and made it impossible for the caravans to move on that side. Added to this, fire started, either purposely or by random cannon shot, and destroyed the big haystacks heaped in the Maratha camp.[39] This misfortune turned the situation from bad to worse and finally into utter helplessness. As a result of this mishap, twenty thousand followers issued from the Maratha camp one night to gather firewood and fodder in the neighbouring woods, but they were overtaken, surrounded and massacred piece-meal by a body of five thousand horse under Shah Pasand Khan who was patrolling that area. After this slaughter, terror struck the Maratha camp and nobody seems to have ventured out.

In the terrible cold of December and January, the Marathas, with their scanty clothing meant only for the cold in the Deccan, suffered terribly in addition to the want of sufficient quantities of good food and firewood. As if this was not enough, it rained heavily that winter, generating biting winds in their wake.[40] Thousands of bullocks, horses, mules and even men died of this calamity. The unburied animals and corpses on the intervening battlefield putrified the air.[41] The crowded camp where within a small area men had to perform all their physical duties made it terribly dirty and full of noxious air. Nana Fadnis vividly describes these conditions in his autobiography.

Such was the condition of the Maratha camp and the state of the men and animals who were to offer battle to the strong, stalwart, efficient and unperturbed Afghans who were well supplied with necessities and fully inured to these climes and circumstances.

As we have said above, we are completely in the dark as to Bhau's aim in not sallying out for battle three weeks earlier when he received the news of Govindpant's death. Such a step would have appreciably reduced the sufferings which the Maratha camp had to endure in the last period. The men and animals would have been found in better condition for a march or a fight, before their reduction by starvation and misery for three weeks more. Even their morale would have been found better and still Bhau would not take such a step. A casual remark in the *Bakhar* (p. 136) also supports the view that "had the Marathas started the next day after the heavy massacre of the Ruhelas in the intervening daily fights, the Afghans had no strength then to overpower the Marathas." "But," so remarks the chronicler, "the fate had ordained otherwise and so the Marathas remained inactive, carrying on the waiting game!" We do not know whether this was a case of fortune first taking away the wit and then striking hard afterwards.

Our wonder increases still more when we find the chronicles reporting the discussion in the Maratha camp previous to the battle. While Bhau, judging that the army could not pull on even for a day more, wanted to offer battle the next day, Malharrao and Janakoji were proposing to postpone the

39 RAJ. 6.406.
40 *Sardesai Commemoration Volume* p. 259.
41 *BDCRI* 4.181.

event by four days.[42] If their argument has any sense in it, we must think the state of the Maratha camp not as bad as it is depicted; otherwise how could they have waited for four days more? Their confidence is curiously found supported by a rare letter of Janakoji, written only ten days prior to the battle, and reaching its destination without being intercepted by Abdali's patrols.[43] He does not betray any sign of fear or hopelessness. He assures his revenue collector not to be troubled at the local pin-pricks of the Rajput princes, as after the chief enemy (Abdali) is defeated, others will fall in the line without effort.

As we have said elsewhere, the tone of the men who escaped from the battle-field was different from their own earlier writing. They charged Bhau with being obstinate, not listening to milder and saner counsels, and casting his last die thoughtlessly and in a haphazard manner. We take these to be afterthoughts only. Had there been not even a thirty per cent chance of bettering their position—and not the hope of defeating Abdali decisively—how the Maratha chieftains could have consented to march out with a hollow square formation, we are not able to comprehend. Let it not be forgotten also that notwithstanding the starvation of the Maratha camp, the Marathas were able to charge so effectively in the forenoon part of the battle that they seemed to carry everything before them. On this central point, all the authorities on the battle are unanimous. This clearly proves that but for some serious disobedience of orders issued after the final decision before the start, or for the sudden demoralisation due to Vishwasrao being shot down, there would not have been that debacle and that stampede which actually took place even to the dismay of such on-lookers as Kashiraj and other reporters of the battle. We have thought it necessary to put down all these facts before the description of the actual battle, because up till now it has been treated by historians in a faulty, not to say malignant, manner.

According to the chronicles, the rank and file of the Maratha army, perturbed at the prospect and desperate on account of starvation, proceeded to the tent of Bhau and besought him not to allow them to die of starvation and disease but to lead them to the battle, whatever be the destiny awaiting them. We have said already that Bhau should have anticipated such a clamour and forestalled it with some continuous preparation spread over a number of days. All the men, high and low, combatants and non-combatants, in the Maratha camp, should have been completely made aware and tutored of their responsibility and actual part in the battle which was to ensue. Clear instructions about the methods of self-protection in the event of a sudden disaster—we do not think inevitable and certain—ought to have been circulated. Nana Fadnis says in his autobiography that Bhau *had* anticipated all possibilities in the conduct of war and provided for them as best he could, and we do not think that Bhau could have failed to take these obvious precautions, consummate master of affairs as he was. The divergence in the military counsels of the Maratha chiefs was the basic cause for the opposite manner of acting on the

42 *Kaifiyat* 0.21; *Bakhar* 0.141.
43 *Shinde* 1.222.

field of battle. But that was no fault of Bhau, but a national misfortune. All the various units and classes in the vast Maratha camp spread over miles were not equally affected by the dearth of grain or money, and that seems to be the reason why some still wanted, and thought it possible, to wait, while others less fortunate had reached the sinking point. Ultimately the clamour of the starved decided the day of the battle and not the convenience or forethought of the commander! This was a calamity, but perhaps there was no help for it. In any case, had the battle been fought a fortnight earlier, it would have been better in all respects, for the Marathas.

The actual plan decided and adopted by Bhau in consultation with Ibrahim Khan Gardi and others was, however, made possible by Abdali's change of camp-site and could not have been devised prior to 30th December, 1760. A battle before that date would have been only a frontal attack or a march with a hollow-square formation liable to be disturbed on the flanks which is the weakest point in such a formation. The direction would have been from north to south and not north-west to south-east. The plan envisaged by Kashiraj and put down in a memory drawing of the field of battle, is correct as far as it goes. Only the direction of the Maratha front he was unable to make out. Kashiraj mistook the longer side of the rectangle on the right-hand side for a front, because guns had been judiciously placed on that side also, and these were pointed towards the Abdali front. The strategy was to march past the right-hand corner of Abdali's camp to the river side with the whole formation, so as to take the river at the back in the evening and then to meet the Afghan army from the right-hand side, which would then become the battle-front. The advantage in this move would have been that the camp-followers would have remained always safe at the back and would have found it possible to run away to the south towards Delhi or to the east across the Jamuna into the Doab in case of a defeat. Had the plan succeeded, the major battle would have come not on the day of the start but on the days following. This would have given double advantage to the Marathas. They would have found the much needed rest, as also time to refresh and recoup at night, and would have been attacking the Afghans on their flank, thus exposing their camp to loot. But the hollow square formation with a long rectangular side made up of mutually antagonistic generals was at best a precarious device, as was proved to their cost the next day.

The Trans-Ganges Raids of the Marathas During the Panipat Campaign

At the beginning of July 1760, Shuja-ud-daulah finally made up his mind and went over to Abdali's side. From that date Sadashivrao Bhau began writing his letters to Govindpant Bundele, Gopalrao Ganesh Barve, Ganesh Sambhaji Khandekar and Gopalrao Bapuji, to foment rebellions in Shuja's dominions beyond the Ganges, and raid them. Many of the big zamindars under Shuja were small chieftains themselves with armies made up of their personal retainers. Balawant Singh of Benares was the biggest and the most refractory amongst them, though there were others like Balabhadrasingh of

Tiloi and Hindupat of Pratapgarh. In fact, the times and the surroundings were such that no potentate could be taken as fully established and free from internal rebellions. Shuja had placed Veni Bahadur with full powers in charge of his dominions during his absence in Abdali's camp. The major portion of Shuja's troops he kept behind him for guarding his dominions, fully knowing the risks to which his dominions would be exposed once he antagonised the Marathas. In fact, his direct help to Abdali was his fine park of artillery and the moral prestige of his name only. Sadashivrao Bhau appears from his letters to be unaware of this important fact. Shuja's troops are found estimated at 20,000 at the beginning of July, but how many of these he took with him to Abdali's camp is doubtful, as none seem to give very reliable figures. But if we take Kashiraj's figures as correct, Shuja had at Panipat 2,000 cavalry, 2,000 infantry and 20 guns with him, thus leaving 16,000 to guard his dominions. All these troops were well disciplined and well equipped. They were engaged on a permanent footing and very well paid with the result that they had no cause to grumble and go against their master. This was possible because Shuja possessed the most fertile lands in India and he could collect his revenues without any hitch. The only possible loop-hole in Shuja's dominions was the danger from his big zamindars who were always ready to rebel and would have liked to become independent. When Bhau is found ordering Govindpant to invade the Ruhela lands beyond the Ganges and Gopalrao Barve to attack Shuja's dominions, he seems to be talking of something which he could not understand. Abdali had sent many of the Ruhelas back to their homes during the rains to lessen the pressure on his scanty supplies of grain and possibly with a view to protect their province, thus making it impossible for Govindpant to move in the matter. Govindpant occupied Ahmad Khan Bangash's lands in Farukkhabad adjoining his, because these were on his side of the Ganges. But beyond the river he could not go. Similarly, Gopalrao found it impossible to move in the face of Veni Bahadur guarding the Ganges in full force. The combined troops of the Marathas under all their captains in this region, are found estimated at only ten to twelve thousand troops. Many of these were possibly infantry corps only, and not very well disciplined. They were fit for collecting revenues from refractory zamindars hiding in their fortalices, but not fit to face regular troops under Veni Bahadur. The rainy season passed in mere manœuvring without any actual invasion. In the middle of November, Govindpant turned towards Delhi on account of Bhau's express orders, with his contingent of some 5,000 troops, and only Gopalrao Barve was left behind in the lower Doab, facing Shuja's dominions. Sadashivrao had ordered Ganesh Sambhaji Khandekar to join his forces with those of Barve, but he does not seem to have crossed the Jamuna from the south at all. Besides, Shuja's wise mother and Veni Bahadur had by this time quelled the rebellions of the zamindars and brought them over to their side by lavish expenditure on them. Gopalrao had written to Bhau in his letter of 22nd November, 1760 that he was presently crossing over into Oudh; actually he was unable to cross before 30th December, 1760, as a part of his army had been sent to Govindpant's help under Bajirao Barve, Ramchandra Krishna and Ghanashyam Pandurang, which he was expecting back. But Bhau could not spare these troops, and so Barve engaged new troops. Ganesh Sambhaji kept on writing that he would come after settling matters in Bundelkhand. Finally, Barve crossed with his new troops and matchlockmen, about 10,000 strong. After crossing, he kept 5,000 infantry for guarding the ghats on the Ganges at his back, and with 5,000 matchlockmen and 1,500 sowars he began his campaign. A thousand horsemen joined him from the lower Doab. With these he attacked Bhojpur (sixteen miles to the north-west of Dalmau higher up the Ganges) which was defended by the Ruhelas by forming a square in the European way. But the impetuous attack of the Maratha cavalry broke their formation and they ran back into their fortalice. In this action, the Marathas killed some fifty matchlockmen, ten horsemen and captured the enemy's flags, themselves losing three horses and one trooper with seven wounded. Next day, the Ruhelas were pursued into the neighbouring thicket where they had taken shelter near the village of Dhuremau, five miles to the north-east of Bhojpur, by the fortalice. When attacked, they again ran away after a little skirmish in which the Marathas captured five horses, losing two of their own. Gopalrao next proceeded to the important fort of Dalmau, which was built on the bank of the river on a prominent hillock. The Marathas first attacked the town adjoining the fort when Haji Beg, the Commandant of the fort, sallied forth two miles with two thousand infantry and one thousand cavalry, consisting of Ruhelas. The attacking Marathas pressed them back into the fort after losing ten horsemen killed and twenty-five wounded. Two hundred enemy Ruhelas were cut off and their fifty horses were killed. The Marathas captured seventy-five horses with the iron drum. The whole town was looted and the Marathas began their march forward, because, had they laid siege to the fort, they would have had to sit there for a long time. Their next camp was at the village of Gaura, on the road to Rai Bareli on the 8th of January, 1761. In this campaign, Balabhadrasingh accompanied Barve, and later on Krishnanand Pant, Faujdar of Karra, joined them near Manikpur in the Pratapgarh district. Many local Rajput landlords joined them with their retainers so as to take part in the loot, if possible. They carried fire and sword throughout the region till they reached Nawabganj, ten miles north-west of Allahabad, to which they set fire after looting it. Next they proceeded to Fulpura to the north-east of Allahabad, and there repeated their performance. Thus, after they had carried their depredations for more than a hundred miles along the northern bank of the Ganges, retribution descended upon them from behind. Veni Bahadur had sent a strong army at their heels, coming into contact with which the rabble, collected in the Maratha camp, broke at once and zamindars, like Balbhadrasingh, who had joined for loot, fled back. The Maratha army under Gopalrao was dispersed and they ran back in small parties by different roads. Gopalrao personally crossed back with some seven horsemen into the Mirzapur district near the famous temple of Vindhyavasini, and then, taking a westerly route along the southern bank of the Jamuna, returned to his seat at Korah-Jahanabad in the Doab. All his broken troops also returned without much mishap. These events took place between 10th to 20th January, 1761. This campaign did not start at the beginning of December as taken by Sir Jadunath,[44] but at the end on 30th December,[45] and ended within three weeks. Bhau had expected this raid into Shuja's territory to have the effect of diverting his forces from Panipat, but it could not have had that effect because the campaign began very late, and ended simultaneously with the battle of Panipat. In joining Abdali, Shuja had insured against any possible attack by Abdali and his allies, the Ruhelas, but had not neglected the defence of his dominion either. Bhau's information on these points seems to be defective. Miscalculation of enemy forces and over-confidence in his own troops led Bhau astray in the whole Panipat campaign. From the dates of the letters giving the news of the campaign, it cannot be said that the rout of Barve's army took place after the news of the Panipat disaster had reached him, or was an outcome of it. It seems, however, that Barve could not rally his dispersed troops to another effort because, by that time, the news had definitely reached him.

* * *

I. Panipat Locality

The Panipat locality did not prove favourable to the Marathas on account of its being nearer to the home-land of the Ruhelas. Panipat itself was —and is—practically a Muslim town and the areas to its east had a larger proportion of Muslim population when compared to the southern tracts of the United Provinces. The road from Panipat to Kairana, Shamli and Muzaffarnagar across the Jamuna farther on, leads to Sukartal, the stronghold of Najib Khan on the Ganges, and crossing the Ganges to the actual home-land of the Ruhelas, in a straight line. In fact it looks as if any place south of Delhi would have been a better locality for the Marathas and worse for the Ruhelas. Their food-supply was assured with the least inconvenience to them. Surajmal Jat's advice was correct on this point, because he knew the local human environment. Bhau's original plan of crossing over into the Doab in the vicinity of Agra was correct, but, on account of procrastination, it was spoiled, and the campaign was unnecessarily lengthened by the four months of the rainy season. This had a disastrous effect from the financial, physical and moral point of view. Shuja would not have gone over to Abdali had Bhau placed himself between Abdali and Shuja's dominions. The miscarriage of that project was the first set-back in the Panipat campaign.

Shakir Khan Ansari's description[1] of the sad condition of Panipat under Maratha occupation must be true as far as it goes. That the Marathas must have felled all the trees in the vicinity irrespective of any consideration for the fruit-trees in the gardens, appears true when we take into account the necessities of the Maratha camp, military as well as personal. Many houses in the city were inevitably demolished by cannon-balls and their residents had to shift to other places. The wonder is not that such things occurred, but that the Marathas had left the inhabitants comparatively free without imposing any conditions on them. Most of the inhabitants were allowed to remain where

44 *Fall* 2.313.
45 *Ait Sankirna Sahitya*, Khanda 3, No. 263.
1 *Fall* 2.309.

they were and carry on their lives as best as they could under the circumstances. We believe that the presence of such a hostile element at their back must have helped the Afghan side much in various ways. Spying and sending news disclosing the Maratha position was easy for this population. Besides these, the two sons of Nejabat Khan Ruhela of Kunjpura were captives in the Maratha camp. What happened to them is nowhere recorded, and there is no ground for thinking that they were beheaded. Perhaps, in the turmoil just after the defeat, they might have freed themselves and joined the populace in destroying the Maratha camp-followers in revenge. That the Marathas had not destroyed any edifice wantonly is clear from the undamaged condition of the splendid tombs of the Saint Bu Ali Qalandar and Ibrahim Lodi with the ancient mosques adjoining. This is a clear proof of the mildness of Maratha rule even under the stress of war. Their civil manners and inoffensive attitude have cost the Marathas not a little in history.

That Bhau, in his Panipat campaign, created a tremendous impression in the Panipat locality is clear from many legends about Bhau, Parvatibai, Janakoji Shinde and Vishwasrao. The Bhau ballad current in the surrounding area, and still sung by itinerant Jogis, Muslim and Hindu, is a living proof of the impression created, and this was natural. The camping of lakhs of men in the locality for about three months was a thing that had never before occurred even in those war-like times. The earlier battles in the Panipat-Karnal-Thanesar locality had been bloody and decisive from the political point of view, no doubt, but they were never fought to the last in the proper sense of the word, nor was there such a massacre of camp-followers after the event. The result is seen in the creation of legends. The Jogi, who copied the Bhau ballad for us (published in the *Bulletin of the Deccan College Research Institute,* 4.3. of 1943), does not record Bhau's death, following in this respect the Maratha chronicles, and says that he went to the village of Bhaopur, some twelve miles to the south-west of Panipat. There he lived for a long time with a Fakir, evidently incognito, hiding his identity. Thence he went to Kairana across the Jamuna after some years, his further life being not known to the men in the Panipat locality. That Bhau did not die on the battle-field and lived long afterwards became the traditional belief throughout India, giving rise to imposters who gave themselves out as the real Bhau, and created political problems adversely affecting the Maratha history. We think that the ballad-singer's account of Bhau living in Bhaopur is a transparent attempt to connect the already existing village of Bhaopur (founded and named after some Bhaosingh, a name common in the locality) with the name of Bhau, the Maratha general. Such a legend is recorded about another place in the *Muzaffarnagar Gazetteer* on page 9 (1920, Reprint) of the U. P. Series. "The Jamuna in the extreme north of the district appears to occupy much the same place as formerly, and on the south also, it washes the high mound on which stood a *Maratha fort still connected with the name of Sadasheo Bhao.* It may further be safely conjectured that the channel of the river has not changed much at this point since Panipat. Between these two extreme points, however, the bed of the river is tortuous and uncertain." We have seen the mound ourselves near the village of Isapur on which now stands not a fort but a bairagi's ashrama and a temple of his household gods; but there was no trace of the fort at least in 1935—nor was the fact of its previous existence known to the inhabitants there. The *Gazetteer*-writer, we take it, must have copied the information from some local report, or the description given by some previous traveller in the locality. As the mound in question is a prominent object in that low-lying river basin, it could have been very effectively used militarily by placing long-range guns on it and guarding or attacking the passage of the Jamuna near that point. As Ahmad Shah Abdali had moved his camp along the river-front just opposite to this mound on the other side of it during the second stage of the Panipat beleagurement, the military use of such a prominent height is not an impossibility. But the idea of the Marathas making use of it during the Panipat beleagurement presupposes that the Maratha line of communication into the Doab was intact during the earlier part of the Panipat siege, or alternately, the Maratha contingents detached by Bhau for cutting off Abdali's line of supply through the Doab, had approached up to this point, though there is very little likelihood of such a thing happening. As the data on which the *Gazetteer*-writer based his statement are not before us, it is not possible for us now to decide the point.

II. Was the Imperial Canal to the West of Panipat Flowing During the Panipat Campaign?

Most of the historians, depending upon the information supplied by such sources as *Gazetteers* whose information is not historically sifted, have taken the Imperial Canal as having stopped flowing eighty years before 1820, when it was again repaired by the British. *Imp. Gaz.* Vol. XIV, p. 234 (1908), under the heading "Jumna Canal (Western)," supplies the information that there were ancient bridges over the canal at Karnal and Safidon and that the Delhi branch ceased to flow sometime during 1753 to 1760. This information the *Gazetteer* has copied from the Persian chronicles, giving an account of the civil war between the Emperor Ahmad Shah and his Wazir Safdar Jang. The canal formed the property of the Wazir and with a view to stopping his income from that source, the canal was broken up by his enemies. But what has been overlooked by the *Gazetteer* has been now brought to light by the deep researches of Dr. T. G. P. Spear of St. Stephen's College, Delhi. Writing in the *Journal of Indian History* (Vol. XIX, Pt. III, No. 57, p. 326, Dec. 1940), he says that the canal was broken up in 1754 in the civil war no doubt, but was repaired by Ahmad Shah. But thereafter sometime, somehow, it was neglected. Taking into consideration the position of Bhau's camp, the major portion of which was situated to the north-west of Panipat, and the description found in the local Bhau ballad,[1] which supplies the information that Bhau's 700 elephants were stationed at the village of Gharaunda, ten miles to the north of Panipat, we assume that the canal was definitely flowing during this period. For elephants require a copious water-supply which would be available only in a place like the bank of a river or a flowing canal. That it was flowing can also be guessed from the fact of the mention of the sojourn of

1 *BDCRI* 4.173.

the various conquerors in the Shalimar Garden (which depended upon the canal water) to the north-west of Delhi. Raghunathrao Peshwa lived there in 1754,[2] Ahmad Shah Abdali in 1756-7,[3] and Sadashivrao Bhau in September, 1760.[4] They would not have preferred the place unless a copious supply of water was available in the vicinity for a big army. We think this to be sufficient proof for taking the canal as flowing during this campaign. When Ahmad Shah succeeded in terrorizing the Maratha troops into huddling themselves in the cramped camp at Panipat during the last fortnight before the great battle, the Marathas seem to have lost their access to the canal water to the west of their camp, for Kashiraj says that Ahmad Shah was able to make a circuit round the Maratha camp from a distance, which we think to be correct for the last fortnight only. On account of this, the Maratha army seems to have suffered terribly for want of water, in addition to want of food. This fact is found mentioned only in the ballad published by us in the *Deccan College Bulletin* Vol. IV, p. 184. If their access to the canal water was not cut off, we think the canal to have been cut higher up in the vicinity of Karnal or Kunjpura at the head of the canal. The ground for such supposition rests on the fact of the reconquest[5] of Kunjpura by the Afghans during the Panipat siege. For the first month and a half, the Marathas were receiving their food-supply from the vicinity of Karnal on account of their friendship with Alasingh Jat, the founder of the Patiala State, but a new army from Afghanistan under Atai Khan came along that route to the help of Ahmad Shah early in December. Dilir Khan Ruhela made common cause with these new Afghan troops and took back Kunjpura from its small Maratha garrison, thus closing the Maratha supply from that side. Taking into consideration the Afghan tactics, it is not unlikely that he might have cut the canal at the head after this event so as to cut the water-supply of the Maratha camp at Ahmad Shah's behest.

Lest it be forgotten, it should be noted that the old Imperial Canal was flowing in those days along a different channel than the present New Delhi branch of the western Jamuna canal. It began lower down on the river Jamuna to the north of Kunjpura. It flowed to the east of Karnal and not to the west as at present. Then it did not take a loop to the west before coming to Panipat as at present, but flowed parallel to the west of the Imperial Road at a distance of three or four miles. Dr. SPEAR in his article referred to above, page 327, supplies the following information: "The canal on its old alignment ran along a depression in the apparently flat Jamuna plain. In some places the bed of the canal was above the level of the land at a great steepage, and waterlogging was the result. The distance between Panipat and Karnal suffered most from this fact." (P. 328.) "Then the alignment was altered to correspond with the lie of the land, and it now sweeps in a great curve from Karnal to Panipat."

This discussion should convince the reader that the old canal—Shah Nahar—was flowing along to the west of Panipat at a distance of some three to four miles during the Panipat campaign.

2 *SPD* 27.74.
3 Ibid 21.106.
4 RAJ. 6.404.
5 *Fall* 2.307.

III. Estimate of the Confronting Armies at Panipat

The chief trustworthy authority on the numbers of fighting soldiers engaged in the Panipat campaign is *Bhausahebanchi Kaifiyat*. It never gives inflated figures. When Sadashivrao Bhau came to Sironj in Malwa and halted there for a week in April 1760, the estimated strength of the Maratha cavalry is given as 27,000, besides Ibrahim Khan's trained infantry which is stated to be 10,000. This figure of the chronicle is testified as correct by figures in some contemporary letters. *Khare* 1.14 gives 25,000 cavalry, starting with Bhau from Patdur. The Maratha army under the Peshwa belonged mainly to the Hujrat division i.e. Peshwa's personal cavalry. *Khare* 1.21 gives a slightly different estimate. It gives the figure of the Telinga Gardis of Ibrahim Khan at 8,000 and the cavalry at some 33,000 total. This figure was made up of the personal squadrons of Vishwasrao, the Peshwa's son, and the nominal Commander-in-Chief of the whole army, the troops of Bhau himself and more than half the troops generally serving under Raghunathrao, who would not lead the campaign himself and remained in the Deccan. The Maratha chiefs of note serving as officers in these regiments were Samsher Bahadar (the Muslim half-brother of the Peshwa), Vitthal Shivdeo Vinchurkar, Manaji Paygude, Antaji Manakeshwar, Damaji Gaikawad, Khanderao Raste, Subhanrao Mane, Mahadaji Naik Nimbalkar, Balvantrao Mehendale and Nana Purandare. This letter written by Gopalrao Patwardhan, a noted general, estimates the numbers on Abdali's side at 50,000 cavalry and 50,000 infantry including the Ruhelas. When the Maratha army had not as yet separated from the main body collected in the Nizam's Dominion, the total strength was estimated at 75,000. Out of this, 10,000 were sent to Karnatak under Visaji Krishna Biniwale, and 25,000 remained with Raghunathrao to check the Nizam. The rest, it seems, were appointed to accompany Bhau to the north. But out of this number some troops probably remained with the Peshwa as his personal guard, and some others lagged behind or would not go as ordered, thus making the figure which went with Bhau near about 35,000. When this army crossed the Chambal at the beginning of June and joined forces with Shinde and Holkar with the remnants of their broken armies, the total number is estimated at 70,000 to 80,000, including the contingents of Surajmal Jat and the Wazir Ghazi-ud-din.[1] The same letter written on 1st July, 1760, estimates Abdali's side at 60,000 troops, besides the contingent of Shuja-ud-daulah which is estimated at 20,000. When estimating the figures engaged in the final battle of 14th January, 1761, we have first to deduct the Maratha casualties in the capture of Delhi at the beginning of August 1760 and the sack of Kunjpura in the middle of October 1760. The Maratha loss before Delhi was only a few hundreds, and before Kunjpura also not much, though the number of wounded was considerable.[2] In short, we need not take the total losses in these two actions at more than 1,000. In the three considerable battles fought during the two months of beleagurement at Panipat, the loss of the Maratha side was similarly very small, not going beyond 1,000 dead.[3]

1 *Purandare* 1.387.
2 *SPD* 21.193.
3 *Aitihasik Patra Vyavahar* 97.

(1) Thus, to calculate the figures left for the final action, we shall have to deduct first the Jat-Wazir contingents which left the Marathas at the beginning of September, numbering possibly not more than 5,000. (2) The troops left in charge of Delhi under Naro Shankar estimated at about 7,000 in all.[4] (3) The total loss at Delhi, Kunjpura and the three skirmishes at Panipat—3,000, leaving 55,000 out of the combined total estimated at 70,000 near Agra at the beginning of July. Out of this also some thousands will have to be deducted for those who died as a result of wounds received in the five actions, as also some disabled on account of serious wounds and starvation. Thus we shall not be far off the mark if we say that the Maratha fighting troops at Panipat were 50,000 only. A writer from Panipat, writing before the three skirmishes, estimates the Maratha number at 60,000, while he reports Abdali's troops at 40,000 only. Perhaps he omits the infantry on Abdali's side, because the word "Fauj" in Marathi is generally used for cavalry only. Abdali is said to have received additions to his troops during the Panipat beleagurement estimated at 8,000. Kashiraj's figures given at the beginning before crossing over the Jamuna to Panipat, are 40,000 horse and 40,000 foot, including the troops of Abdali and his allies. For Bhau he gives the figures as 55,000 horse, 15,000 foot (including 9,000 Gardis under Ibrahim Khan), besides 15,000 Pendhari horsemen. As against this the irregulars on Abdali's side are estimated by Kashiraj at four times the number of the Durrani horsemen on the muster roll of the Shah. Even if we take the actual Afghan cavalry at 33,000 only, this estimate would give one lakh and twenty thousand as the figure of irregulars, which we think very much overestimated. It is true that there possibly would be more soldiers from amongst the camp-followers on Abdali's side than there would be on the Maratha side, on account of the very character of the two peoples and their usual mode of life. An average Afghan camp-follower would be a good horse-rider even when he had no horse of his own. Similarly, he would be more adept in using arms than possibly an average camp-follower in the Maratha army. But it is incorrect to think that none of the camp-followers and non-combatants following the Maratha army would have horses of their own; we rather think that many of them had the Deccan ponies with them serving as baggage carriers for their masters. Unfortunately for the Marathas, most of these ponies seem to have perished of starvation during the beleagurement of Panipat, due to want of fodder, while the irregular horses on Abdali's side were still serviceable. Satvoji Jadhav, writing after the battle of Panipat,[5] definitely says that many a cavalryman had lost his mount before Panipat, and even the rest had become unserviceably weak. If we deduct 20 per cent on this account, then Sir Jadunath's estimate[6] of 40,000 horsemen actually present in the field seems to be a tolerably correct figure, though arrived at in a different manner. Kashiraj's estimates of the two armies given in round figures seem to be based on heresay reports, and not on official figures as he would make us believe by his mode of writing. His only strong point is that he clearly distinguishes between trained government-

4 RAJ. 6.406.
5 Ibid. 1.406.
6 *Fall* 2.287.

paid soldiers and camp-followers or irregulars. The figures given by Shamlu and others are inflated because they include all the camp-followers also. An average of four camp-followers for each professional soldier would make a fair estimate[7] of persons gathered in the two camps, and on that basis it looks as if each camp had two and a half lakhs of people in it. The Maratha camp had many pilgrims also in its entourage. Some sardars had brought their families for this very purpose with them, so as to facilitate their travel in comfort and safety. Many priests had gathered in the camp from Benares and Prayag with the hope of getting good fees and alms by plying their trade. Many candidate clerks had joined with the hope of getting some temporary work or civil appointment in the newly conquered territories. This was almost a normal and permanent camp-following class in the Maratha armies ever since the days of Shivaji, as is attested by Martin, the French Governor of Pondicherry. Incidentally it shows the nature of the Maratha camp. The chartered bazar accompanying the army supplied all the needs of the people in it. People felt "so little danger in following their camp that life in camp is spent as happily there as in towns." (MALET'S *Memoranda Relative to the Maratha Army at Kharda,* Maratha-Nizam Relations, No. 202, p. 272.) Major DIROM writes that the Maratha army on march "resembles more the emigration of a nation guarded by its troops than the march of an army only to subdue an enemy."[8] The women camp-followers in the Maratha army were a necessary element for doing certain duties which men thought it derogatory to perform in those days. Cooking their food and cleaning the vessels could be done by males, but grinding the corn was thought to be an exclusive duty of the female sex, for performing which a number of them accompanied the army. It is difficult to estimate the number of females in the Maratha army, but we think there were some 20,000 all told. Most of these were slaves of their masters, who served in various capacities and also as concubines. Very few married women had accompanied their husbands in this long-drawn-out campaign. Because Bhau, Balvantrao Mehendale, Nana Fadnis and possibly a few others had taken their wives with them, a wrong impression is formed about the total number of such women accompanying the army. *Mirat-i-Ahmadi* states that 12,000 women in good position among whom 700 travelled in palkis, were taken prisoners.[9] We think this statement a gross exaggeration. There could not be more than 100 women carried in litters, nor could the 12,000 women belong to the married class. A few other sardars had also taken their women-folk with them, no doubt, for pilgrimage along the route, but their number was not more than a few hundred at the most.[10] The rest of the women belonged to the slave-concubine class. Nuruddin Hasan's mention of "handsome Brahman women" being sold after the defeat can only be treated as a figment of the brain, and as to the "rose-limbed slave girls" mentioned by Sir Jadunath,[11] their number could be infinitesimally small, if such were to be found there at all. Had the

---

7 DIROM p. 242.
8 DIROM p. 243.
9 *Sardesai Commemoration Volume* (English) p. 260.
10 *Purandare* 3.209.
11 *Fall* 2.348.

Peshwa's army been going on after Shivaji's pattern, there would have been no impediment like this in the camp at all. But Shivaji led few campaigns lasting more than a few months at a stretch or far away from the homes. The Peshwa's army was modelled after the Mughal pattern with all its drawbacks, which proved fatal here as they had proved fatal to Aurangzib in his campaigns against the Marathas.

IV. Imperfect Sense of Time and Direction

Indians of pre-Panipat days had no maps before them to judge properly of the directions of places, etc., and so we have to take their descriptions of events cautiously. Bhau writes "Abdali has come to the *south* by crossing the Jamuna at Baghpat." Nana Purandare takes Kunjpura as situated on the *south* bank of the Jamuna. "Panipat lies 40 kosa from Delhi *towards the west.*" With these examples from contemporary documents before us, we have to accept Kashiraj's directions with correct visualisation. Sir Jadunath has bungled in his attempt to connect Kashiraj's translation with the Browne's map of the battle. This is also due to his non-visualisation of the path of the sun during the days of its highest southern declination. A man from the Maratha camp talking of Abdali's position or Kashiraj writing from the Abdali's camp about the Marathas was sure to confuse correct direction during December-January. Kashiraj has *naturally* taken the Maratha army as facing eastwards and so described the Afghans facing westwards on the day of the battle. Another thing incorrectly calculated by Sir Jadunath is the hours of the day. The sun rose at Panipat (latitude 29° 23′ 30″ North, longitude 76° 58′ 30″ East) on 14-1-1761 at 7 A.M. and set at about 5.20 P.M. (local time). The day thus consisted of about 10 hours and 20 minutes and the battle has to be described accordingly. The day was, in lunar calendar, 8th of the bright half of the month. The moon would set about mid-night on such a day and not at 9.15 P.M. as taken by Sir Jadunath. (Vide *Fall* 2, pp. 369, 346, etc.)

CHAPTER VI

THE BATTLE

FINALLY, as decided at night, the Maratha army rose in the early hours of Wednesday, the 14th January, 1761, and prepared itself to march out of the beleaguered camp at Panipat. After going through the morning round of physical duties, Sadashivrao Bhau and Vishwasrao bathed, worshipped the gods, had a hurried breakfast and then dressed themselves in full armour for the ensuing battle. The whole camp was agog throughout the previous night. They had collected all their little belongings and tied them in bundles to be carried away by securing them to their backs or on the bullocks and other pack animals which had survived. Some carts and other heavy goods, found either difficult to arrange properly or as absolutely unnecessary on the march, were left behind in the camp in order to facilitate the march. With the first call of the trumpets, the whole camp started and arranged itself in marching order as best it could.[1] To the front were placed the heavy cannon, behind it the infantry of Ibrahim Khan followed in triangular formation so as to make the artillery in front, the spear-head of the march. To their rear were placed Damaji Gaikawad, Yashwantrao Pawar, Vitthal Shivdeo, Antaji Manakeshwar, Samsher Bahadar and other small units. Then followed Bhau and Vishwasrao with their personal troops. After them came non-combatants and baggage. On the right flank of the rear were appointed the Shinde and Holkar contingents. The lighter artillery was placed mainly on the right of the marching square, though a few were placed on the left and at the back also, to scare away any surprise attack on those sides. The hollow square thus formed marched out step by step and stood three miles in front of Abdali. Their position at nine o'clock (local time) was: Ibrahim Khan's infantry in the village of Nimbdi to the south-west of Panipat; Bhausaheb with the centre one mile behind him to the north of Ugrakhedi; Malharrao Holkar at the rear directly one mile to the south of Panipat. The non-combatants and camp-followers were standing between Panipat and Ugrakhedi, their left-hand side reaching the outskirts of Rajakhedi to the north. The distance between Malharrao Holkar's rearmost contingent and Abdali's left under Shah Pasand Khan was more than three miles, his contingent probably standing in the field to the east of Siwa.

The Afghan army when arranged stood roughly in a crescent-shaped curved line from Siwa to Chhajpur Khurd. Barkhurdar Khan's Risala was standing there with the *nullah* at their back. Dunde Khan and Hafiz Rahamat Khan were standing between Chhajpur Kalan and Ujah. Ahmad Shah was somewhere between Risalu and Dhadaula, while Wazir Shah Wali Khan's cavalry stood ready between Risalu and Ujah. Ahmad Shah's baggage and camp were between Dhadaula and Nurpur. Najib-ud-daulah and Shuja-ud-

[1] The front originally was spread from Kabulibagh to the north-east of Panipat, to Chandani Bagh to the west of it, where Ibrahim Khan's corps were camping. This was the head of the Maratha marching order. The direction it took was to the south-east of Panipat.

TO FACE PAGE 87

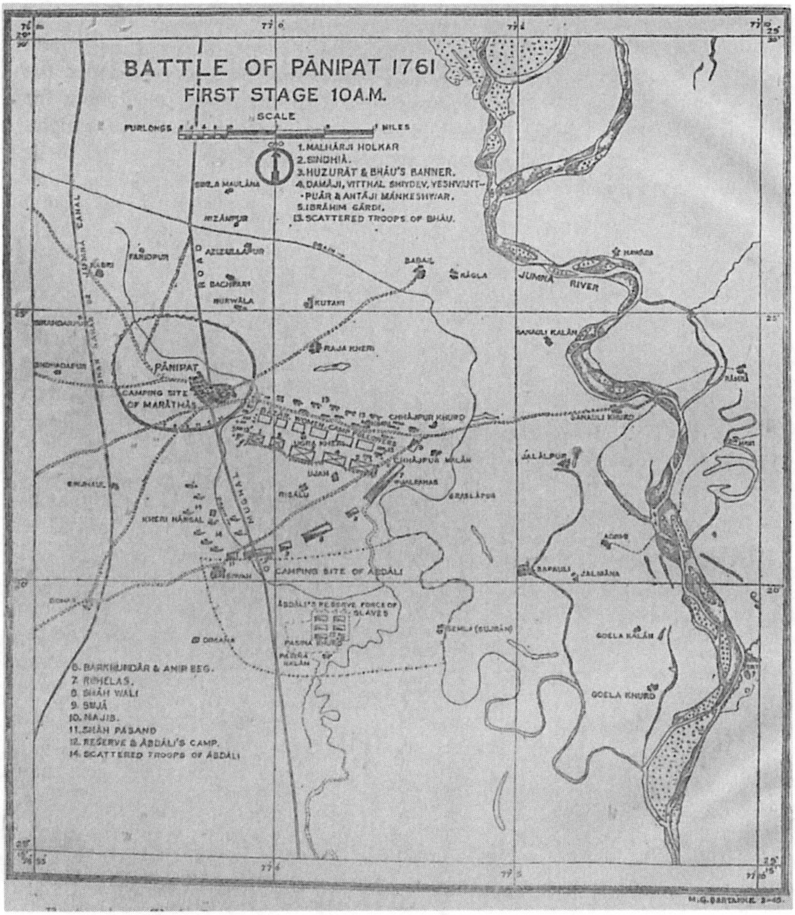

Foot-note:—Shah Pasand Khan was standing with five thousand troops at the left flank of Abdali's line of battle across the Mughal Road to the northeast of Siwa.

daulah were on the plain between Risalu and Siwa. We do not think that the Afghan army was standing in a continuous line along the whole front between Chhajpur and Siwa.[2] There were gaps between the various contingents which were ordered to the front, though none so wide as to allow a Maratha corps safely to thrust itself between. Najib-ud-daulah had to cover full three miles before he could come into contact with the Shinde division to the west of Ugrakhedi. The army was spread on a front some seven miles in length from Chhajpur Khurd to the west of Siwa. The right-hand side of the Maratha square was not more than three miles in length, and spread from Nimbdi to Chandni Bagh (to the east of Panipat) in almost a straight line.

The battle began with a cannonade as usual. Within an hour Ibrahim Khan's corps touched the Abdali front at the point where the trans-Ganges Ruhelas were massed in front of the village of Chhajpur Kalan. On the right-hand side of these Ruhelas Barkhurdar Khan and Amir Beg were standing ready to cover the Maratha flank on that side. Ibrahim Khan ordered two corps to stand in front of them so as to stop their advance with a view to cut off the gunners in front of the corps of Ibrahim Khan. The rest of his infantry engaged with the Ruhelas. His quick firing muskets soon began to have their effect on the opposite side. The infantry advanced step by step fighting for each inch of ground, but the heavy siege-guns seem not to have kept up the march and soon lagged behind. This was probably due to the difficulty of dragging them on an uneven ground, and also to the advance of the Ruhela cavalry to cut off the gunners as is usual in this kind of battle. For three hours the combat went on, and the Ruhelas were pressed back with heavy slaughter. Only a few hundred match-lockmen remained with their chiefs Hafiz Rahmat and Dunde Khan. This was the result of the battle at twelve o'clock. But before this the Maratha cavalry, detailed for supporting Ibrahim Khan and standing half a mile at his back, had acted injudiciously, not understanding the kind of battle they were engaged in. In their impetuosity they seem to have acted on their own initiative and broken the marching order absolutely necessary when the army is to advance in a square formation. They advanced rapidly at a trotting pace and soon overmarched the infantry corps of Ibrahim Khan. But they met with the sharp fire of the Ruhela infantry and had to run back with broken spirits. Vitthal Shivdeo and Yashwantrao Pawar then galloped back and stood behind the heavy guns fixed in the ground and possibly chained together so as to obstruct the advance of the enemy cavalry to cut off the gunners. Damaji Gaikawad also met with a similar check from the Durrani cavalry to his left, and he, too, returned back and stood behind as at the beginning. This disobedience of orders was the chief cause of the Panipat disaster. Before starting, Bhau had clearly placed his plan before his officers and asked them to march straight without breaking the order by swerving to the right or left. The aim of the march was to gain ground and reach the river Jamuna before evening and not to offer battle. If the enemy would step aside and allow the Marathas to press forward with their whole mass, then the Marathas were not to engage with them at all. Only if and when the

2 *IHQ* 10.259, 60.

enemy would not allow them passage in their march, the cavalry was to charge and press forward, beating the enemy back so as to break their order. As at the very beginning this breach of order occurred, it had a disastrous moral effect on the frontal troops. The first cause of the break in the ordered march was due to the heaviness of the Maratha guns which, on account of their long range, fired their shots in a faulty manner so as to fall at the back of the enemy. Thus their ammunition was wasted without gaining the desired effect of breaking the enemy line of battle and creating a gap in it for the troops to advance. Ibrahim Khan had then to cease fire and order his infantry to march with bayonets in their hands to break the enemy line and make a breach. The Telinga infantry under Ibrahim Khan was formed of well-trained corps with experience of such battles. Their resolute advance made the Ruhelas fall back, leaving few soldiers with the chiefs as stated above. But in this effort Ibrahim Khan lost half his troops in killed or wounded, and then the preponderating number of Ruhelas began to tell. The Ruhelas were in the proportion of three to one of Ibrahim Khan's musketeers. Their match-locks fired heavier bullets and were even more effective on account of their steady aim due to their long barrels. Their range also exceeded that of the comparatively light muskets of French-make used in Ibrahim Khan's infantry. If, at this psychological moment of apparent stale-mate, the Maratha cavalry had advanced again, galloping to support him, there would have been no further slaughter amongst them, and the battle would have been carried on in the intended order. But, as said above, the cavalry ordered for his support had foolishly advanced first, and then coming back stationed themselves behind the chained heavy guns, with their strength exhausted and spirits broken. Damaji Gaikawad who was to the left of the Maratha thrust—thus adjoining Barkhurdar Khan's out-flanking cavalry—behaved better than Vitthal Shivdeo and Yashwantrao Pawar. He supported the two corps left by Ibrahim Khan to meet the enemy on that side. As there was no infantry facing them, they repulsed the Ghilzais on that side as often as they advanced with their scathing fire. But Damaji was himself wounded in the action and he also returned to stand in the company of Vitthal Shivdeo and Yashwantrao Pawar.

Until now we have said nothing about the Maratha centre under Bhau. He was standing to the right of the (middle) centre of the Maratha march. Behind him to the left were standing the non-combatants and camp-followers. The attack on Bhau's side seems to have been begun not by Bhau himself but by the Durrani Wazir who advanced farther than the main line, firing his camel-swivels manned by Persian bombardiers.[3] The Maratha light artillery placed on the right of their march and facing the Durrani line obliquely was gradually receding back from the Durrani line. Its fire would not reach the Durrani line at all, except at the front under Ibrahim Khan. At nine o'clock the distance between Bhau's right-hand side and the Durrani Wazir's front was a mile or so. According to the Maratha plan, Bhau would not swerve to his right unless it was attacked by the enemy. The Wazir on whom naturally the main responsibility fell and who was stationed at the centre, advanced him-

3 MUNDY p. 215 (note).

self and soon came into contact with Bhau's right wing. As the fire from the camel-swivels supported by Persian infantry at its back was both quicker and sharper, they seem to have soon overpowered the Maratha light artillery on that side and silenced it. As there were no infantry battalions to support it, Bhau had himself to swerve to the right to its rescue, and thus the Peshwa's Huzarat came into contact with Shah Wali Khan's troops. The ground where they met was to the south of Ugrakhedi and to the north of Risalu. The troops surrounding Bhau belonged to the select group and were possibly in the best of condition. Working under the eye of the commander-in-chief himself, and themselves possessing a high sense of duty with patriotic fervour for the name of the Marathas, they came sweeping down and would not stop even in the face of the sharp fire from the swivel-guns. Now a cavalry battle fought with lance and sword on the Maratha side and musketry and archery on the other side began in good earnest. It is certain that the Afghan cavalry under Ahmad Shah had more musketeers, match-lockmen and archers amongst them than were to be found in the Maratha army.[4] Each Maratha of note had possibly a hand-gun by his side but he had neither love for it nor expertness at its use. He preferred lance and spear at a short distance to the clumsy bow and arrow or heavy, long matchlock of those days. "The fighting was so violent that earth and sky could not be seen and the eye of heaven became dazzled at beholding this spetacle." (Kashiraj.) The Afghan army was composed of 12,000 horsemen and 8,000 foot-soldiers, besides 1,000 camel-guns. "The Marathas drank them up like the water of a river." Atai Khan, the son of the Wazir's paternal uncle, (who had carried the raid against Govindpant Bundele and slaughtered him) was slain. 3,000 Durranis were put to the sword and the rest fled back at the fury of the Maratha charge. Only 200 troops stood surrounding the Grand Wazir with fifty camel-guns in his front. He was clad in full armour from head to foot, still dismounting from his horse he sat down on the ground, saying to his followers, "Comrades! Vilayat is far off, whither are you going?" He asked Kashiraj (who himself reports this) to take a message to Shuja-ud-daulah that he was dying and that Shuja should come to his aid. Shuja did nothing of the kind, however, excusing himself with the plea that it was not proper to break the line of battle at that stage and thus allow the Marathas a possible chance to pierce past the Afghan line through the gap. As a matter of fact, though Shuja stood ready with all his troops and guns throughout the day, none moved from the Maratha side against him. This clearly shows that the oblique Maratha line never came by itself into direct contact with the Afghan line at the left throughout the main fight, a distance of more than a mile still intervening between the two armies.

But though Shuja would not come to the Durrani Wazir's aid, Ahmad Shah was not unaware of his plight. By this time it was twelve noon, and it seemed for a moment at the centre that the Marathas were triumphing. Ahmad Shah who was some three miles to the back, received intelligence of

---

[4] Even in 1795 match-lock seemed to be daily gaining ground of the long spear according to MALET. In 1760 it must have been comparatively rare. *(Poona Residency Correspondence* 4.270.)

the dispersion of his troops from the right flank to the centre. As a precautionary measure he asked his zenana to mount on horses and camels so as to be ready to run away in case of emergency. At the same time he took the stern measure of beating back his run-away troops who had now crowded themselves in the Afghan camp. He called in his *nasaqchis* (military provosts) and ordered 500 of them to go to his camp and striking with their axes all the camp-followers great and small, drive them back to the battle-field, caring for nothing else. By this method he brought within an hour 8,000 armed men, mostly foot-soldiers, to fill in the gap created at the back of the trans-Ganges Ruhelas. The remaining 1,500 military provosts were sent to the battle-field with orders to kill every man who ran away from the battle and refuse to return to the charge. This order they executed so effectually that after killing a few they compelled the rest to stand in battle array again behind the Grand Wazir's line. Ahmad Shah sent some 4,000 fresh troops to reinforce the Wazir from his retinue. Thus, within an hour, by one o'clock, 10,000 horsemen stood ready behind the Wazir to charge again, while on the right-hand side of the Afghan line 8,000 soldiers supported the Par-Ruhelas in their efforts to stop the march of Ibrahim Khan's successful Gardi troops.

Let us now take stock of the military position at noon. At the very beginning the Maratha cavalry under Vitthal Shivdeo and Yashwantrao Pawar had acted impetuously and gone beyond their orders, attacking the Ruhelas before Ibrahim Khan had created a gap in their ranks by the fire of his artillery and the attack of his musketry. The result was they had to run back exhausted and stand behind the chained heavy artillery to escape an attack from the enemy. Thus their fighting power was neutralized when it was most necessary to take advantage of the gap created by Ibrahim Khan Gardi two hours later. Damaji Gaikawad, on the other hand, had succeeded, for the time being, in warding off the flank attack on Ibrahim Khan's troops by Barkhundar Khan and Amir Beg, by supporting the two Gardi corps left by Ibrahim Khan on his left side. In the centre, Shah Wali Khan's quick advance had obliged Bhau to break the line of the marching square and advance to meet the Wazir, with what result we have already seen. Twelve noon to one o'clock was the most crucial period of the battle. Had the beaten horsemen under Vitthal Shivdeo, Yashwantrao Pawar and Damaji Gaikawad courageously rushed out and marched past the chained guns in front of them to support Ibrahim Khan, it is very likely they would have succeeded in marching past the Ruhela line with the help of the Gardi troops, and outflanked them. But they do not seem to have done anything of the kind. Perhaps there was a distance of one mile or so intervening by now between the advanced corps of Ibrahim Khan and the heavy artillery behind which their troops stood, with the result that no correct news of the condition at the front was available to them. For the time being they stood safe behind the chained guns, Barkhurdar Khan and Amir Beg finding it impossible to assail them. Perhaps these Persian Mughals did not advance from their flanking position, with a view to cut off the advancing Marathas if they tried to create a breach on that side. Thus it so happened that the Maratha troops reaped no tactical advantage from the an-

TO FACE PAGE 90

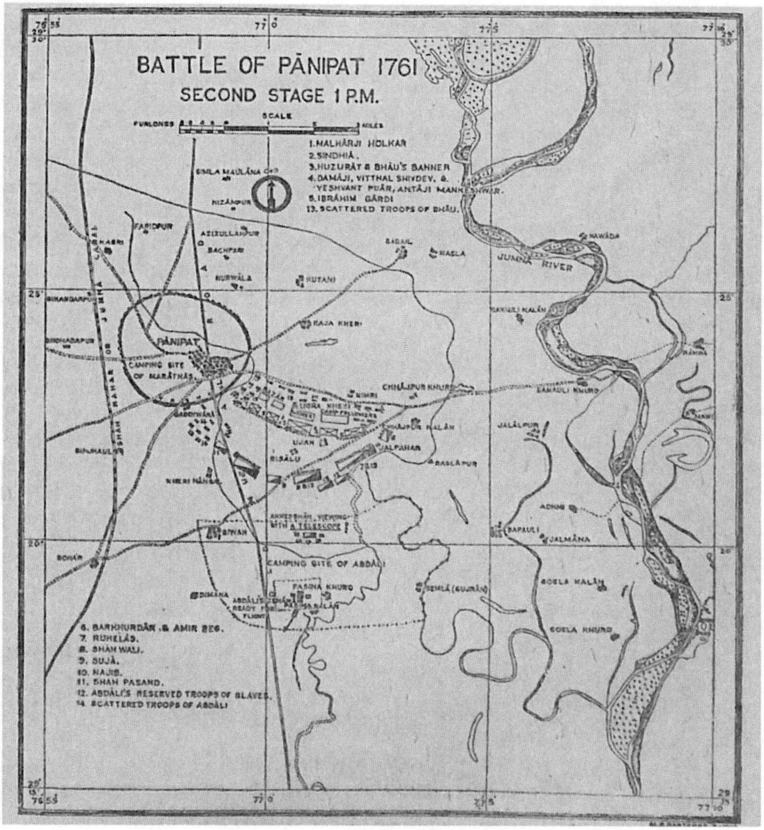

Foot-note:—Ahmad Shah was viewing the Maratha line, it seems, with a telescope (durbin; vide Irvine p. 246, note 1.)

nihilation of their five Gardi troops, nor could they succeed in reinforcing Ibrahim Khan in his time of need and distress.

The right centre under Bhau also could not, or rather would not, reap a tactical advantage, being encumbered with the women-folk. There was a distance of about a mile between Ibrahim Khan's vanguard troops at the left of the Maratha line and the centre under Bhau. It is not clear from the scanty descriptions of the actual battle whether a line of communication was maintained from the one end of the line to the other, whether Bhau knew the condition of Ibrahim Khan's corps or the behaviour of Vitthal Shivdeo and others. Had he with his remaining victorious troops galloped at full speed for one mile to the left and stood behind Ibrahim Khan's hard-pressed musketeers confronting the broken Ruhelas, it is certain that he would have succeeded in creating a breach there, and run behind the Ruhela camp. Had he cared to save his life together with that of Vishwasrao and his nearest womenfolk, he would have possibly taken such a line of action, and escaped along the river Jamuna past the Abdali camp. But that would have meant a breach of promise he had entered into with Ibrahim Khan. The previous night he had told on oath to Ibrahim Khan that he would under no circumstances flee away from the battle-field forsaking the Gardi infantry under Ibrahim Khan, but would rather stand as if entrenched behind him and take the risk of being cut to pieces rather than leave the field. Secondly, it would have meant a break of the marching square formation, leaving the non-combatants, camp-followers and the bazar people to the tender mercy of the Afghan troops. Looking to the result, however, it seems as if that would have been a better alternative, because, after all, the camp was left to be looted and slaughtered by the Afghans at the end of the day. By it the Maratha defeat would have been felt less, as it would have resulted in the survival of politically and militarily the most important people in the army.

The behaviour of the Maratha rear-guard under the Shinde and Holkar contingents is not known. When, actually, Malharrao Holkar and the captains in the Shinde cavalry left the field is not recorded. But we take it that they never came in contact with the enemy throughout the main period of the battle from 9 A.M. to 3 P.M. Exception must, however, be made for the personal troops under Janakoji, Tukoji and Mahadji Shinde. They kept their eye on the movements of the centre under Bhau and, after Vishwasrao's accidental death, ran to his rescue. It was an unfortunate necessity of the plan that these veteran troops practically did nothing in this final battle. They merely neutralised the opposite camps under Shah Pasand Khan, and Shuja. But many of them escaped the last slaughter by taking to their heels just in time to get their way westwards.

The main difference in the position of the two armies was created by the necessity of the Marathas. They had, if they wished to move from Panipat, to come out in a body all together, leaving no base with reserves behind. Ahmad Shah's position was the reverse. He stood on his ground well entrenched. He was not out to carry his bag and baggage with womenfolk past the enemy line, as the Marathas had to do. His defensive position was now as strong as that of the Marathas at Panipat. Ahmad Shah took full advantage of this situation. Only the fighting force was first sent to the front, the rest doing all their duties in the usual manner. They could cook their food and have their meals before the Maratha onslaught could reach them. The Shah's personal troops had, as usual, been kept as a reserve. Ahmad Shah seems to have taken the precaution to keep his main body of troops intact in all his battles and not only at Panipat. He would make the second-rate troops face the enemy first and wear them out. Later on, at the critical juncture, he would rush in with his fresh, unexhausted troops and complete the victory. His methodology was thus quite different from the Indian practice since the days of the Mahabharata battle. In all the noted Indian battles in history, the chief general was always at the fore-front, and at his fall the battles ended in a rout. The battles were fought for the general, and with his fall no motive remained for the troops to fight any longer. Ahmad Shah, in fact, was the precursor of the European mode of warfare, wherein a general seldom takes a personal part in the fight. In a composite fight he would make his allies face the brunt of the battle and expose them to severe casualties. He himself would come in last when the result hung in the balance, thus leaving a preponderating force with him to take charge of the spoils and not leave an upper hand to others in case of a dispute later on. The original Hindu practice of fighting with a general at the head of the army had been handed down even to the Muslim rulers of India. They also followed the same mode. The Marathas revolutionised the old system by their guerilla mode in which a face-to-face battle was to be avoided. But Sadashivrao Bhau had now again brought the original vogue into fashion with the help of the trained infantry and its park of artillery. Unfortunately for him he had to practise this mode under very adverse circumstances now.

Thus the critical hour of the battle, when the Marathas could possibly have given a different turn to it, passed away with the army standing exhausted and bewildered by the very first effort. Sir Jadunath thinks[5] that because "Bhau had no squadron of cavalry in heavy armour and mounted on powerful horses ready to charge in close order and cut its way like a solid wedge through the shaken Durrani ranks," he could not complete his initial success. He also thinks that because the Maratha troops did not carry roast meat and dry bread in their saddle bags and water in leather bottles to refresh and reinvigorate themselves easily in the field on account of their caste susceptibilities with its dread of its defiling touch, they could not recoup themselves in time so as to follow their initial success with further advantage. Though these causes are true so far as they go, we do not think that these decided the line of action taken by Bhau. He knew that Ahmad Shah with his entrenched camp was behind the Wazir's line, and the possibility of marching through it was very remote. At the same time he was neither prepared to expose his camp to Afghan butchery as long as he lived, nor would he break the square formation decided upon the previous night, and run past Ibrahim Khan's in-

5 *Fall* 2.335. See the appendix on food arrangements.

fantry through the gaps created by it and forsake him, going back on his promise. Anyway, the possibility of saving the main centre with the most important personages on the Maratha side, passed away by one o'clock when the Wazir rallied his troops and began the fight again.

Now the battle entered its most desperate stage. The fight was a close combat with sword, spear, lance, dagger and knife, both sides vehemently charging each other. This went on for an hour or so, and then "by Ahmad Sultan's good fortune" an arrow struck Vishwasrao, killing him outright. He fell from his horse. The news of Vishwasrao's death spread like wild-fire throughout the Maratha camp in a very short time, and it had a very disastrous effect on the morale of the fighters thenceforward. When Bhau heard of it, he also was very much affected. He ordered that the corpse should be placed on an elephant so as to keep it safe from being trodden upon, and then ordered a last charge. But by this time the news was beginning to have its effect. Timid men, it seems, fell back and began to leave the field, saving themselves as best as they could, and in a short time Bhau's flanks seem to have completely deserted. Kashiraj writes that, all of a sudden, the field became clear, the Maratha army having vanished entirely, and none remained in the field except heaps of corpses here and there.

Besides the news of Vishwasrao's death, another cause which created panic in the Maratha camp was the behaviour of 2,000 Afghans, employed by the Marathas and working under Vitthal Shivdeo. The sentiment and aim of the Marathas in this war under discussion is incidentally well illustrated thereby. They were not fighting against the Muslims, not even the foreign Afghan Muslims, but against Ahmad Shah Abdali who wished to interfere in Indian politics and bring foreign pressure on the solution of Indian problems. This existence of the Afghan troops serving under the Marathas is not mentioned by Kashiraj at all. But it is found in both the *Kaifiyat* and *Bakhar* of Bhau in Marathi.[5a] It is also testified by Bhau's correspondence with Govindpant Bundele.[6] It is not clear to which of the Afghan tribes these dissatisfied, renegade troops belonged. They may even be Indian Ruhelas. Be that as it may, these troops, employed without forethought, became a source of great havoc at this critical juncture. To distinguish them from the Afghans on Abdali's side, they had been given a badge of an ochre-coloured headdress[7] after the Maratha fashion. They were standing behind Vitthal Shivdeo's troops to the left-hand side of Bhau. As soon as they heard of Vishwasrao's fall, they treacherously threw away their badges and began to loot the Maratha camp adjoining them, circulating the news of the Maratha defeat with exaggerated accounts. The non-combatants, consisting of two lakhs of persons, naturally thought that the Afghans had now penetrated the Maratha lines, and they took to their heels. Vitthal Shivdeo also began to fall back as a result, instead of trying to check these Afghans in their nefarious activities. Thus it was that Kashiraj found the Maratha side suddenly deserted and the field

5a Pp. 23 and 148 respectively.

6 Raj. 1.237, 242, 244.

7 *Bhau Bakhar* 148; *Bhau Kaifiyat* 23

cleared. Now only a few hundred troops surrounding Bhau remained at the front in the centre of the line.

On the left-hand side the Ruhelas, now reinforced with fresh troops, began their attack simultaneously with that of the Wazir at the centre. In the consequent battle, Damaji Gaikawad, Antaji Manakeshwar and Yashwantrao Pawar fell back defeated, unable to stand the heavy slaughter by the consecutive rounds of match-lock fire from the Ruhela side. They could not make a united stand in one place. Ibrahim Khan went forth and mixed his troops amongst the Ruhelas, heavily firing his last salvoes, but was himself wounded and carried a prisoner by the Ruhelas. His son and brother-in-law died in the effort. Practically the whole of his corps seems to have died on the battle-field fighting to the last. Yashwantrao Pawar also was cut to pieces. Damaji Gaikawad received three wounds, but retreated safely with his immediate civil assistants.[8] Antaji Manakeshwar also with his usual cautiousness retreated just in time to save himself, uncovering the left side of the Marathas. The Ruhelas now closed upon the left flank of Bhau's personal cavalry.

On the left-hand side of Bhau, Samsher Bahadar was standing. He behaved on that day as a worthy scion of the Peshwa family and fought to the last. To his right were standing the Shindes, Tukoji, Mahadji and Janakoji. Their opposites on the Abdali side were Shuja-ud-daulah and Najib Khan. At the beginning of the battle at 9 A.M. the distance between the Ruhela front and the Shinde line was more than three miles. Najib was the coolest brain on the Abdali side, never losing his head and never acting impetuously. On this day he seems to have acted with perfect calculation. As the Maratha plan of the battle was to march on to the river-side before the evening and not to fight a battle, naturally no one from the Shinde side advanced to attack Shuja or Najib. Besides, there was a great distance intervening between them. Najib used this respite to act in a systematic manner. He turned all his troops into infantry, dismounting even his cavalry from their horses. Then with his 15,000 troops he slowly advanced on foot, throwing up earth-works in front at each quarter of a mile. That is to say, the sappers and others raised a breast-work of sand and earth a few steps in front of the line, one cubit high, which afforded a shelter to the stooping infantry and prepared trenches where the Ruhela infantry advanced and crouched down. Najib had a vast quantity of rockets with him. He would fire a volley of 2,000 rockets all at once from his advanced trenches. This had the effect of darkening the ground and the sky with their smoke, and their noise created a sort of terror very useful for frightening away any advancing force. Kashiraj says that the troops of the Shinde contingent wanted to attack Najib, but they got no chance on account of this fire. We think otherwise. Bhau had wisely kept the Shinde and Holkar contingents with their beaten troops—beaten by Abdali himself in three or four fights during the last two years—to the rear flanks of his advancing square so as not to demoralise other troops by their chicken-hearted behaviour in an

[8] SPD 21.200

emergency. In one sense they were in a position to act better than others, having a first-hand experience of the Abdali tactics. This time they were acting accordingly, never breaking their line and never acting impetuously as in a Maratha charge. It means they obeyed the orders of the Commander-in-Chief and would not offer battle themselves unless attacked. Najib could gain only one and a half *kos,* i.e., not more than two miles in four hours by this method, according to Kashiraj's measure. By one o'clock, he came within the firing distance of the Shinde contingent and began his attack on it. This had the effect, it seems, of pushing the front ranks of the Shinde line to its left towards the centre and separating them from their rear. The news of Vishwasrao's fall by this time had created terror in the Shinde contingent also. Janakoji and Tukoji, as the most intimate and loyal servants of the Peshwa, pushed themselves to Bhau's side to see what had happened and rally the centre. Sabaji and Mahadji turned back towards Holkar's contingent and thus created a gap in the line through which Najib's Ruhelas pressed forward. Shah Pasand Khan, who was to the left-hand side of Najib and had been ordered to support the flank attack of the Ruhelas on that side, followed close at the heels of Najib so as not to allow the Marathas to run that way. It is not known when the Holkar and Shinde contingents, which fled away from the field of battle, actually left the field. Certainly it was not before the news of Vishwasrao's fall became known, i.e., 2 P.M. But after that they seem to have soon taken to their heels,[9] and never once came into direct contact with the Afghans or the Ruhelas. We have no faith in the widely expressed belief that Malharrao had an understanding with Najib who allowed him to escape unscathed. He had, perhaps, selected his own position in the rear, or Bhau had wisely and knowingly placed him there. Fortunately for him, the opposite side under Shah Pasand Khan would not leave their original position at the front astride the Mughal Grand Trunk Road near the village of Siwa. Had Shah Pasand Khan left his place he would have allowed a clear passage to the Maratha troops at the rear along the easiest road. Shah Pasand Khan could not break the battle array, and Malharrao would not swerve to the right and break the marching square. But after 1 P.M., when Ahmad Shah ordered simultaneous flank attack on Bhau's centre to aid the frontal attack of the Wazir, Shah Pasand Khan naturally swerved obliquely to the right. As Najib had also by this time advanced systematically on the flank of Shinde, there was no problem for Shah Pasand Khan to break the fighting line and create a gap for the Marathas to escape, though its natural result was to free the Maratha right rear from the watch of Shah Pasand Khan's flank advance. Malharrao's whole life philosophy was based not on honour and prestige but on profit and escape. The Marathi adage which says that "if the head remains whole, one can have eighty-five turbans to wear," seems to have been old Malharrao's guiding principle which he naturally followed at this juncture. Half the Shinde contingent under Sabaji Shinde, Khanaji Jadhav and Janrao Wable, which had separated itself from Janakoji and Tukoji, also joined Holkar in his flight. Unless they had a clear start of two hours, it is difficult to believe that they could have escaped unhurt to the extent they did. Malharrao was

[9] RAJ. 6.409.

very old now and had scarcely strength to ride swiftly enough to save his life.[10] It was only because of his early start that he was not overtaken by the pursuing Afghans after the final rout.

In the meantime at the centre, Bhau tried to rally as many of his troops as he could, and fought to the last. Janakoji and Tukoji joined him in this last effort. Najib had succeeded in separating half the Shinde contingent from the other and closing upon its heels. His position at 3 P.M. was in the gap created by the escape of the Shinde contingent, and Shah Pasand Khan was immediately at his back. This position meant that Bhau's escape was now closed. The main attack on Bhau came from the personal slaves of Ahmad Shah. He had divided his 6,000 slaves into three parties, and placed each of them on the flanks of Bhau. Bhau's front was now closed by the Wazir and the rear by Shah Pasand Khan and Barkhurdar Khan. On the flanks, the 6,000 fresh troops began to fire incessantly and simultaneously. This, combined with the frontal fire of swivel-guns, made it impossible for the centre to swerve to any side, and they were turned into a knot which twisted itself this way and that at each attack until completely withered away by death. Nana Fadnis reports that Bhau was fighting to the last, till fifty horsemen remained by his side. After that Nana Fadnis was separated from Bhau and went back towards Panipat. What happened to Bhau afterwards nobody exactly knows. Tukoji Shinde, Sonaji Bhapkar and many other captains of note lost their lives in the last desperate fight. Bhau would not take even a last chance of escape though advised to do so by Tukoji Shinde, and was thus slaughtered by someone somewhere at last. We take Kashiraj's account of the finding of Bhau's trunk first and his head afterwards as true, though we do not believe in the story of Bhau's last struggle as reported by a Durrani soldier and put down in writing by Kashiraj, because it would not stand criticism. Janakoji was wounded and was made a prisoner by Barkhurdar Khan.

The battle seems to have ended finally by 4 P.M., when Nana Fadnis, separated from Bhau, turned his face towards Panipat. Already many of the civilians had gathered there after early separating themselves from the centre. Thus it was that Ramaji Anant Dabholkar, Bapuji Ballal Phadke and Nana Fadnis met together. These three had good horses and therefore they were able to cut their way back to Panipat. When Nana Fadnis reached Panipat it was already 5 P.M. Taking the advice of experienced Ramajipant, all of them left their horses and baggage and donned the garbs of ill-clad beggars. As Ramajipant knew the geography of those parts well, he led the party out, going west. After it was dark they started their trek, but before they could cover one *kos* they were attacked three or four times and searched by the Afghans. Each time they could they cut off ten or twenty of the party till they covered a great distance, some twelve or more miles to the south-west. Upto this point the three had kept together. But again the Afghans came and wounded Ramaji and Bapuji who thus fell behind. Weak Nana Fadnis swerved into tall grass and was thus saved, his frail figure probably creating compassion

10 Ibid. 3.516, dated 11-3-1760.

TO FACE PAGE 96

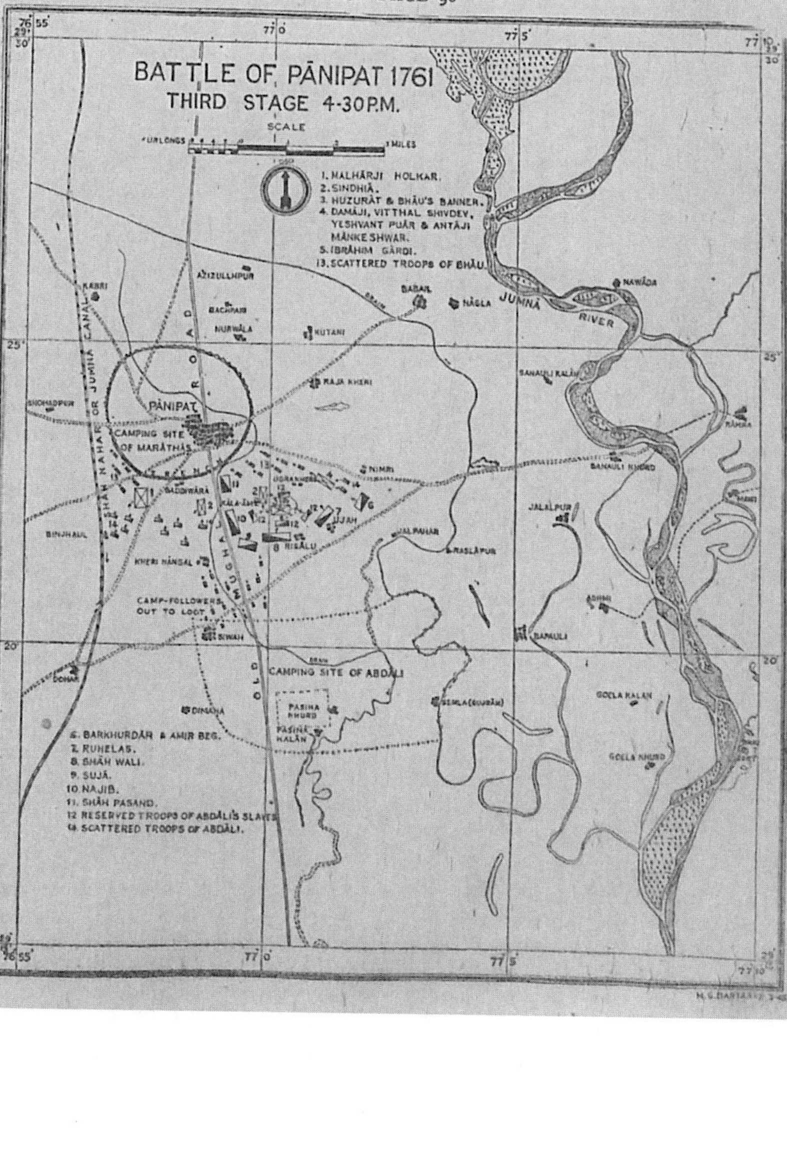

amongst the assailants. He proceeded still farther when again a party attacked him, drawing him out of the tall grass where he was hiding. Here again some old soldier took pity on the boy and thus he was finally saved. Because it was the eighth day of the bright half of the lunar month; the moon was shining overhead in the evening till she set after midnight. This circumstance, while it was useful to some in covering their flight, was also responsible for the long pursuit by the Afghan troops over that plain and the heavy slaughter of non-combatants running on foot for their lives. But many more were killed by the surrounding villagers who had suffered terribly during the last three months by the constant tramp of soldiers. The *Karnal Gazetteer* has recorded that the villages of Phurlak (twelve miles to the north), Bala (fifteen miles to the north-west), and Dahar (six miles to the south-west of Panipat) had migrated to other areas forsaking their sites. This will give an idea of the devastation wrought in the surrounding area. It is not recorded as to when the elephant on which Bhau's wife, Parvatibai, Nana Fadnis's mother and wife were seated, got itself separated from the other troops. From the Maratha chronicles it appears that this elephant was not far behind Bhau's line of battle. Once her elephant touched the elephant on which Vishwasrao's corpse had been placed, covered under some cloth. Then only she came to know of Vishwasrao's death and began to weep and wail. If this fact is truly reported, it means that she was half a mile behind the fighting line. The chronicles report that one captain with 500 shepherds[11] had been specially appointed for the protection of Parvatibai. The name of this captain is given as Visaji Krishna Jogdand, a name which is not found mentioned in any original document. He had been ordered to follow the army to Delhi if it successfully cut its passage through the Afghan lines; but if the battle turned into a defeat, as soon as Bhau's fall was reported, he should cut off Parvatibai so as to avoid her falling into the hands of the Afghans. But neither this Visaji nor his shepherds seem to have done anything according to order. They ran away at the first shock and tried to save their lives! Only a personal servant, Janu Bhintade, never left her for a moment and tactfully brought her back to Panipat out of the turmoil[12] when only half an hour of the day remained. She got down from her elephant and followed Janu Bhintade for some time on foot. Fortunately they met one Virsingrao Baravkar with his good horse. He took her on his horse and fastening her at his back, carried her out of a sea of Afghans with rocks of corpse-heaps in the middle. Being a skilful horse-

11 Why the Marathi chronicles have reported the fact of 500 shepherds (Dhanagar in Marathi) as specially appointed for the protection of Parvatibai is a Mystery. Many of the followers of Malharrao Holkar were by caste like him Dhanagars (shepherds). Was it is to suggest that Malharrao had a hand in the protection of Parvatibai? If so why is the name of the captain specifically given as Visaji Krishna Jogdand? The mystery of this reference is rendered still more mysterious by the tale of Parvatibai as we found current in the region surrounding Panipat. A septuagenarian Gaud Brahmin told us the same fact of shepherds (Gujars) being specially charged with the protection of Parvatibai. We think that Bhau, who was prepared for all eventualities, had done some such thing for extricating his wife out of the turmoil by some safe, comparatively unfrequented path only known to these local Gujars, many of whom must have been certainly serving in the Maratha camp during all these months. It is not unlikely that because some of them acted as guides through the jungle to the south-west of Panipat that Janu Bhintade and other loyal Marathas were able to cut their way out of the danger zone.

12 *SPD* 2.149 (p. 171)

man, he carried her safely across. When his horse was exhausted by its double weight he got her down, when another cavalryman, Piraji Raoot, got her on his horse and thus carried her twelve miles farther on. When his horse became exhausted he also left her behind, but all along Janu Bhintade kept her company, walking or riding along by her side. No Maratha would refuse her a place on his horse on the road, and thus she was thirty miles to the south of Delhi when she met Malharrao Holkar and Nana Purandare. We have related this event in detail because it falsifies Malharrao Holkar's plea as put down in Holkar's *Thaili*.[13] Malharrao Holkar was neither charged by Bhau with the special defence of Parvatibai nor did he himself of his own accord do anything to bring her out of the field. Only casually and accidentally they met to the south of Delhi, a circumstance of which Malharrao took full advantage in preparing his apology.

The description of the actual battle is very scanty in Marathi, that given in the chronicles being more or less personal and not useful for military study. The only eye-witness who speaks of the last effort of Bhau is the truthful Nana Fadnis who was only nineteen years old at the time. His autobiography is a document by itself throwing considerable light on the whole campaign. It clearly sets forth his own prejudices but none can say that he is anywhere untruthful. From his writing it seems that Bhau was not unaware of the possibility of defeat, and had, therefore, made provision for the special protection of the women-folk. As a last resort, it had been decided to kill them before they should fall into the hands of the Afghans. From Nana Fadnis's words, it looks as if Bhau had prepared himself for death. But this was personal. As a general he had taken care that none other should have any scent of his personal decision except Nana Fadnis and one or two other persons like Nana Purandare. He had made every provision that was humanly possible for the ensuing battle with minute care for all eventualities, but all his precautions came to nothing because the plan was not understood, and, if understood, not followed by anyone with zest, except by Ibrahim Khan Gardi who was the author of it. It is clear that the last fight was fought between the Maratha cavalry and the Afghan infantry. But the majority of the Maratha generals had, it seems, no faith in Ibrahim's plan and its possible success. They were expecting defeat rather than victory, and as such were more prepared for immediate flight than for a fight to the finish by sticking to their posts. At the same time they knew that precipitous flight at the very beginning was quite impossible, the other troops being engaged at the front. It is curious to note that of all those who survived the battle, there is an overwhelming majority of old men amongst the notables. Malharrao Holkar, Vitthal Shivdeo, Satvoji Jadhav, Damaji Gaikawad, Antaji Manakeshwar, Sabaji Shinde Khanaji Jadhav, Janrao Wable and Gangoba Chandrachud were all aged sixty or more, and as they were able to run away with some of their troops comparatively unscathed, it means that they had had a clear start of two or three hours before the final pursuit on all sides by the victorious Afghans. The civil officers who were at the back of the fighting force also escaped to a

[13] RAJ. 3.172.

certain extent, though they were massacred on the way, like Antaji Manakeshwar and Baji Hari Supekar who were killed[14] by the Baluch Zamindars near Farukh-nagar to the south-west of Delhi. Not all who ran away survived; rather the majority died as a result of slaughter or by starvation and cold. It is certain that some two lakhs of people died during those two or three weeks, but more died from hunger and cold than by wounds in the battle. We do not believe that the Maratha camp had five lakhs of people as reported in BROWNE's translation of Kashiraj, much less can it be ten lakhs as translated by Sir Jadunath.[15]

Another important thing to note in this affair is the absence of any detailed account of the campaign or of the final battle from the pen of any of these renegades. Malharrao Holkar's supposed confession is only an example of specious pleading specially written to order by some clever scribe. Otherwise no one else even tries to give the whole account. Nana Purandare who was very intimate with Bhau and was supposed to belong to his party in politics, is ominously silent about the battle, though he had occasion to write of the event. From the whole tenor of the various writings about the battle, it is clear that the survivors had come to an understanding among themselves to report it in a particular manner. Their additional excuse of doing so was on account of the personal and political necessities of the case. The personal necessity arose out of the respect for the feelings of Parvatibai, Bhau's wife, who survived and returned in the company of the renegades, as well as anxiety for the health of the Peshwa. Though Nana Fadnis, Nana Purandare, Malharrao Holkar and others seem to have been convinced very early of Bhau's death by the letters they receivd from Kashiraj, Anupgir Gosawi, Purushottam Hingne, Ganesh Vedanti and others, they were afraid to disclose the fact for its effects on Parvatibai and Nanasaheb. The political necessity was still greater. The Marathas tried as far as possible to minimise the disaster by starting rumours about the safe running away of Bhau, Janakoji and others, thus trying to keep an atmosphere of expectancy for the sudden emergence of Bhau and Janakoji at any time and from anywhere, as long as they could. By this method they did succeed in rallying the survivors and making a bold stand from the base at Gwalior. Its definite political effect is seen in the return of Ahmad Shah Abdali after waiting for two months at Delhi, and still more by his political arrangement. He bestowed the Wazirship of the Mughal Empire—be it noted—not on his ally Shuja-ud-daulah but on the regicide Ghazi-ud-din Khan, a protege of the Marathas. He tried to conciliate the Peshwa by sending condolence messages couched in an apologetic tone, and also by opening negotiations for a political settlement.[16] In response the Peshwa also tried to look at the matter in a political manner without revengeful feelings. He also sent Mir Anvarulla Khan Trimbakkar to Delhi with dresses of honour for Abdali and his Wazir Shah Wali Khan.[17] But by the time Anvarulla Khan had reached Kota, he got the news of Abdali's sudden return to his own

14 KHARE 1.71.
15 *IHQ* 10.265.
16 *SPD* 21.202.
17 Ibid. 2.168.

country due to the rebellious attitude of his Durrani troops, and had, therefore, to come back with the elephant which was being carried as a present to Abdali.[18]

ESTIMATE OF THE LOSS OF HUMAN LIVES IN THE BATTLE

The last trace of resistance on the battle-field ceased at 4 P.M. on that day, when two hours of day-light still remained. This fact, together with the fact of the day being the eighth of the bright moon on which the moon was overhead in the evening casting no shadow and setting after midnight, gave ample time and scope for the Afghans to pursue the fugitives and kill as many of them as possible. It is difficult to estimate the number of Maratha soldiers and non-combatants slaughtered, but the total was not less than one lakh. Out of the 60,000 soldiers, possibly half the number died on the battle-field fighting face to face. Some 10,000 more must have died in the pursuit. Of the remaining 20,000, 10,000 definitely reached Gwalior in safety after a fortnight. The rest died on the way fighting with the villagers or on account of heavy wounds, exhaustion, starvation and disease. Of the survivors, too, half only had run away with their horses, the rest had slowly trudged back on foot losing their horses to the robbers on the way. Amongst the soldiers who lost their lives, Bhau, Vishwasrao, Samsher Bahadur (who had extricated himself out of the final struggle after receiving heavy wounds and run back upto Deeg in the Jat's dominion to die there), Yashvantrao Pawar, Janakoji Shinde (who was slaughtered in captivity), Ibrahim Khan Gardi with his brother-in-law and son, Santaji Wagh, Manaji Paygude, Khanderao Nimbalkar, Sonaji Bhapkar, Tukoji Shinde, Dadji Darekar and Narayan Bapuji Rethrekar were the most notable, though practically all the soldiers who died on the battle-field were experienced men who had fought in more than one battle.

In the camp were probably one lakh and a half of non-combatants. Of these some 6,000 found their way to the non-hostile camp of Shuja-ud-daulah and got a shelter there. They were protected from the fury of the Afghans and safely sent back to Jatwada after the return of Ahmad Shah to Delhi. Some 22,000 persons were captured as slaves by the Afghans the next day. Of these a considerable number were women belonging either to the servant or concubine class with perhaps a few hundred of married women, who had accompanied their husbands for pilgrimage. These were sold by their Afghan captors to Indian soldiers. Of the rest, possibly some 50,000 were slaughtered in cold blood by the Afghans on the day after the battle for religious merit. According to Kashiraj, every Durrani soldier slaughtered a hundred or two in this way, which is obviously a gross exaggeration, because if we take even 10,000 Durranis to have done this, it would bring the total slaughter to 10,00,000! Many persons who had foolishly returned to Panipat in the evening of the battle and taken shelter in the walled town, were, the next day, hunted out and put to the sword by the hostile townsmen themselves. The *Bhau Bakhar* reports a curious permission granted by Ahmad Shah to the sons

18 RAJ. 6.472

of Mian Qutb Shah and Abdus Samad Khan who were beheaded by the Marathas at Kunjpura with ignominy. They sought permission to slaughter captured men to avenge their fathers' deaths. Ahmad Shah gave them the permit to go upto 20 kos and slaughter for four ghatikas only, but not more. Thus permitted, Qutb Shah's son slaughtered 4,000 fugitives near Sonepat and Samad Khan's son killed 5,000 near Bahadurgad to the west of Delhi. None of those who were captured alive at Panipat on the next day were slaughtered. Their property was looted but they were allowed to get themselves freed by paying a ransom. Shuja-ud-daulah and his Hindu officers, like Anupgir Gosawi and Kashiraj, paid the ransom for many and sent them back with a safe escort. Many of the fugitives possibly lost their lives because they would not part with what they possessed on their body. Only those who like Nana Fadnis threw away all property and assumed the dress of beggars were able to return unmolested, unless they were caught in the cold massacres related above.

The loss on the Afghan side can be estimated at some 20,000, practically all dying on the battle-field. Three-fourths of this number were possibly the Indian Ruhelas, the rest being Afghans and other foreign allies.

The Spoils of the Battle

If it is impossible to estimate the total number of men who died at Panipat, it is still more impossible to estimate the spoils which came into the hands of the Afghans and the Ruhelas. The definite loss on the Maratha side as stated by Nana Fadnis[19] was 50,000 horses; the number of all the elephants and camels and bullocks is nowhere definitely stated. 300 elephants, 3,000 camels and about a lakh of bullocks would be, we believe, a fair estimate. All the artillery as well as the weapons possessed by the various soldiers and non-combatants fell into the hands of the victors and brigands. The total number of cannon, great and small, heavy and light, should be some 300; 25,000 match-locks and muskets of the French pattern wielded by the Gardi troops of Ibrahim Khan must have fallen into the hands of the Ruhelas and the Durranis. One lakh of swords, shields and spears in the possession of both combatants and non-combatants must have been looted by the victors. A similar number of javelins, axes, daggers and knives of many varieties also must have been captured from the camp by the victors. A few thousand armours, worn by some of the noted Marathas and the Gardis of Ibrahim Khan also must have fallen into the hands of the various captors. This is as far as the war material is concerned. Of these, most of the horses and bullocks and elephants were in a half-starved condition, unable to walk even a short distance. These were sold by the Afghans to the Indian soldiers at almost nominal prices. Many of these must have perished before reaching the homes of their buyers as no fodder was available anywhere in the vicinity of Panipat and Delhi. Many of the bullocks must have been slaughtered for food by the victorious Muslims.

---

19 *Purandare* 1.417.

How much property fell into the hands of the captors is very difficult to estimate. The personal kit of an average Maratha soldier was very meagre. It would be one big brass lota and a small vessel for drinking water, an iron pan for baking bread and a brass plate on which to dine. A few hundred big vessels for storing water or cooking rice and vegetables in volume would naturally be found in this big camp where occasionally even Brahmins must have been fed on religious occasions, or when on visits to places of pilgrimage on the way. The clothing and bedding of an average Maratha soldier and camp-follower could not have been worth much, except for some big sardars and officials who were probably well clad, wearing costly apparel. The tents, big and small, screens and other material of an official nature, worth some lakhs, also came into the possession of the Afghans. What the bazar accompanying the Maratha army possessed on the last day, it is difficult to say. But taking into consideration the famine conditions subsisting in the Maratha camp, there could not have been much of corn, grain and other articles of food and drink. The only item left worth noting was cash and jewellery. A certain amount of accumulated coin should have been found in the possession of the bazar merchants and artisans who had received fabulous returns for their goods. But most of the army and camp-followers, as well as the state treasury accompanying the army on the march, had possibly exhausted their treasure in buying things at fabulous prices, and many had to sell their jewellery and trinkets in order to subsist, thus leaving comparatively very little in their pockets or on their persons. Possibly the accumulated sales money of the merchants had been borrowed by the starving individuals in the camp and also perhaps by the state. If this surmise is true, then even the merchants' money must have disappeared from the camp in buying victuals and fodder or other necessities. Only the unsold and unsalable articles must have remained in the camp and fallen into the hands of the Afghan soldiers. Some 20,000 slaves, male and female, were also appropriated by the victors.

Taking into consideration what has been said above, we do not think the estimate of various writers about loot as correct. "Every trooper brought away ten or even twenty camels laden with money" is the description of Kashiraj. We think it a gross exaggeration. It is true that the Marathas lost everything they possessed, but no Maratha soldier would have on his person or in his pocket precious metal worth more than a hundred rupees on an average. It is doubtful whether even this much had been left with him after ten months of march through a foreign country, when looting had been forbidden, salaries and wages not paid for the most part, and all subsisted by selling what they possessed. We know the aftermath of war. Ahmad Shah Abdali found it impossible to pay the accumulated salaries of his soldiers and hence they mutinied. They were, so reports Nur-ud-din, completely dissatisfied with what they had received as spoils, which they considered very meagre after two years of hard campaigning. The conquered territories were bestowed on the Ruhelas. The booty had also to be sold to them at nominal prices on account of the want of cash with which to buy the necessaries. The captured horses were worth only ten or twenty rupees each! As a result, the unruly Durrani troops were on the point of plundering the camp of Shuja-ud-daulah who decamped from Delhi without even taking leave of the Afghan monarch! It will be seen from these descriptions that this great victory had not brought much cash into the coffers of the Afghans, and was thus a financial failure. While the Marathas had lost their all in the immediate as well as distant sense, there was no commensurate gain to the victors. Verily it was a Pyrrhic victory!

Food Arrangements During the Battle

Sir Jadunath's charge (*Fall* 2.337) that the Marathas did not carry "roast meat and dry bread" in their saddle is due to his ignorance of the Maratha manners. Roasted gram and rice were generally carried by the Marathas when on travel, together with raw sugar (gur) to be eaten before drinking water after a long journey. Flour for baking bread was carried on the person to be used at halt. The Marathas were vegetarians to a great extent, but they also knew the sustaining power of meat in preference to bread. At least one reference mentioning its use is available in Rajwade 10-59, during the war between Janoji Bhonsle and Madhavrao Peshwa in 1769. Janoji for one month was continually on the march every day with Madhavrao close at his heels. During a march of three or four days in succession, he could not make a halt so as to bake bread. The Bhonsle army subsisted on mutton only and thus gave the slip to the Peshwa. This clearly proves that occasionally, when available, the Marathas made use of roast meat to subsist on. Of course, it is more than we can say whether the Marathas on the field of Panipat were actually carrying ready-made food on their persons, but our surmise is that they did.

Maratha Mode of Warfare

That the historic Marathas had perfected an individual mode of cavalry movement is clear from its adoption by Col. Skinner in his later famous "Skinner's Horse." General G. C. Mundy[20] who accompanied Lord Combermere, the Commander-in-Chief in India in 1830, on his tour through northern India, writes of it in the following manner:

> "The peculiar evolution of the 'Skinner's Horse' and which is most striking to a European eye is *the Maratha charge.* In this movement, the whole corps advances in line, two deep, at a canter or trot, which, like John Gilpin's, becomes 'a gallop soon'; and as they approach their object, the files open out, and every man, uttering a wild, shrill scream, comes thundering on with his sword waving above his head. In spite of the apparent disjointed irregularity of the charge, and the amazing speed of their approach, at the word 'halt' every horse is brought upon his haunches within ten paces of the reviewing General. The Maratha charge is certainly well calculated to strike terror into a foe already wavering, but its real physical effect upon staunch troops must be far inferior to the close combined charge of our cavalry." (Page 165.)

The Marathas were known as superb spearmen and their mode can be judged from the Skinner's Horse trained in the same tradition.

---

20 Mundy's *Pen and Pencil Sketches in India*, 3rd ed. (1858).

"On our way thither we were preceded by a band of chosen spearmen, who played their elegant exercise before us with long lances tipped, like foils, with a button. The combatants kept in constant motion, caracoling and circling about, and dealing pretty heavy blows upon any one who happened to wheel within reach. Sometimes one fellow retreated at full speed, trailing his long spear after him with a point on the ground, and skilfully warding off the thrusts aimed at himself or his horse by his pursuer; then when he thought his assailant was off his guard, he would make a sudden wheel and assume the offensive; and in the midst of a cloud of dust, the too confident pursuer was thrust from his saddle and rolled on the ground."

The descriptions of warfare in Marathi *Bakhars* and papers are similar. They say that they attacked, as in the play of "Hututu" going forward, attacking with force suddenly and then returning again, repeating this mode a number of times in succession. Each attack was styled "Hiriri."[21]

The Impression Created by the Marathas—Their Arms[22]

"The personal appearance of the Mahrattas is mean and unprepossessing. They have neither the fair stature and noble bearing of the Mussulman, nor the delicacy of feature and elegance of figure of the southern Hindoo; and they appear to greater disadvantage in our eyes, that we have just left the territories of two of the finest races of people in India, the Seikhs and the Rohillas. Their acknowledged character as brave and skilful soldiers, however, amply makes amends for their personal deficiences."

Maratha Arms: "The chief weapon of the Mahratta is the spear, which is formed of the male bamboo, and from 12 to 18 feet long. He is also skilful in the use of the matchlock. The troops are for the most part mounted on mares, which, although, like the cossack's horse, lanky and ill-fed, are, like him, capable of going through a great deal of work."[23]

Maratha Camp

"Pursuing our march, we crossed another small river, and found the camp pitched on an extensive sandbank, enclosed by two arms of the stream and surrounded by deep ravines. The red and white striped tents of the Mahratta party were spread out on the farther banks; and in a few minutes after our arrival, their wild-looking steeds were picqueted around them, their long lances standing in up-right clumps in the ground, and every man, with a diligence worthy of a German hussar, preparing forage for his horse or himself."

"The swarms of horsemen marched totally without order, and might be seen in straggling parties caracoling and circling their well-broke horses, as far as the eye could reach. The plain looked like a Birnam wood of spears!" (Page 211.)

"The cavalcade of the Mahratta sovereign whose glittering spears and floating pennons we could distinguish even as far as the foot of the rock: and each elevation of ground was thickly thronged with spectators. Every invention of barbaric pomp was lavished on the elephants and equipages of the Raja's immediate suite. The elephant of the Hindoo Rao, in particular, was the most beautiful animal I ever saw, and caparisoned in the most costly style; the whole of his head and trunk was painted in the richest colours; he wore a deep frontlet of solid silver network, and each of his huge tusks was fitted into a sheath of silver richly embossed; massive silver chains encircled his legs (which were about circumferent with a forty years' oak tree), large and sonorous bells of the same metal depended from his sides; his ears were decorated with silver ear-rings about 6 feet long; and his

---

21 *Bhau Bakhar* p. 146.
22 Mundy, pp. 206-7.
23 Ibid.

housings, the fringe of which reached nearly to the ground, were of velvet embroidered in gold and silver.... The Mahratta elephants have a style of gait and carriage peculiar to themselves, and are as superior in appearance to ours, as the English thorough-bred racer is to the earth-stopper's hack. The Company's elephants, probably from having been rode too young, and oppressed with burthens, shuffle along with short steps, their necks bent, and their heads hanging with the melancholy air of an Oxford-street hackney coach-horse. The Mahratta elephant strides majestically along, his head elevated far above his shoulder, and his tusks standing out horizontally. The chiefs pride themselves greatly on these animals, and take pleasure in teaching them a variety of tricks." (Pages 213, 4.)

Though these descriptions are dated seventy years after Panipat, they can as well serve for the visualisation of the Maratha army on that fatal field.

CHAPTER VII

THE JUDGMENT

THE RESPONSIBILITY OF THE PANIPAT DISASTER

THE MARATHA survivors from the Panipat disaster seem to have combined in taking advantage of the death of the commander-in-chief and ascribing the defeat to his incorrect strategy, wrong tactics and, in general, to his conceit, arrogance and blindness to the facts of the situation. Our narrative should have made it clear by now that most of these grounds of condemnation are flimsy after-thoughts. As Bhau was not a free man in diplomatic talks, the responsibility is shifted to the shoulders of the Peshwa. Sadashivrao Bhau's strategy or planning was not incorrect, but its execution devolved upon persons who were not strong enough or wise enough to carry it out. Bhau certainly cannot be pronounced a first-rate general in history. Three-fourths of his mental mould was civil in composition, and only one-fourth can be treated as military in form. Ahmad Shah Abdali, his rival, bore a reverse proportion in his mental make up. The sort of expertness in any matter which comes to a man by single-minded absorption in one kind of work only, is not possible in a man whose life is divided and shared by various interests. Sadashivrao was, no doubt, trained as any other Maratha sardar of the day for war, but that does not seem to be his favourite occupation. His mind was diplomatic in formation and his expertness was to be seen in his management of finance and administration. Ahmad Shah had led the life of a slave under such a military master as Nadir Shah from his childhood, and spent practically every minute of his life amidst war. His expertness was born of this long, all-absorbing experience. Such an experience and such period of candidateship seldom fall to the lot of an average man. Certainly none of the Marathas could boast of such training. The historic Marathas were war-like no doubt, but when compared to the Afghans, must be judged more as civil than military. Civil men can also become good soldiers if they are imbued with high ideals. If the cause for which a man fights is after his own heart, he can put all his faculties into the affair and see to it that it ends in success. Unfortunately such was not the state of the Maratha army at Panipat as a whole. Bhau and others siding with him fought for the name of the Marathas, but there were many others, perhaps the majority, who thought otherwise. Malharrao Holkar and others, who escaped by running away from the battle-field in good time, held a different opinion. They thought that they were not fighting for a supreme cause like the defence of one's motherland. It was the life-long conviction of Malharrao and men of his type that the Marathas outside Maharashtra were fighting for profit and not for a cause. If they succeeded in the attempt without scratching their skin, so much the better. But if they had to fall back in face of higher odds, there was no disgrace for the name of the Marathas in case of a reverse. Sadashivrao Bhau's declared ideal—India for the Indians, governed by the Indians themselves—was scarcely understood by anyone besides a few near friends, and none in the enemy camp believed in his professions at all. This was the real tragedy of the Panipat campaign. Actually, it was Malharrao who, in the company of Raghunathrao, had gone to the Panjab and stretched the Maratha sphere of influence upto Attock and even beyond. It was this expansion by driving Abdali's forces out of the Panjab that had caused Ahmad Shah Abdali to seek revenge. But Malharrao had stretched the line only when Ahmad Shah, after first looting Delhi and Mathura, had returned back to Afghanistan. Taking advantage of the absence of the main forces of the enemy in India, Raghunathrao and Malharrao had proceeded to Lahore. Even in the Panipat campaign, Malharrao's idea was similar. He had advised Bhau to remain behind the Chambal in the Maratha dominions and wait till the departure of Abdali. Afterwards he would have accompanied Sadashivrao Bhau even to the Panjab, had he so desired. Malharrao and most of the Marathas thought this as the real guerilla mode coming down from the days of Shivaji. Fighting open, face-to-face, pitched battles on the result of which the fate of the Marathas would depend, was against the fixed tenor of their minds. They would never run such risks. On the other hand, it was the intention first of the Mughals and later on of the Afghans under Abdali to bring the Marathas to a pitched battle so as to decide the issue in a single fight. As long as the defence of their home-land and the breaking up of the enemy's power were the primary aims of the Marathas, their old mode was all right; but now that the Marathas had spread over the length and breadth of India and aspired to take the reins of Government of the whole continent in their hands, the original mode was out of place and time. Sadashivrao Bhau had understood this point, especially after coming into contact with the French under Bussy in 1751, but Malharrao had not. Malharrao followed his life's conviction even after Panipat and succeeded when not confronted by the new type of infantry. He received his *coup-de-grace* finally at the hands of the English at Kora on 3rd May, 1765, and fled back to Kalpi to save his life! Thus it will be seen that a conflict of ideals and long cherished modes of warfare cut at the root of Panipat.

The late Vishvanath K. Rajwade in his oft-repeated and uncritically accepted criticism of the Panipat campaign,[1] puts the whole blame for the failure on two persons in the main, Malharrao Holkar and Govindpant Bundele. We have seen above how a fundamental conflict of ideals and modes was at the root of the whole difference. Just as Bhau's mind was already prejudiced against Govindpant long before his starting for the Panipat campaign, similarly Bhau's opinion about Malharrao from the beginning was anything but favourable. Malharrao's way in politics was to keep on speaking terms with all and not to antagonise anyone completely.[2] He had kept a similar attitude towards Najib Khan for the same reasons. Such an attitude was possible for a secondary potentate like Malharrao, but impossible for men of Bhau's position who had to take a decisive step one way or the other. In 1750-51 the Peshwa had suspected Malharrao and even Jayapa Shinde of trying to free themselves from the Peshwa's service and accepting service under the

[1] Raj. 1. Introduction.
[2] *Purandare*, 1.287, 293.

Wazir Safdar Jang.* Malharrao was head-strong but he had also the knack of neatly and vigorously carrying out a piece of work on which he had set his heart or on which a challenge was offered to him. In the dispute for succession at Jaipur he had taken a different attitude from the Peshwa and Ramchandra Bawa, but ultimately he forced his will on the others and executed the thing in his own manner. Similarly, after Ghazi-ud-din's poisoning in 1752 when the Peshwa went back on his promise to his sardars, Malharrao and Jayapa were suspected of being in collusion with Tarabai and Mahadoba Purandare so as to checkmate the Peshwa's plans for the governance of the Maratha Empire.[3] Even that suspicion was ultimately found to be wrong. These examples will show the tenor of Malharrao's previous life, and can account for the suspicion which fell upon him during the Panipat campaign, of acting hand in glove with Najib, Shuja and Surajmal. In popular mind, this suspicion proved correct as Malharrao could escape from the disaster unscathed with most of his troops, but we have no faith in this judgment. Sadashivrao Bhau very well knew Malharrao's ways in politics, but had decided to take a different line in this campaign on his own responsibility. Not only Malharrao but other sardars also were dissatisfied with Bhau on account of his financial exactions. To balance his budget after Raghunathrao's deficit campaign of the Panjab, Bhau had put the burden of the Peshwa's debts on the shoulders of the various Saranjamdars and Jagirdars. Malharrao had to pay 30 lakhs for this debt-tax,[4] but due to the debacle after Dattaji Shinde's death, Malharrao had not found it possible to pay it in time before the Panipat campaign. Holkar's Diwan Gangoba Chandrachud is found putting excuses[5] for the non-payment of this accepted debt-tax. Bhau was naturally dissatisfied with Malharrao and other sardars for their non-payment of this tax which had put a strain on his treasure-purse. Malharrao was always a man of tight purse, but there does not seem to be any ground for suspicion that there was any bickering between Bhau and his sardars on this point during the Panipat campaign. Those who think him acting in collusion with Surajmal Jat should note the fact of his behaviour after the disaster. Holkar's *Kaifiyat*,[6] ostensibly written to represent Malharrao's side, positively tells us that he would not put his faith in Surajmal and remain in his territory to recoup himself. When one Jat zamindar tried to stop him in his flight by catching hold of the reins of his horse, Malharrao asked his companion, Govindrao Bule, to cut off the Jat's hand, and drove away precipitately for fear of treachery. This anecdote represents Malharrao's mind. He would not put faith even in his friend, for who could guarantee that the Jat Raja had not changed his mind as a result of the disaster? Malharrao's whole manner was that of a very suspicious and overcautious man taking no risks. The anecdote is supported by the fact of his flight through the Jat's territory south of Mathura without sojourning in it. He took a road skirting on the Jat dominion, but not through it, and went direct to Bhind via Agra, crossing the Chambal and the Kuwari along the river

---

* *Shinde* 3.25
3 *Purandare* 1.311
4 *Satara*, 2.292.
5 *SPD* 21.184.
6 *Kavyetihasa Sangraha* No. 18. 2nd Ed. 1930. p. 23.

Jamuna to avoid the oft-trodden and direct road to Gwalior. After Panipat he fought against the rebels in Malwa and Bundelkhand.. In November 1761, he decisively defeated Madhosingh of Jaipur, getting a wound himself. He fought in the Rakshasabhuwan campaign and helped in defeating the Nizam in 1763. Returning to the north, he again joined Jawahirmal Jat against—be it noted—Najib. All these incidents make it difficult to believe that Malharrao was treacherous towards Bhau or the Peshwa. A man's character ought to be judged as a whole and not by his suspicious behaviour in one incident only.

Govindpant Bundele has been made the chief scape-goat for the Panipat disaster. One third of RAJWADE's renowned introduction to his first volume of letters is devoted to an analysis of Govindpant's behaviour and his downright condemnation, making him solely responsible for the miscarriage of Bhau's plans. RAJWADE's charges against Govindpant are as follows: Firstly, he was not successful in bringing Shuja-ud-daulah to the Maratha side. Next, he had not made proper arrangements for Bhau's transport into the Doab. Thirdly, he had not sent the monies called for. Fourthly, he would not invade Shuja's dominions and create a diversion in that direction. And last, but not least, he did not cut off Abdali's supplies coming through the Doab, thus making Bhau's plan futile. We have seen in the course of the campaign how none of these charges can be substantiated. RAJWADE, and following him other critics also, have wrongly assumed that Govindpant was a military captain. On page 19, RAJWADE puts Govindpant in the list of renowned generals of the time! The suffix Pant as opposed to Rao appended to the name of Govind is itself a proof that the man was taken as a civilian and not a soldier. He was not a Saranjamdar or Jagirdar maintaining troops out of the income of his Jagir. He was an ambitious mamlatdar who on account of a boastful temperament, aspired to be a captain. He had to call in various military captains like Antaji Manakeshwar, Naro Shankar, Gangadhar Bajirao, Manaji Payagude and others for helping him in meeting the rebels in his districts. Occasionally he had himself acted as a captain, but that was against insignificant opponents and in the company of regular troops. Even Bhau looked towards him as a mamlatdar first and a military sardar afterwards. In RAJ. 1, Letter No. 244, Bhau specifically says, "You are not now only a Mahalkari. You have with you as many troops as with a sardar." This means that Bhau was bolstering up Govindpant and asking him to take upon himself work which was normally not his. His age (sixty-five) and habits of life were against Bhau's expectation. This was not a question of ordinary times but of a fight to the finish. Only exceptionally good captains could have done what Bhau asked Govindpant to do. The argument that as Bhau asked Govindpant repeatedly to do certain things, it must have been in his power to do it, is faulty. The fact is, geographically, Govindpant was living in a region to the rear of Abdali, and as such he was the only man who could have done anything in the matter. Bhau could not detach a part of his army and send it to Abdali's rear, as Abdali was sitting across the path. Upto October, Sadashivrao had ordered Govindpant not to come to the north[7] but to invade the enemy dominions be-

[7] RAJ. 1.258, 260.

yond the Ganges. The original plan of Bhau when proceeding towards Kunjpura in October was frustrated by Abdali's daring in crossing the Jamuna at his back. This fact changed the strategy in such a manner that Bhau had to fall back on Govindpant's support because he found it impossible to return to Delhi in the face of Abdali. Herein Bhau was completely non-plussed. Abdali's daring could have been met only by a counter-daring on the part of the Marathas. Bhau's original plan was to proceed farther north from Kunjpura and replenish his army. He expected Abdali to follow him towards the north in a parallel line across the Jamuna through the Doab, as his calculation for the subsidence of the Jamuna waters made him believe. When he heard on his way to Kurukshetra that Abdali had begun crossing above Baghpat, he should have proceeded farther north and crossed over into the Doab by the Budhia Ghat as first intended. Instead, he returned by the same path and found to his dismay that it was impossible to pass by Abdali towards Delhi or to defeat him by direct attack in an open pitched battle. Because he received this first check, he had to fall back on Panipat and dig trenches there so as to follow a different mode of warfare to suit Ibrahim Khan's Gardi troops. Looking historically, it seems that in this Bhau took a wrong decision. Once taken, the only strategy which remained open was to make Abdali attack him in his strong, almost impregnable, entrenched position; but who was to make Abdali attack? No single valiant captain could have succeeded in the move. So Bhau expected hunger to do the work. If somebody in the rear could cut off Abdali's supplies he would have to move and either attack the Marathas as Bhau wanted him to do or return to Afghanistan without offering a battle. Placed in such straits, Bhau was found urging Govindpant to do the needful. Govindpant came into the rear as ordered and tried his luck. He lost his life in the attempt, proving that the work was beyond his strength and that Abdali was a far more consummate general than Bhau imagined him to be. This discussion should prove that Govindpant cannot be charged with not obeying orders and doing his best. We believe that any other captain would have met the same fate and could not have succeeded in cutting off the supplies, as the Ruhelas in that region were well organised and vigilant.

The charge of not sending the sums called for stands on a different level. There is no evidence available on the point of Govindpant's ability to pay. As a Kamavisdar of thirty years' standing, the public as well as the Peshwa probably took him to be a rich man. Whether he had funds at his disposal when Bhau called for them is a moot point. We suspect that the ideas about his riches were ill-founded. Like all other mamlatdars of the time, he was also very cautious in money matters and would not easily part with money. But there is no external evidence, as in the case of Naro Shankar, for Govindpant's having spent money lavishly on any work or in any matter. There are no temples or ghats or forts built by him, which would prove his ever having been an opulent man. On the other hand, complaints about non-realisation of Government dues in his rented Mahals is a theme found repeated throughout the period under discussion. We do not suggest that Govindpant was above board in all his money dealings. But the Peshwa's estimates about his vast riches seem to be ill-founded. Nor do we think him to be an efficient mamlatdar. There is evidence of troubled times and consequent non-realisation of Government dues by him from 1750 onwards. In 1755 a similar condition is found repeated.[8] From the unpublished Dabholkar papers (Nos. 159, 163, 164, 165, 166) it is clear that Sadashivrao Bhau and even Raghunathrao who was in the north at the time, were very suspicious of all the sardars and the mamlatdars in the north.[8a] Gangoba Chandrachud the Holkar's Diwan, Ramaji Anant Dabholkar the Shinde's Diwan, and Govindpant were supposed to be acting in collusion, and grabbing Government dues by an understanding among themselves. Bhau seems to have threatened Govindpant with an investigation into his revenue dealings even then. Govindpant had not submitted accounts for some five years. So he was peremptorily called to Poona and Govindpant was very apprehensive of the result. He wrote to Ramajipant his fear of losing the credit and the fruit of his thirty years' service if the investigation against him went wrong. He asked Ramaji to help him in his difficulties as both were sailing in the same boat! His visit to Poona was delayed for a year more on account of local difficulties. After defeating Sayyad Ali Askar Kubda sent by the Wazir Ghazi-ud-din to occupy the Mahals granted to the Marathas at the beginning of 1756, settling the affairs in the north and making arrangements for his absence, he came to Poona at the end of the year and remained there for some ten months. He seems to have satisfied the Peshwa and his exacting Diwan, Bhau. Bhau sent back with him two auditors, Janardan Apaji Erande and Trimbak Krishna Kanitkar, to check his accounts and, in general, to control Govindpant in his revenue matters. They lived in the north for three years till Panipat, and still they could not succeed in doing what they had been appointed to do! Govindpant became entangled in other political matters and went with Dattaji Shinde to the north. The auditors, becoming hopeless, were on the point of returning to Poona at the end of 1759, but somehow they were prevailed upon to remain in the north on Govindpant's promise to come and settle the accounts to their satisfaction. The correspondence between Govindpant and the auditors proves that Govindpant was not efficient in keeping his accounts nor could he be treated as blameless or above suspicion. Why he was not dismissed for his negligence before Panipat is again a moot point. It may be that while Bhau was charging him with embezzlement, the Peshwa was perhaps shielding him in the affair. Even after the Panipat disaster, the Peshwa is not found condemning Govindpant or calling his sons to account for their father's negligence. Thus it appears that there was something wrong in the system of administration devised by the Peshwa. Every Government officer of some standing looked upon himself as a small chief in those days. Sardars like Shinde, Holkar, and Pawar, thought themselves more as partners in the empire than as servants of the Peshwa. What was allowed by the Peshwa to these higher men out of necessity, was usurped by lesser men. Antaji Manakeshwar, Naro Shankar, Vitthal Shivdeo, Gopalrao Barve, Govindpant Bundele, and the Hingne brothers tried to pose as equals in some way with the fortunate sardars. Their rivalry had vitiated the whole atmosphere, and it was difficult for the Peshwa either to dis-

---

[8] *SPD* 2.29,30; RAJ. 3.158, 159, 160.
[8a] *Shinde* 3.316.

miss an unwanted officer or to replace him by a better one. If Govindpant did not prove serviceable enough during the Panipat campaign, the result must be attributed to the defective system and not to the individual. But supposing that Govindpant did not send the funds to Bhau even though he did possess them, his non-compliance had little to do with the military side in the Panipat affair. Ample funds in the hands of Bhau at Panipat would not have brought him the necessary supplies which depended solely on the military strength to fetch them. Even Bhau, writing to his son after Govindpant's death, is not found speaking anything against him. The Peshwa heard the news of Govindpant's death after his crossing the Narmada in January 1761. Writing a letter[8b] of condolence to his son, the Peshwa eulogised his faithful services unto death, a befitting end to a long life of faithful service. The Peshwa wanted to treat the sons of Govindpant as children in his own family. This shows that the Peshwa had no information or suspicion of Govindpant's dereliction in the Panipat camgaign. Balkrishna Dikshit, writing from Benares about Govindpant's end, remarked,[8c] "A great man has passed away." Thus it would seem that contemporary opinion did not condemn Govindpant. It was only when survivors from Panipat, who wished to absolve themselves from all blame, began to put the whole responsibility on those who had died, that Govindpant came in for his share in the condemnation along with Bhau and Balvantrao. The *Bhau Bakhar* puts the whole affair in such a dramatic form as to lead to the inevitable disaster. It has made Govindpant a friend of Najib Khan[9] from the beginning of the campaign, where he is shown as an accessory of Malharrao in shielding Najib against Dattaji Shinde's wrath! Govindpant is the agent who made Dattaji accept Najib's treacherous proposal of building a bridge over the Ganges, so as to delay the affair till the arrival of Abdali! Later on, Govindpant is represented as having refrained from attacking Najib's family and treasure in his trans-Ganges raid by accepting five lakhs as a bribe. Ultimately Govindpant is killed, according to the *Bakhar*, not by Atai Khan, but by Najib's Ruhelas! Now from what we know of Govindpant's relations with the Shinde family from the very beginning, it cannot be imagined that he would do anything of the kind, especially against the Shindes. There is positive proof in his letters to Ramaji Anant, the Diwan of the Shindes, that Govindpant favoured Jayapa Shinde in preference and perhaps as against Malharrao Holkar.[10] In Dattaji's campaign against Najib, Govindpant is throughout acting under his orders. He escorts the women in the Shinde family after Dattaji's death. It will be seen from these antecedents that there was no likelihood of his acting in collusion with Najib as stated by the *Bakhar* and by RAJWADE. The *Bakhar* is thus proved to be a prejudiced and partial document. It is worth noting that the *Bakhar* does not condemn Holkar for the Panipat disaster, though earlier he is shown as acting against the Shindes as well as the Peshwa. Beginning with a prejudiced mind against Govindpant, mainly on the presentation of the *Bakhar*, RAJWADE was simply carried away in his thought when he alighted on a big

8b *Bundelkhand Prakarana* p. 147.
8c RAJ. 3.511.
9 *Bhau Bakhar*, pp. 50, 60, 130.
10 *Shinde* 3.314-15-16.

sheaf of papers connected with Govindpant. He thought that here was the key to the understanding of the whole Panipat disaster! He so far forgot himself as to change the dates of the original documents in his hand published in his first volume (Nos. 175, 181, 183, 184). He even went to the length of entering into a discussion of a possibility of changed Eras[11] to suit his antedating of the said letters! Even Govindpant's caste came in for criticism and was tagged on to a letter of Naro Shankar, a Deshastha brahmin and not a Karhada! When a critic is obliged to fall back on the caste of a man for explaining an affair, he has fallen very low indeed! Govindpant as one of the most successful Karhada brahmins of his time was naturally taken as a leader of his community. In Benares, a large number of Karhada brahmins, well-versed in brahmanical lore, were residing during these times. They formed, it seems, more than half of the Deccani brahmins resident in that holy city. During the Panipat campaign and even before, a rivalry existed between these Karhada brahmins and the Chitpavans headed by the Dikshit Patankar family, the members of which acted as bankers, diplomats as well as the spiritual gurus to the Peshwas! Sadashivrao wrote to Govindpant to settle the dispute as best he could.[12] The language used by these spiritual gurus against other castes was offensive and derogatory to their status. Even the Peshwa is once found using a word[13] for the Karhadas (Ambhasta) which makes them rank lower in the scale. As an individual, the Peshwa Balaji Bajirao, was a mild type of person, paying attention mainly to politics and ignoring other squabbles. Sadashivrao Bhau, like his father Chimaji Apa,[14] seems to be somewhat different, with caste consciousness at the back of his mind. Even the Peshwa Nanasaheb was charged with being caste-conscious by such an intimate family friend and servant as Mahadoba Purandare,[15] his Diwan during the first half of his rule. Govindpant always tried to be on good terms with the Peshwa family from the very beginning as he was a personal servant under Bajirao. He was probably introduced into the Peshwa family by Radhabai, wife of Balaji Vishwanath, who came from the Barve family of Newre from which Govindpant also hailed. Or it may be that he came to Bawdhan, near Wai, in the company of Ramajipant Kolhatkar who also hailed from Newre. But his previous intimacy with the Peshwa family had by this time no value in the eyes of Sadashivrao who was a strict task-master. The Peshwa was so overpowered with the sense of indebtedness, that he had allowed a free hand to Sadashivrao in all state matters, and Sadashivrao Bhau seems to have antagonised one and all by his line of conduct. His opinion about Raghunathrao Dada and men of his persuasion seemed to have steadily deteriorated for at least three years before he undertook the Panipat campaign.[16] Both military as well as civil sides in the state were disaffected towards him. Govindpant's statement in his letter to Janardan Apaji that the Peshwa had then begun to search in small things, and that at

[11] Rajwade 1, note 265; Raj. 1, Introduction, p. 68; Raj. 1,282, note 325.
[12] Ibid. 1.185.
[13] Ibid. 3.501.
[14] *Purandare* 1.146.
[15] Ibid. 1.275.
[16] Original letter in the Parasnis Collection.

the Poona Court nobody's reputation was safe, are true not only as far as Govindpant himself was concerned, but are applicable to one and all. The whole trouble had arisen from the precedent of the Peshwa's own doings. A state servant (albeit the first minister) who had risen by flouting the orders of his master could not hope to secure the willing obedience of his servants. The Peshwa had broken the unity of the state by concentrating power in his own hands by all kinds of machinations and subterfuge, by relegating his co-ministers in the state to a corner. Now the same game was tried upon him by his servants. What is clearly seen by studying all the material and taking a comprehensive view of the whole affair is that, both military as well as civil servants in the Maratha State thought themselves in spirit more as partners in the state than as servants who could be dismissed at will. The trouble had been growing for a long time, but seemed to be coming to a head just at this awkward time when the state was engaged in a life and death struggle with a first class enemy. All the sins of commission and omission committed by the Peshwa knowingly or unknowingly before, now came to visit him like the ghost at the table of Macbeth. Panipat thus proved to be the culmination of all previous defects in the Maratha system, and was not the result of one man's misbehaviour or default. That Sadashivrao Bhau was already prejudiced against Govindpant, we have seen. The Peshwa was conscious of this fact and so had written to Govindpant, early in May 1760, to go to Sadashivrao Bhau personally and satisfy him about the accounts, so as to get into his favour;[18] but it was too late. Govindpant was now acting on the defensive. Sadashivrao Bhau might have tried to assure him that there was no fear of dismissal in store for him but his words had then exactly the opposite effect on Govindpant's mind.[19] Even after this Govindpant did not turn a traitor. He tried his best, but perhaps he could not put as much heart and energy into the affair as he otherwise might have done.

To sum up, RAJWADE's charge against Govindpant is proved as far as his keeping of accounts goes, but not on any other count. That the Peshwa should have kept a man of Govindpant's type in such an important border region as the Doab, was wrong and injudicious. A far better and younger sardar was necessary at such a key-post. A clerk grown into a mamlatdar and exaggerated into a sardar was not a fit man for the post. But it seems that no better men were available to the Peshwa, which means he had neither trained nor had engaged better men for the post, showing a defective system of recruitment for filling in various posts. To appoint men simply because they are near at hand somehow, is not a proper mode for running an empire. Those who think of the rise of obscure and ill-educated men into imperial diplomats, governors and generals as an achievement of the Peshwas should bear this point in mind. The machinery devised by the Peshwa was not fit and sufficient for carrying on an empire; even the constitution and machinery of a trading company like that of the English East India Company was found better adapted to cope with the times and emergencies, but the Maratha system proved in-

17 RAJ. I.143.

18 RAJWADE I.182.

19 Ibid. I.242.

effectual in the end. Individuals, however great and towering, do not make a nation. It is the level of the whole populace that ultimately tells.

SADASHIVRAO'S PERSONAL FACTORS

In the treatment of the Panipat campaign, Sadashivrao has been shown as proud, capricious, self-willed, harsh and offensive in his dealings with others. In this, both Kashiraj and the Marathi chronicles have combined in the condemnation of Bhau, because both write after the event, keeping their eye on the final disaster. But this seems incorrect. The personal letters of Bhau in the *Purandare Daftar*[1] bear testimony to the quite different mould of his mind. He seems to be a straightforward, shy and guileless man in his correspondence with his equals in the first half of his life before he became the Diwan of the Peshwa in 1752. He is found referring every matter to Dhondopant Purandare[2] who seems to be his *guru* in the beginning. Dhondopant advised him on the points referred to for some time, but later on became weary and stopped giving advice. A man who can write in the way he has written to Dhondopant cannot be taken as proud or self-willed. He fears social obloquy[3] and is found currying favour with the Peshwa his cousin and his wife Gopikabai, as well as Sakharam Bapu, Baburao Phadnis and Mahadoba Purandare. These secretaries would not initiate Bhau into the state affairs for fear of being ousted from their positions, as well as from their unwillingness to interfere in the family squabbles of the Peshwa. Sakharam Bapu, the wisest among them, clearly writes to Dhondopant that "Bhau is neither proud nor easily led by anybody.[4] Whatever wrong he does, he does through ignorance." Of course Bhau naturally felt that he belonged to the Peshwa family and was thus to some extent a master and not a servant like the other ministers, though the Peshwa seems to have treated Bhau at first as only one of the secretaries. Only after Bhau had shown his capacity for administration and had played a trick with the advice of Ramchandra Bawa, the Peshwa was brought to understand the real situation and consented to appoint him as the sole Diwan, lest Bhau would go to Kolhapur and become a rival Peshwa there. As a Diwan, Bhau is found to be an expert in financial matters and strict in administration. He antagonised most of the sardars and mamlatdars by his strictness, since they were loose and undisciplined in their dealings. Nevertheless the various Kamavisdars trembled before Bhau and would not get his confidence. This had a disastrous consequence in the Panipat campaign. One and all had to obey his orders, but none did it willingly. All would have liked to run away from him at the first opportunity. A general must inspire not only awe and respect, but should also be loved by his followers, a thing which was not possible, it seems, in the case of Bhau. Bajirao with all his weaknesses was loved by his followers; Sadashivrao was not. This was the result not of his

---

1 *Purandare*, 1. 168, 169, 180, 181, 182.
2 Ibid. 1. 171-3, 178, 180-1.
3 Ibid. 1. 170, 176-8, 197, 211.
4 Ibid. 1. 182, 184.
Ibid. 3.196.

behaviour during the ten months of the Panipat campaign, but of the impression he had created during the previous ten years. It was singularly unfortunate for the Marathas that such should have been the case at this most critical juncture. The respect and awe with which Shivaji seems to have been looked upon by his contemporaries was not felt in the case of Bajirao and Bhau. Bhau was not strict in his sex-life, as was wrongly assumed by SARDESAI in his Panipat Campaign.[5] The *Purandare Daftar,* Part I, bears ample testimony[6] to Bhau's extra-marital sex life. Perhaps this fact had affected the contemporary opinion about Bhau in an adverse manner to a certain extent. We do not know whether Kashiraj's statement[7] that "one of the Bhau's wives escaped" from Panipat on horseback was made under this misapprehension.

SADASHIVRAO BHAU AS A GENERAL

Sadashivrao Bhau has become the scape-goat of both the sides. He is criticised not only by the opponents but also by his compatriots. The majority of the Marathas thought that the strategy he followed at Panipat was wrong. The Marathas till then had never encamped behind the trenches and arranged their fight on the basis of infantry tactics. The critics on the opposite side think that the whole Maratha system was loose, insubordination being ingrained in the Maratha ranks; there was no proper gradation, no link between the commander-in-chief and the common soldier. But if we compare Bhau with another renowned general of his times in Europe, there does not seem to be any great difference in their ideas about the strategy and tactics of those days. In the battle of Panipat, Abdali had definitely a superiority in the Ruhela infantry under such a consummate captain as Najib Khan. His infantry it was that decided the day by its last tactics. Bhau's infantry under Ibrahim Khan had been used decisively in the beginning of the battle. But it was not followed with advantage by the cavalry at the back. Bhau's personal effort was mainly based on his devoted cavalry, in the use of which he seems to have followed the innovation attributed to Fredric the Great. "Fredric had learnt its value, against the musket of those days, by experience; and he believed that Seydlitz in the open, at the head of 70 squadrons, was a thing which no infantry could resist."[1] But unfortunately for Bhau he first came across the Afghan cavalry under Shah Wali Khan and not against the infantry under Najib Khan, due to his formation of the oblique order in the march out of Panipat. Had the cavalry divisions kept behind the infantry of Ibrahim Khan to support it and take advantage of its invincible attack acted in a valiant and correct manner, there would have been no occasion for Bhau to deliver his side-attack on the Afghan front. Damaji Gaikwad, Vitthal Shivdeo and Yashwantrao Pawar had been placed behind Ibrahim Khan to do their duty. They inadvertantly rushed forward, before the full effect of Ibrahim Khan's grand effort had reached its culmination and created a wide

5 SARDESAI, *Marathi Riyasat, Panipat Prakarana,* p. 253.
6 *Purandare* 1.212, 241, 289, 293, 311, 345, 364.
7 KASHIRAJ, p. 50.
1 ACTON p. 298.

gap in the weak infantry under the trans-Ganges-Ruhelas. Their duty was silently to wait for some two hours, though keeping themselves ready on horse-back for any eventuality. Had this order been properly carried out, Bhau and the magnificent Hujrat cavalry which was behind them would have had no occasion to offer a front battle to the Durrani Wazir. They would themselves have followed the rushing cavalry of these three sardars into the gap created by the Gardi fire. Bhau's generalship failed not because his strategy was incorrect, but the tactics were not properly understood by his captains and they seem to have acted as if it was only a cavalry battle. Bhau had till then followed "the school which taught that actual fighting must not be resorted to until the use of brains has been exhausted, that the battle comes in when the manæuvre has failed, the seizure of the strategic position is the first defence of the armies, so that a force which is tactically inferior may be strategically superior."[2] Now when all these alternatives had been tried and failed, Bhau was following Fredric in his new doctrine "to act on the principle that nothing can destroy the enemy except a pitched battle, and the destruction of the enemy, not the weakning of the enemy, is the right object of war," knowing that "even a successful defence weakens the victor." Unfortunately for Bhau he was possibly the only person in the Maratha camp who had understood this principle and the overwhelming majority of his lieutenants were trained in different tactics. They thought Bhau almost a madman to follow this method, their heart was not in it and they deviated from the order of the battle at the first shock and followed their own mind in the later half of the day. Those who were loyal and devoted died with the Commander-in-Chief, while the rest fled back from the field as soon as it was possible for them to quit the field unnoticed by Bhau.

Not Individuals But the System Responsible for the Panipat Disaster

Panipat was a national disaster. A national disaster exhibits all the weak points together with some of the good points of a nation. A national war fought for the prestige of a nation is like an examination for a student. Though the examination lasts for less than a week it is supposed to show the preparation of a year. The physical, the intellectual and the moral capacities all have their play in an examination. Weakness on any of these sides is likely to prove fatal. There are good students who fail in the nick of time or are too weak to complete a paper. There are clever students whose intellect often fails them at the proper time. There are nervous students who have shown their capacity throughout the year but still are found leaving the examination hall all of a sudden. War is a similar test for a state. All the weak points exhibited in the Panipat campaign had not cropped up all of a sudden, but were inherent in the Maratha system under the best of the Peshwas. These inherent defects have been very convincingly pointed out by a deep student of Maratha history, Vasudev Vamanshastri Khare in his invaluable introduction to the

[2] Ibid. p. 298.

book *Marathe va Ingraj* by N. C. KELLAR, in 1918. The Marathas in the 18th century had nothing original to contribute for the benefit of the Indian people. They were imitators and not inventors. They tried to imitate the foreign model in war, but never made it their own in all its details. The Maratha Constitution was very loose. Their military system was no better. The policy of nurturing strength by consolidation had given place to wayward wandering on the basis of the line of least resistance. The result was as KHARE has tellingly put it: "In peace times the Maratha empire was everywhere, but during times of turmoil it was nowhere." (Page 15.) Sadashivrao Bhau and the Peshwa were depending upon the sympathy and help of the various states which had paid them tributes, but not one amongst them actually helped the Marathas during the critical Panipat campaign, exemplifying the truth of KHARE's indictment. The Marathas tried to imitate the European war-machine by engaging Bussy's pupils Ibrahim Khan and Muzaffar Khan, but the danger to the Maratha State of this procedure has been clearly exhibited in history. Muzaffar Khan was all along a self-willed, arrogant and treacherous person. Once he left the Peshwa's service and joined the Nawab of Savnur and was, after his defeat there, on the point of joining the Portuguese at Goa or any one else who would engage him. In 1759 he tried to assassinate Sadashivrao Bhau for personal or political reasons and was beheaded for the attempt. Ibrahim Khan was personally loyal, faithful and expert, but all along he remained unassimilated in the Maratha mode of warfare. The various Maratha officers never felt any comradeship with him and treated him as a foreigner. Instead of co-operating with him and supporting him in his difficulties, they would sit on the fence and see his effort wasted; all this because he was paid punctually in cash after the European manner, because Bhau treated him with special favour and tried to depend upon him to the heart-burning of others! Because he was treated only as an adjunct to the Maratha cavalry, his system was never understood, much less made their own, by the Maratha Shiledars. The result was seen in the battle of Panipat where his superb effort was wasted because the other Maratha sardars never tried to defend the square formation nor would they reap the harvest by taking the proper advantage of his initial effort. The Marathas did not try to assimilate the foreign system then, nor have they done it subsequently. Their political effort and initiative were then, just as they are even now, individual and not collective. The end to be secured was personal rise, prosperity and aggrandisement. The leader is the sole loser in the effort, his followers having no concern with it except temporary loss of employment. The Europeans have perfected their system in such a manner that their united effort does not depend on individual caprice. Even amongst them incompetent and selfish individuals occasionally come to the top, but they have little power to play mischief in the perfected system. With us the reverse is the case. Occasionally good people come to the top amongst us, but still they have no power to change the system or rather the absence of system existing amongst us. Amongst us the individual effort of the best of men is only temporarily and partially effectual for some time and ultimately wasted, the nation never deriving permanent benefits therefrom. Viewed in this philosophical light, it seems idle either to boom up or condemn downright an individual, however great personally. The final result must be attributed to the static system and cannot be attributed to any one actor in history.

DEATH OF NANASAHEB PESHWA

The Peshwa's death six months after the battle of Panipat on 23rd June, 1761, is treated as the last event of the Panipat campaign. It is almost thought as a consequence of it. That the unexpected disaster unhinged his mind by that tremendous shock, by the loss of all that was dear and valuable, was natural enough, but it is utterly wrong to say that his death was due to it. As a matter of fact there seems to have been some hereditary defect in the Peshwa family which made its members prone to sudden collapse of health and wasting diseases. The uneven life of camp and war had something to do with it. Nor were they free from vices. Peshwa Nanasaheb particularly seems to have been inordinately fond of the company of women. He loved ease and pleasure. Beautiful young girls[1] from northern India were always requisitioned by him. This trait of his life had become known throughout India and even the distant Kashiraj, living far away in the north at the Lucknow Court, knew of it and thought it necessary to mention it at the beginning of his account of the battle of Panipat. The Peshwa had started from Poona in November and had made known his plan of proceeding to the north to set the matters right at the Delhi court in the company of Nizam Ali, the younger brother of the Nizam Salabat Jang. But his march was delayed on account of the "wait and see" tactics of the Nizam brothers. Though it was a condition of the peace treaty after the battle of Udgir in the previous year, that the Nizam should join the Peshwa whenever there was any urgent need[2] and now definitely such a need arose due to the beleagurement of Bhau at Panipat, the Nizam brothers would not move from their cantonments even after the cessation of rains. The need for taking Nizam Ali with him to the north arose in a double sense. Firstly, his Gardi troops with their fine park of artillery would have been invaluable in a fight against Abdali and the Ruhelas; next it was dangerous to keep such a mischievous man behind, with power to do what he liked when the Peshwa had moved north with all his troops. But this was a political excuse. The Peshwa was entangled in other domestic matters also. For some time, it seems, he was not keeping on good terms with his wife and had taken it into his head to marry a second time, though three sons from the first marriage were available as heirs. Match-makers had been dispatched far and wide from the one end of Maharashtra to the other. He was prepared to marry a girl from any of the three[3] sub-castes of Maharashtra Brahmins, Karhada, Deshasthas or Chitpavans, to which last caste he himself belonged. The Peshwa's diary shows expenditure incurred in this search for suitable girls where half a dozen girls have been noted. The Peshwa had become so weak, irritable and listless that his memory was failing and he could not devote him-

[1] RAJ. 1.214; 3.158.
[2] *SPD* 40.128.
[3] *SPD* 2.133

self to any business with full attention. This was natural when we take into account the decline in his health which is noted in many places. In 1755, he was suffering from toothache[4] which is a sure sign of declining health. In 1758 Sadashivrao Bhau[5] notes that the Peshwa's health is not what it should be. When at the end of 1759, Bhau started for the Udgir campaign, the Peshwa's health had already become a state problem. He was not in a position to follow the campaign himself[6] with its daily marches. Bhau's one anxiety throughout the Panipat campaign was for the Peshwa's health. He writes[7] from Delhi on 16th September, 1760, that all problems would be best solved when the Peshwa's health improved. We are at a loss to know why, when things had come to such a pass, the Peshwa was thinking of marriage. It could not have been for mere sex satisfaction, because he had any number of concubines and dancing girls at his service. Three things are suggested as probable causes for marriage. (1) The advice of the Hindu Vaidyas who prescribed young girls as a cure for venereal diseases. A Sanskrit verse states that a tender girl below sixteen adds to the strength of the husband; a youthful one makes her husband youthful like herself,—an elderly woman drains away the strength of her partner; and an old woman leads her partner on his way to death. *(Bala tu balada prokta taruni tarunayate, praudha s'aktihara prokta vrddha mrtyuvasam nayet.)* It is not unlikely that some such advice might have been offered to the Peshwa, though we do not know whether it falls under the category of medicine or sexual science (Kamasastra). But we have already suggested that this remedy could have been followed even by having extra-marital relations with girls, and so we reject this cause. (2) The second cause which is more probable comes from astrological advice. It is thought that the stars of certain girls so ordain that a person marrying them cannot possibly die, as it is written that these girls have no widowhood ordained for them in their horoscopes. Of course there is the possibility of the girl herself dying before her husband so as to justify the stars. We presume that the inquiry for girls was possibly based on this point. Though this cause seems more probable, even this is not completely satisfactory, because had the inquiry been only based on horoscopes, it would not have been found necessary to bring all these young girls from distant places, and there was no particular necessity for seeing them unless men who judge horoscopes from bodily features wished to view and examine them. We would have believed such to have been the case, but the Peshwa is found in a somewhat playful mood in marrying, as he not only marries, but makes two of his bosom associates, Aba Purandare and Vireshwar Dikshit Manohar,[8] marry, side by side. (3) The third cause is equally likely, namely, his quarrel with his first wife, Gopikabai. For one reason or another, they had not been on good terms for some time. The difference of opinion had arisen on account of domestic causes as well as state policy. The episode at Patdur, described in the *Bhau Bakhar* and *Kaifiyat* before Sadashivrao's appointment for the Panipat campaign, illustrates one phase of this difference.

4 *Purandare* 3.206.
5 Ibid. 3.193.
6 *SPD* 1.10.
7 *Purandare*, 1.389.
8 *SPD* 2.149. pp. 162. 171.

Nana Phadnis, than whom no veracious and correct writer can be found, writes definitely about this difference in his autobiography.[9] The irritability of temper and in general the loss of balance of mind, which is ascribed to the Peshwa during his last illness, was not a sudden growth after Panipat, but was a gradual development. Govindpant Bundele[10] notes this change in the Peshwa's temper even from the north. It will be seen from this detailed discussion that the death of the Peshwa had little to do with the shock of Panipat. He would not have survived it long, even if it had ended in a victory. We have thought it necessary to enter into this detailed treatment of the problem as all historians have fallen into the trap by treating it as a result of Panipat.

We agree with Sir Jadunath[11] in thinking that the Peshwa's marriage at Hiradpuri had nothing to do with the issue in the north, because we do not think that the Peshwa was at this time in a fit physical or mental condition to help Bhau by proceeding post-haste to the north. It was a national misfortune of the Marathas that the supreme head of the state should, in these critical years, not be in a fit condition to direct the affairs of the state with a single-minded devotion to the cause of the nation. A Shivaji or Santaji Ghorpade or Bajirao would have possibly relieved Bhau by marching to Delhi in the rear of Abdali in about a month with all the spare troops. Such an exploit was beyond the capacity of Balaji Bajirao (alias Nanasaheb), to judge from his whole life.

Historical Opinions About the Battle of Panipat

That the disaster of Panipat ultimately led to the destruction of the Maratha power, was understood by Rajwade more than forty-five years ago.[1] Even before him, other historians had also said the same thing. But while the foreigners were conscious of this result the Marathas were not, which only means that they had no proper understanding of the situation and were thus living in a fool's paradise. On the other hand, the English writers after Plassey seemed to be perfectly conscious of the things shaping in those times. Their knowledge and their self-consciousness ultimately made them the masters of India.

A national disaster of the type of Panipat has naturally resulted in casting a shadow of gloom over the Maratha nation. But the defeat has been treated differently by various students of history, who have given quite a different turn to the whole discussion. Evans Bell wrote long ago that "even the battle of Panipat was a triumph and a glory for the Marathas. They fought in the cause of 'India for the Indians,' while the great Muhammedan princes of Delhi, of Oude and the Deccan, stood aside, intriguing and trimming. And though the Marathas were defeated, the victorious Afghans retired and never again interfered in the affairs of India." Prof. Rawlinson writes,[2] "A defeat is

[9] *Ait. Patre Yadi* 192; Raj. 6.415.
[10] Raj. I.143.
[11] *Fall*, 2.364.
[1] Rajwade 1. Introduction, p. 46.
[2] Kashiraj, Introduction, p. xiii.

under some circumstances as honourable as a victory; and never, in all their annals, did the Maratha armies cover themselves with greater glory than when the flower of the chivalry of the Deccan perished on the stricken field of Panipat, fighting against the enemies of their creed and country.... But, after all, the general who wins a campaign is the one who makes the fewest mistakes. The Bhausaheb did not commit a tithe of the blunders of both Wellington and Napoleon in the Waterloo campaign. He lost not because he was a bad general, but because his opponent was a better one."

We have shown above that these opinions are correct as far as they go. But that is beside the point. The wisdom for the Marathas lay in not coming to grips with such an awkward enemy as Ahmad Shah Abdali. Had Panipat resulted in a defeat of the Afghans, it would not have meant the same thing to them or to others. Nobody was going to invade barren Afghanistan and try to rule over it. Instead of consolidating and making sure of what they had got, the Marathas had no business to march forward, lengthen their lines of communication and multiply their responsibilities. This wrong policy had begun already with Bajirao's invasion of Delhi in 1736. Geographic factors were completely ignored, because they were completely misunderstood by the Marathas. The Marathas boasted all along that "the Deccan was as good as theirs," but had never once understood the implications underlying that statement. Even in their hey-day before Panipat, others had coolly stolen a march on them. The implication of the destruction of the Angre's naval power seems to have been understood by Alivardi Khan[3] in Bengal just before his death, but not by the Peshwa. The short-sighted policy pursued by the Peshwa even after his experience in the Vijayadurg affair resulted in his directly playing into the hands of his enemy and assured Clive's success in Bengal. A similar thing occurred at Mysore and made the line clear for Haidar Ali. It should never be forgotten that Surat and Janjira never came into the hands of the Peshwa, much less could he have hoped to touch the European citadels on his coast, Bombay and Goa. While the Marathas were exhilarated by their march beyond the Indus, the English were silently entering Surat by the back door of the sea. A big army of the Marathas was encamping outside Surat and their navy had also entered the Tapti estuary. Diplomats were coming and going and taking sides in the civil struggle at Surat, but still the English could carry on independent correspondence with the Wazir Ghazi-ud-din (a so-called creature of the Marathas) and get a Firman from the Mughal Emperor (who thought himself a protege of the Peshwa) appointing them the keepers of the Surat fort and admirals of the Mughal fleet. This neglected Surat episode throws a flood of light on Maratha politics during its most triumphant days. Sadashivrao's defects have been well pointed out by the English envoy John Spencer[4] four years before Panipat. He knew him to be a man with great capacity for business, but as hasty and avaricious, too. The impatience mentioned by the English Vakil was born of ignorance. The ignorance was due to the defective educational system or rather absence of a progressive system marching with the times and adequate for making its votaries able to cope with

---

[3] S. C. Hill, *Bengal in 1756-57* (1905), Vol. II, pp. 16, 65, 6.
[4] G. H. Forrest, *Selections*, Vol. I, p. 121.

any situation arising around them. Balaji Bajirao's studies in Sanskrit were advanced to the extent of writing verses in that language, but there is no evidence to prove that the Peshwa had enough geographical information to cope with that of the contemporary Europeans. RAJWADE's statement[5] that the Peshwas possessed maps of the various provinces in India is not borne out by any positive proof till after the First Maratha War. What knowledge they possessed was gained from gossipy news or orally from visitors to their Court, but it was not sufficient to make these aspiring conquerors of India visualise either the shape of their country or correctly point to the directions of the various parts of the continent, nor an understanding of its correct extent. This had a disastrous effect on the policy of the Marathas. Their avarice made them grab everything which their hands could reach, but the political repercussions of that grabbing and the pressure it would exert on their military machine they were unable to comprehend. The non-comprehension of political and military facts surrounding them is the chief defect which made the Peshwas act as waywardly as they did. No other reason can explain their actions otherwise. The contrast can be best understood by studying the English documents and publications of those times. All their military campaigns, naval fights, political aggrandisements, are found fully reported, discussed threadbare and lines of policy deduced therefrom for future guidance. Not an iota of knowledge once gained, not a point of vantage once secured, not an inch of ground once occupied was wasted or lost by them. The Marathas in their career had to go through many a campaign, to enter into diplomatic talks, to carry on political controversies and to devise various ways and means for securing their end; but scarcely any of these things are found published for public edification, for the use of the younger students in various walks of life. A nation which carried on wars in all directions over a wide continent for more than a century, has not produced a single treatise on warfare. That is the basic defect in the nation. Its want could not be supplied by any other means. When one finds such a book published in English in the very year of the Panipat disaster with detailed maps, plans of battles, illustrations of the positions of forts giving a visual demonstration of their military situation, naval manœuvres with drawings of the anchored ships, together with their full political and diplomatic background, one is forced to exclaim that want of such training led to the Panipat disaster (Vide R. O. Cambrige's *War in India*, etc., 1761).

THE CONSTITUTIONAL BASIS OF THE PANIPAT CAMPAIGN

The Panipat campaign takes away the charge against the Marathas that they were not the rulers of India, but only robbers in the dominions of other rulers. This one campaign bears evidence not only to the military organization developed under the Peshwas, but also to the fact that they were waging war not for aggrandisement but for the defence of a principle, India for the Indians, governed by Indians. The Peshwa had accepted the responsibility of defending the Mughal Empire, from its internal and external foes through his

[5] RAJWADE, op. cit., p. 99.

agents in 1752. From that date they had waged war against practically all the potentates in India, great and small. Jayapa Shinde had waged war unto death against Bijesingh of Marwar as a Mughal Subahdar of Ajmer and Malharrao Holkar had fought against Madhosingh of Jaipur and Surajmal Jat, as a Subahdar of Agra, in order to bring these recalcitrant chiefs under the rule of the Mughal Empire. In the campaign against the Nizam in 1760, Bhau had actually talked with him on the same basis. Bhau had received the Imperial Firman[1] from Alamgir II through his confidential secretary Kamyar Khan sent in August 1759, three months before that Emperor's assassination. In it, the Emperor had besought Bhau's help against his unprincipled and unscrupulous Wazir Ghazi-ud-din whose behaviour had become unbearable to the Emperor. The Emperor had given a *carte blanche* to Bhau to take over the sole charge of the Mughal Empire, with power to appoint his own Wazir and Mir-Bakshi or any other official. The Emperor wished Bhau to arrange matters in such a way as to leave him in the position of the Maratha Chhatrapati at Satara. Those who are ticklish about the constitutional procedure cannot criticize the Marathas with high-handedness in their dealings with the various Indian chiefs, if they bear in mind this important fact often overlooked by the historians. There was no need for the Marathas to take upon themselves the onerous burden of running the Mughal Empire, had they wished only for self-aggrandisement. As a matter of fact, matters became difficult for the Marathas by the acceptance of this burden, because they had to become enemies of all and sundry by this procedure. But they wished to preserve the grand fabric of the Mughal Empire in so far as it was possible. They had no wish to sweep away all trace of old rule and begin their rule anew. They did not wish to create anarchy throughout the length and breadth of India. But they were counting against the time. None of the chiefs and potentates who had risen in India during the 18th century, had a wish to lose what they had grabbed or usurped. The selfishness and machinations of these rulers foiled the attempts of the Marathas to run the empire on its Mughal basis. It looks as if it would have been far better for the Maratha state to have run its own course without getting into this entanglement with the Mughal Empire. But this is by the way. The critics of the Marathas cannot charge them with not knowing the constitutional ways or want of principles. They tried to follow the constitutional way, they fought for a principle. They understood the responsibility devolving on them by the acceptance of a treaty, which they did not treat as a scrap of paper, to be torn when it did not suit them. They would not sign away the rights of the Mughal Empire even when these had been usurped by such a potentate as Ahmad Shah Abdali. Raghunathrao would not part with Kabul and Kandahar[2] in 1758, Bhau would not accept the boundary of Sirhind in 1760. In these instances, the Marathas were fighting for regions and rights already lost by the Mughal Empire. Can any one say with this history before him that the Marathas had no idea of a state, that they did not know the constitutional ways, that they had no respect for treaties or had no regard for principles? They certainly aspired to be the Regents of the Indian Empire and

1 *BISMQ* 1.1 p. 44.
2 *Itihasa Sangraha—Ait. Sphuta Lekha.* 4.11.

none can say that they were inferior to any in India of those days. With all their internal quarrels, no other state in India could muster so many troops for war under a unitary command. No other nation was less bigoted or more tolerant in religious and social matters, as is proved by their behaviour towards their Muslim neighbours or their rule over Muslim subjects. There is no instance of their having fabricated a document like Clive, none where they tried to gain a point by assassination or intimidation. They did not hire mercenaries for slaughtering their opponent in an unguarded moment. They would not murder persons by calling them for an interview. They would not kill foreign emissaries at their Court. No other war-like nation is known to be milder in their peace-time actions. There are no instances where the Marathas entered into the slaughter of civilians after a victory, or during conquest to have created terror. It is nowhere noted that they slaughtered disarmed prisoners, like the Durranis after Panipat, or uselessly cut off the head of a fallen soldier as in the case of Dattaji Shinde at Buradi. They did not apply torture to extract hidden wealth like the Afghans at Delhi in 1757. In fact, one feels many a time that their comparative mildness, their humane behaviour, their civil manners, their unwillingness to gain their ends by back-door machinations or solve their problems, internal or external, by swift unscrupulous actions such as murdering an opponent, or doing away with their unwanted brethren like the Mughals, has had the effect of their not succeeding in history. Be that as it may, none can charge them as being morally condemnable in comparison with many other military nations in the world. When a responsible historian of India like Sir Jadunath SARKAR charges the Marathas with being "lesser breeds beyond the law,"[3] one does not know how to characterize such a statement and what standard of conduct and morality he wants to apply. He seems to belong to that category of historians-*cum*-moralists "who justify Providence by the event and hold nothing so deserving as success. To them there can be no victory in a bad cause; prescription and duration legitimate; and whatever exists is right and reasonable; and God manifests His will by that which He tolerates. Men must confirm to the divine decree by living to shape the future after the ratified image of the past."[4] These writers should learn to know that there are many Marathas—perhaps the majority—who think it better to have lost the Empire than to have followed a line of conduct after the manner of a Clive or Najib or Abdali.

GENERAL THOUGHTS ON WAR

Mankind since it began to think and take a retrospective view of human affairs, has been sharply divided on the moral basis of war, and it will probably remain so divided for all time. Indian civilisation, at least after the Aryan imposition, has not only sanctioned war but has consecrated a particular class for that work and given it the second rank in society. This is in sharp contrast with the neighbouring Chinese civilisation which had relegated the soldier to the last place in society and only tolerated him as an unavoidable

[3] *Fall* II.291.
[4] Lord ACTON, *Lectures on Modern History* (1907) (Inaugural Lecture) p. 25.

evil. Turks who conquered India and held their sway over it for half a millennium were a moving nation in arms. In addition, the Islamic teachings which they followed had charged them with waging an incessant war upon the infidels till they were converted to Islam. When the Marathas rose upon the horizon of history they had perforce to take to the military profession for solving the Indian riddle. It was a necessity imposed on them by the Epoch and they had no choice of refusing it. How mild and inoffensive the Marathas otherwise are has been proved after the extinction of their sovereign power, for by the end of the 19th century they were relegated to the rank of non-martial races in India in the Indo-British political phraseology. It means that the Marathas as a race take to arms only when they are insulted or forced to, as the Chinese monk Yu'an Chwang remarked long ago in his itinerary. Spilling of blood never became a pastime with them as with the Afghans. On the whole, the battles fought by the Marathas were the least bloody, the casualties on both sides being as few as possible. Their so-called guerilla mode of warfare was nothing more than seeking to gain their ends by manœuvring and strategy more than by actual crossing of swords face to face. Having acted throughout their career in this spirit, they naturally felt intensely such a disaster as Panipat on account of the heavy massacres following it. When estimating the effects of Panipat on the Marathas, this fact should not be lost sight of.

The best of political thinkers have allowed war as a human necessity in solving uncompromising questions. Some go so far as to call it a moral necessity. Taking the historic view, certainly the recorded history of mankind is mostly a history of wars waged by the various races of mankind between and amongst themselves as Sir John FORTESCUE says, but all would not agree with him in thinking the military force of a nation as a manifestation of its moral force. At the same time it is certain that in history the military force has stood as the test of material civilisation if not of moral. The best soldier has always manifested the highest human virtues personally, but collectively it is difficult to characterise war as a school for virtues. If sometimes the best qualities of a nation are called forth and mobilised by war, it is also true and much more often true that the worst side of human nature is exhibited and given a licence as a result of war. Whether a state lapses into degeneracy as a result of long peace is also a debatable point, because for counteracting such a possibility someone else has to suffer. The cruelty and the futility of war for final settlement of human world problems has become more and more manifest with the progress of modern civilisation and coming together of mankind. Be that as it may, speaking about Panipat, it is very correct to say that the inferiority of the Marathas, in the material sense, became very manifest. But on the moral side their record is very clean. Thy had not fought for the three primary (and also primitive) aims of war as given by HOBBES, viz. (1) material gain, (2) fear, or (3) glory. It means they fought for a fourth cause unknown to that political philosopher, viz. principle, the sanctity of the contract they had entered into with the Delhi Emperor for the guarding of his Empire. On the other hand Ahmad Shah Abdali individually was also fighting for a cause he thought right, viz. the cause of Islam in India. He triumphed by his superior power, won glory, freed himself from the fear of the Marathas once for all;

but did not gain anything, materially speaking, thus proving the futility of war in the material sense to any party, long before Sir Norman ANGEL wrote his *Great Illusion.* Incidentally it also proved the correctness of the Maratha stand in the political sense. The Marathas lost the Panjab no doubt, but it was gained not by Abdali a foreigner, but by the Sikhs in the long run. The treacherous Najib-ud-daulah, the arch-villain of the piece, outwardly succeeded in warding off the Marathas, but found himself thrown between two mill-stones—the Sikhs from the north and the Jats from the south—never getting a moment's rest till his death a decade later. The hated Marathas again ruled in Delhi and uprooted Najib's family together with his buried bones in the grave at Najibabad.

The trans-Ganges Ruhelas under Hafiz who had joined Abdali as Afghans, also experienced the scourge of the Marathas after Najib's death. Shuja-ud-daulah who had been enticed away into joining the side of Abdali by cajoling and threatening, not only left the Afghan side just after Panipat, but became the annihilator of the Ruhelas with the help of Warren Hastings, thus historically proving that he had acted under "duress" the wrong party. He himself had escaped falling under the suzerainty of the Marathas, only to find himself obliged to fall a victim to the utterly foreign English. In fact, the ultimate result of Panipat was to make the way smooth and clear for the English, a result which could have been avoided only by a victory for the Marathas. History thus vindicates the correctness of the Maratha stand and exposes the basic hollowness of their critics. Further, it also proves the complexity of the Afghan border problem, which has not been satisfactorily solved by the British even after a rule of 150 years. The irony of history can have no better illustration than Panipat.

A CRITICAL AND COMPARATIVE ANALYSIS OF THE SOURCES (PUBLISHED AND UNPUBLISHED)

1. *Kashiraj:*

Persian account of the battle of Panipat and the events leading to it (Oxford University Press, 1926). Corrected by the translation of Sir Jadunath SARKAR, published in *Indian Historical Quarterly,* 1934 and 1935.

Kashiraj Shivdev was a Deshastha Brahmin (native of the Nizam's Dominions) at the court of Shuja-ud-daulah of Oudh, who was present throughout the campaign in the camp of his master. His narrative is taken as the best authority on the battle of Panipat. He seems to have been working in the north for some twenty-five years before Panipat since the time of Safdar Jang. He had occasional correspondence with the Peshwas[1] for more than twenty years. His exact status at the court of Shuja-ud-daulah is not quite clear. He is called a *Vaki* r a diplomat, but is scarcely sent anywhere as an emissary with full powers. In his account he is found assuming superior airs, standing tightly on his dignity. But there is no mention of him in the whole range of Marathi political correspondence,[2] an omission which seems to us rather significant. His account was written nineteen years after the battle of Panipat, and from memory. It appears to have been purposely written for someone inquisitive on the point, possibly a British official at the Oudh Court. In 1780 when this account was written, the British power in India was already combating with that of the Maratha power. The glory of the Maratha power was on the wane. Kashiraj, though racially a Maratha, had culturally, by this time, become by his long sojourn in northern India, almost a U. P. Kayasth with all that it means. When he wrote his account he was almost seventy, an age when the mental faculties are on the decline. He seems to have been, at first, a disappointed candidate for service under the Peshwa,[3] and later on moved to the north in search of employment, which he secured on account of his proficiency in the Persian language. That there was no particular love lost between him and the Maratha nation or their Empire is evident from the tone of his account. According to him, Sadashivrao Bhau was defeated on account of his arrogance and pride.[4] Throughout his narrative, he seems to have been convinced that fate had ordained the miscarriage of the Maratha enterprise.[5] On the other hand, whenever he had occasion to write about Ahmad Shah Abdali, he is found completely over-awed by his superior prowess and his divine role of punishing the Marathas for their wicked pride; for in the eyes of Kashiraj, pride is sin. This much for the mental make up of the man.

Bhau's munshi once wrote a letter to Kashiraj at which Kashiraj was offended on account of some deficiency in the proper form of address due to his station. It means that the Maratha Court did not think Kashiraj to be

1 *SPD* 40.25 dated Feb. 1741.
2 KASHIRAJ 14.
3 *SPD* 30.329.
4 KASHIRAJ 52.
5 Ibid. 8; *IHQ* 11.552; 10.266.

a superior official, but thought him to be an ordinary munshi. Kashiraj is self-contradictory in his account of Bhau's behaviour. On the one hand, he condemns Bhau on his pride and obstinacy, on the other he depicts Bhau as ready to submit to any conditions mediated through the agency of such persons as Kashiraj himself. Now to judge Bhau from his own letters, one thing is certain about him and that is that he was never proud, though his tone was often harsh and his manner peremptory. Bhau should be the last person to assume a cringing role before a man of Kashiraj's position or to be over-confident about him.

There seems to be some discrepancy in the account of Kashiraj, as is acknowledged by Sir Jadunath SARKAR who has carefully studied the original manuscript. He thinks it due to lapse of memory or loose narrative of events.[6] We cannot treat it so lightly. Kashiraj tells us of Bhau's writing his last chit just before the battle of Panipat, a thing which no thoughtful person will be ready to believe. A commander-in-chief intimating in his autograph the last desperate movement of his army, just before the commencement of the fatal battle, is a thing which cannot be inserted or allowed in fiction or poetry, much less can it be believed in a primary source of history. Was Bhau such a fool as to believe and hope that his last note would bear any good and immediate results, after his experience in diplomacy for six months? Would he not rather fear the fatal consequence of pre-intimating his movement to such a consummate general as Ahmad Shah Abdali? It was a matter of astonishment to us when we tried to study this point deeply and found none of the previous writers even suspecting the full import of this, to us, a cock-and-bull story. We call it such because fortunately for the historian there is the clear evidence of a contemporary letter directly falsifying Kashiraj's narrative. Sir Jadunath in his new translation of Kashiraj's narrative has given the name of Bhau's valet who took the last chit to Kashiraj as Balakram, who is styled as Bhau's betel-bearer, and is taken as the most confidential servant of his master.[7] Anybody with an acquaintance with the Maratha names knows that Balakram is not a common Maratha name. On the other hand, a letter from the Purandare Archives published by RAJWADE in his sixth volume clearly gives the name of Bhau's valet as Balaram, a common name amongst the Marathas.[8] Anupgir Gosawi writes in this post-Panipat letter to Nana Purandare that the Peshwa's valet, Balaram Vaghoji Naik, and some others also had gone to Shuja-ud-daulah's camp on some errand on the Sunday prior to the battle of Panipat, fought on Wednesday, 14th January, 1761. This proves that the chit Kashiraj is talking of as having been dramatically sent three hours prior to the battle had been actually sent (if at all) three days previous to it. We suggest from this small but vital point that Kashiraj had not only forgotten the days and their proper order, but was narrating the whole story with a dramatic touch, as the battle of Panipat is a good theme for such treatment.

[6] *Fall*, 2.369.

[7] Ibid. 2.320.

[8] RAJWADE 6. No. 407, p. 472.

Bhau Sahebanchi Bakhar,[9] on the other hand, gives quite the opposite story. It tells us of Abdali's Vakil coming to Bhau just before the battle and asking him to postpone the fight for the day in order to give a last chance for peace-talks. Bhau is reported to have unceremoniously driven him back, beginning the fight at once thereafter. Sir Jadunath, though he considers the Marathi *Bakhars* "as later gossipy fabrications no better than opium-eaters' tales,"[10] has still to acknowledge that "there are some true traditions (as proved by authentic records) and some statements which have every appearance of being true though unsupported elsewhere." We do not know whether Sir Jadunath would like to believe in this *Bakhar* story, which, we think, as most improbable and written to suit the whole tenor of the author, who was out to condemn Bhau and make a scapegoat of him.

Kashiraj was on the battle-field that whole day, no doubt, but that fact cannot make any person see the whole line of battle with his own eyes, much less can it give him a correct idea of the order of the battle on the opposite side. Kashiraj, with all his sagacity, was a civil official and not a soldier who could judge military matters correctly. For the most part, he was standing ready in his own camp throughout the day of the battle. He himself confesses that Shuja's side was the least affected part in the line of battle, because none came to attack it. The whole line of battle is taken by Sir Jadunath to cover some seven miles. So it was physically impossible for Kashiraj to see anything but a small part of the actual battle, and that, too, from a distance. His value as an eye-witness must, therefore, be discounted to a great extent, and his version of the battle must be taken as gathered after the event from the general reports which came to his ears. This work of collecting news from various sources and afterwards collating and correlating it into the form of a running narrative could be done by others also, and, therefore, we have no valid ground to reject the version given in the Marathi *Bakhars* and letters only because we are unaware of the status of the narrators. We have shown in the detailed description of the battle the various points wherein Kashiraj is proved to be wrong.

2. *Bhau Sahebanchi Bakhar* (1922) and 3. *Shrimant Bhau Saheb Yanchi Kaifiyat* (1887).

These two are the most important primary sources about the battle of Panipat in Marathi. Their authors are unknown but they were certainly much nearer to the event than Kashiraj when they wrote, as can be proved from the language, the tone and the textual criticism of their manuscripts. Certain passages in the narration of the events in the *Kaifiyat* are found bodily incorporated in the *Bakhar*[11] which is a bigger narrative of the event. From this we can say that the *Kaifiyat*, small and to the point, was the earlier narrative of the two, of which the *Bakhar* was an amplified edition with enlarged paraphrase. The *Kaifiyat* gives the life of Bhau from the point of his start for the Udgir campaign of 1759-60 and closes with the retreat from Panipat. The *Bakhar*, on the other hand, narrates the Maratha activities in the north from 1753 on-

9 *Bhau Bakhar* (1922). p. 115.
10 *Fall* 2.367.
11 *Cf. Kaifiyat* 21 and *Bakhar* 141; *K.* 22, *B.* 144; *K.* 23, *B.* 148.

wards. It is ostensibly written to glorify the achievements of the Shindes and these have no direct connection with the battle of Panipat. The author is evidently a biased person and on that account tries to supply and explain the genesis, the events and the activities behind the scenes of actual narration with all the personal bickerings of the actors in their full gusto. The reports of these bickerings and their actual wording may or may not be true in their full import; but it is clear that they throw a necessary light on the seamy side of history. We shall have to discount much of this report due to the bias of the author. Another thing which has to be borne in mind is the fact that these reports must have necessarily come from the persons who ran away from the field of battle and as such were dubbed as renegades by the people at large. The odium of this obloquy and the guilty conscience of having failed to be with their leaders in the thick of the fight, made the reports from these survivors naturally colourful and excusatory. Most of these persons had direct blame attached to their conduct and in sheer self-justification they gave such a retrospective turn to their own and Bhau's conduct as to lead to the disaster which would then appear inevitable. If we compare the tone of the letters[12] which some of these survivors sent previous to the battle with those they wrote after it, we can understand the difference worked out in the minds of these writers by the fatal disaster. When the authors of the *Kaifiyat* and the *Bakhar* wrote their accounts after a few years, the public in Maharashtra had come to form some sort of plausible opinion about the great disaster, after hearing, explaining, accounting and guessing about the various reports brought from the distant field. The boiled essence of all these is found written in the *Bakhar*. Sadashivrao Bhau was out to give a new turn to the ancient mode of Maratha warfare which was taken to be of the guerilla type. Bhau had introduced the trained infantry tactics and tried to combine them with the original mode. The good result of this innovation had been reaped in the Udgir campaign. The Udgir victory had naturally increased the prestige of Ibrahim Khan Gardi and his mode of warfare. Throughout the Panipat campaign, Bhau had put his main confidence in these infantry corps and they also gave a very good account of themselves. The idea of entrenching at Panipat was a result of these tactics. It made the Marathas unassailable so long as they remained within their entrenchments. Bhau expected Abdali to attack them in this strong position, as he was sure of victory in the event of such an attack. But Abdali had understood it equally well. He himself never once tried to attack, and had strictly forbidden any one from his camp to go out with a view to attacking. He played a game of waiting and hoped to get a victory when the Maratha army would come out due to starvation. That is why Bhau is found raging and almost railing against Govindpant Bundele for not attacking Abdali from behind and making him compulsorily fall on the Maratha entrenchments to his sure destruction. When, due to the failure of Govindpant and due to starvation, Bhau himself had to come out, that combination of artillery, infantry and cavalry tactics which it was necessary to keep

12 RAJ. Vol. 6. Cf. Satvoji Jadhavrao's letters No. 404 dated 18-9-1760 and No. 409 dated 10-3-1761; also cf. Nana Purandare's letters No. 391 of 14-11-1760 in *Purandare Daftar* Pt. I. and No. 118 in Pt. III.

with an army on the march with all their camp-followers, could not be kept up and the disaster inevitably followed. The Maratha army was mainly composed of veteran horsemen with a life-long belief in the guerilla mode of warfare. It seems they neither understood nor had a mind to follow the correct orders of their commander based on the tactics advised by Ibrahim Khan Gardi; and when the inevitable disaster followed, due to their misunderstanding and faint-heartedness in the fight, they laid the whole blame on the new mode of "entrenched warfare." On this point the whole opinion in Maharashtra seems to be unanimous and it is reflected in these chronicles.

Notwithstanding these prepossessions, however, the *Bakhar* correctly reports Bhau's plan of the battle which was unknown to Kashiraj Pandit on the other side and which was not followed to the end. Unaware of the plan and the aim, Kashiraj reports the battle in an inexplicable way, while the author of the *Bakhar* charges Bhau himself with breaking the plan decided on the previous night and thus becoming the author of the disaster. All the historians up till now have been so much obsessed with the idea of the complete reliability of Kashiraj's report that they have never stopped to inquire how the account in the *Bakhars* is to be explained and why it should be disbelieved and set aside. The full import of the intended plan in the *Bakhar* cannot be understood unless one studies the detailed maps of the battle-field in their complete environment, and tries to construe a connected idea with the help of every line reported in the *Bakhar* in combination with it. The authors of the chronicles seem to be well acquainted with the topography of the battle-field and its surroundings, and they might have been personally present in the Maratha camp themselves. The chronicles correctly report the changes in Abdali's camping ground during the two months and a half, while the impression created by Kashiraj's account fixes Abdali's camp once for all, a very serious discrepancy on the part of this eye-witness.[13] When one begins to re-read the *Bakhars* in the light of the original letters, one is impressed by the substantiality of their account.

The Common Points in Kashiraj's Narrative and the Bakhar

Comparison:

That Kashiraj wrote his account after reading some other accounts is proved by certain curious coincidences in the arrangement of his writing and that of *Bhau Bakhar,* which was definitely a northern Indian production. The short *Kaifiyat* was definitely written earlier than the *Bakhar.* But what seems strange to the reader is that the correct consecutive narration of events is followed by the writer of the *Kaifiyat,* and an absence of the sense of time characterises the writer of the gossipy *Bakhar.* Thus the *Bakhar* gives Govindpant Bundele's death as the first event while it was actually the fourth during the beleagurement. Similarly, the cutting off of Parashar Dadaji's treasure-carrying party was the last event which is subsequently dealt with by the *Bakhar.*

13 *Bhau Kaifiyat* pp. 14, 21

The first event of the Shinde-Ruhela fight is given next and Balvantrao Mehendale's event the last! Kashiraj is found following the incorrect order of the *Bakhar* in his narrative, giving the events of Govindpant, Parashar Dadaji, Shinde and Balvantrao consecutively. We cannot treat this as a mere accident in writing. Either Kashiraj had the *Bakhar* in his mind when writing his narrative, or both the *Bakhar* and Kashiraj copied from a third unknown, common source. This is further proved by Kashiraj's attempt at giving dates of certain events which are proved to be utterly wrong by other direct evidence. The *Kaifiyat* gives the correct dates wherever it has given these, while Kashiraj is found to be wrong—even in his date of the great battle, reckoning by the Muslim calendar. Sir Jadunath treats these points as "lapses of memory or hurried writing." But no serious student of textual criticism can be satisfied with this explanation. Kashiraj tries to foist authenticity on his hearsay narrative by introducing dates into it, thereby impressing upon the reader the correctness thereof. We do not think he had kept a diary of the events. Had there been no verifying proofs for the events he narrates, he would have passed on as the writer on Panipat, eye-witness as he was for the events from beginning to end. Unfortunately for Kashiraj, a few Marathi papers have survived the ravages of time, exposing him to the hilt. A man who treats the whole episode as a sort of play of destiny; who charges Bhau with pride; who though a Maharashtra Brahmin himself, cannot properly know Bhau's relationship to Balvantrao Mehendale; a man who could not understand the constitutional thread behind the Maratha politics in the north; a man who treats Surajmal's episode without understanding the politics behind it; who introduces rumours to heighten the romantic effect of his narrative; a man who omits important facts which militate against the tenor of his narrative (e.g. Bhau's deposition of Shah Jahan Sani and the proclamation of Shah Alam as Emperor); a man who gives incorrect dates; a man who does not report Abdali's shifting of camps; a man who is incorrect even in his narration of the actual battle in certain particulars; and finally a man who would not mention the important fact of Abdali's appointment of the regicide Maratha-protege Ghazi-ud-din as the Wazir with full powers before his departure because it would mar the effect of his whole narrative, shedding a powerful light as it does on the whole of the Panipat episode from beginning to end,—to call such a man's narrative as the most trustworthy authority on the Panipat campaign and to say that "no other author can be set against him in point of authenticity," is something beyond the range of historical research.

The main points on which the chronicles differ from Kashiraj's account are the following:

(1) Changes in the sites of Abdali's camp.

(2) Bhau's plan of battle.

(3) The directions of the rival armies on the battle-field.

(4) The cause of the so-called Maratha right wing and the Durrani left wing never coming to grips throughout the battle.

(5) The actual site of the battle.

On all these points Kashiraj is proved to be wrong and loose in his account by the evidence of original letters. Because Sir Jadunath and others have placed their faith in Kashiraj, they have been completely misled in their account of the battle. Kashiraj's account should be relied upon only in so far as the Durrani side is concerned. The Maratha side cannot be understood unless we rely upon the evidence of the Marathi chronicles and original letters.

4-5. *Purandare Daftar* Vols. 1 and 3 (1929 and 1934): These form a valuable primary source not only for the events after the battle of Panipat, but also for the events prior to it, because they throw a rare flood of light on the mental make-up and character of some of the chief characters in the Panipat episode. What Sadashivrao Bhau was really like cannot be understood without his early personal letters. The characters of Nanasaheb Peshwa, Nana Purandare, Sakharam Bapu and Raghoba Dada are properly understood in all their setting by a study of these volumes of intimate personal letters. Sir Jadunath has missed this point and so cannot properly appraise their part in the great drama of history.

6-7-8. RAJWADE *V. K. Marathyanchya Itihasachin Sadhane* Vols. 1, 3 and 6: They are the basic sources containing original letters direct from the scene of the battle as well as throughout the campaign and for events leading to it from the very beginning. When RAJWADE published his first volume in 1898 after accidentally getting possession of a number of original letters addressed to Govindpant Bundele, it was the only, and therefore, partial side of the campaign that was open to him. He should have corrected it when his own third and sixth volumes were published later on. But RAJWADE, after his own manner, left the scathing criticism of Govindpant in the first volume untouched throughout his life, though he lived twenty-eight years thereafter. Whatever excuse he had in his day for obstinately sticking to his own view based on one source only, we in 1946 have none. After the publication of the *Peshwa Daftar* in its forty-five volumes a decade ago, a flood of light has been thrown on the Maratha activities in the north in all their bearings. It is clear from evidence adduced in these volumes that Govindpant was not the only culprit, if culprit he was, who should be made the scapegoat for the whole disaster. How historical perspective is blurred when only a part of the material is available and historians try to draw a complete picture out of it, is best exemplified by RAJWADE's classical introduction to his first volume on the Panipat period. We shall have occasion to point out how far RAJWADE had been carried astray[14] in his attempt. Psychological proof for it is available in that volume itself though none of his deep students uptil now have either detected it or have shown the candour to point it out openly.

9-10-11. Selections from *The Peshwa Daftar* Vols. 2, 21, 27: These directly deal with the north Indian activities of the Marathas for a period of almost two decades previous to the battle of Panipat, though cross-references

---

[14] RAJ. 1.175 and Note, 170, 183, 184, 181, 182, Note 325.

will be found interspersed in many other volumes also. For studying the characters of the main actors in the Panipat drama it is necessary to study most of the other volumes for the pre-Panipat period, and sometimes even the later volumes. The characters of the individuals are the one sure and constant guide from which we can correctly judge their activities in a proper perspective. A man's life is never compartmental, and it is unjust and unhistorical to judge events in the lives of these individuals, from the bare data concerning particular events and, therefore, from a partial angle. What a man will do under given circumstances mainly depends on his past, which is reflected in his character. Historians are not the advocates of the historical characters but their post-mortem judges. Unfortunately, very few historians correctly understand their proper role and praise or blame the historical characters in detail. We have tried to study each single character separately, completely and in detail, and then come to form certain notions about the proper manner of judging their actions in this study, a procedure we think absolutely essential. To attain this end, we had to utilize all the available material in the various volumes of original letters concerning these individuals.

12-13-14. *Shindeshahi Itihasachin Sadhane* Part I (1929), Part II (1930), and Part III (1937): These contain a few original letters from Panipat itself. Others throw a flood of light on the inner workings of Shinde affairs. Specially valuable is the correspondence of the diplomats connected with the Shinde family which is collected for publication in the third volume. Ramaji Anant Dabholkar who was the Diwan of the Shindes from 1750 to 1761, and died after Panipat, was the chief director of Shinde affairs and his correspondence is the most valuable of all. Sir Jadunath has overlooked these volumes and his description of the battle is deficient on that account.

15-16-17-18. *Four Incomplete Manuscript Bakhars* about Panipat were examined by us but they contain no authentic or new material. They are gossipy in their contents and their burthen is all the same. Malika Zamani is given as the chief instigator in calling Ahmad Shah Abdali. Bhau and Balvantrao Mehendale are depicted as proud and bad. Holkar and Shinde were against the war, but Bhau was adamant and bent on honour. Only three persons remained fighting to the last, viz. Bhau, Jankoji and Tukoji Shinde. A portion of these *Bakhars*, especially that containing Malika Zamani's part in it, is found incorporated in *Bhausahebanchi Bakhar*, the *Bakhar* published by Parasnis in his *Marathyanche Parakrama* (Bundelkhand-part) and similar other attempts. The theme was a favourite one with all Maratha clerks of the Peshwa times and they copied the story from wherever they could.

19. *A few pages of Bhausahebanchi Kaifiyat* were supplied to us by Mr. K. V. PURANDARE. These pages contain a few verbal changes but no new information. We note this fact here to show that even the *Kaifiyat*, though it was over-shadowed by the more complete and the enlarged *Bakhar*, was still copied by a few in Maharashtra. Rao Bahadur SANE was able to get only one copy of this *Kaifiyat* and had to rely on that one alone. He concluded therefrom that the *Kaifiyat* was a rare brochure. But this does not seem to have been the case.

20. *Raghunāth Yadav's Panipat Bakhar:* Though ostensibly written by a court-clerk and that by order of a member of the Peshwa's family, this is the most worthless of all the Panipat *Bakhars.*

21. *Aitihasik Lekha Samgraha* Vol. I (1897) by V. V. KHARE contains a few letters on the Panipat Campaign.

22-23. *Chandrachuda Daftar* Vol. I (1920), and Vol. II (1934) also contain a few letters dealing with the northern India affairs and bear evidence to the Maratha advance and rule upto Attock on the Indus.

24-25. *Holkarachin Kaifiyat* (published in the Kavyetihasa Samgraha by K. N. SANE (1886), and Holkarachi Thaili (RAJ. III, No. 172 and *Itihasa Samgraha):* These are both explanatory after-thoughts, to justify Malharrao Holkar's conduct in the Panipat affair. That he ran away at the previous behest of Bhau in order to escort Parvatibai, the wife of Bhau, is now proved to be false, on the authority of contemporary letters. How an imaginary turn can be given to historic events is proved by these attempts.

26. *Aitihasik Partren, Yadi Vagaire Lekha* (2nd Ed. 1929): This contains the autobiography of Nana Phadnis which we take to be written sometime soon after the event when the author was extremely grieved and repentant and almost on the point of forsaking the world to lead the life of a recluse, and not after thirty years as assumed by Sir Jadunath. There is nothing incorrect in it when compared with the original letters. Other letters in this volume are also important for the northern Indian affairs of the Marathas.

27. *Aitihasik Patravyavahara* (1930): This volume also contains valuable correspondence, amongst them being an important letter by Nana Phadnis from the Panipat camp. Sir Jadunath has wrongly understood it, as his translation of a line in it gives exactly the reverse meaning.

28. *Persian Akhbars* (news letters) in manuscript form existing in the archives of the Bharat Itihasa Samahodhak Mandal contain valuable material not found elsewhere about the Panjab campaign of the Marathas, ending in the far-famed carrying of the Maratha banners beyond the Attock to Peshawar.

29. *Bhau's Ballad* (published in *BDCRI* 4.3) in the Jatki dialect of Hindusthani copied for us after the dictation of a Muslim ballad-singer of Siwa, five miles to the south of Panipat, contains a more complete version of the ballad than that published in the *Sardesai Commemoration Volume* by Dr. KANUNGO and also one given in pieces in the Marathi publication "Bhaunchya Virakatha." Our copy which contains both prose and poetry, gives valuable information in deciding the field of battle, the environment and the actual point on the river Jamuna where Abdali crossed.

30. ELLIOT and DOWSON, *History of India* (1877), Vol. VIII, contains selected translations of

(i) *Tarikh-i-Alamgir-Sani,* (E. & D. CII).

(ii) *Manazil-ul-Fatuh, by Md. Ja'far Shamlu* (E. & D. CIII).

(iii) *Nigar-nama-i-Hind,* of Saiyid Ghulam Ali (E. & D. CXLIII).

(iv) *Ibratnamah* by Faqir-ud-din Md. of Allahabad (E. & D. CXIX).

(v) *Tarikh-i-Ibrahim Khan* (E. & D. CXXI).

Of these *Ibratnamah* and *Tarikh-i-Alamgir-Sani* are used for Ghazi-ud-din's acts, especially the assassinations of the Emperor and others. *Tarikh-i-Ibrahim Khan* and *Nigar-namah* practically copy their accounts of the Panipat battle from Kashiraj. But Shamlu was present on the battle-field as a servant of Shah Pasand Khan who commanded the left wing of Abdali's army. His figures are inflated no doubt but certain casual references of his are helpful in deciding a few controversial points. Though both Kashiraj and Shamlu were eye-witnesses, present on the battle-field during the battle, both could see only a corner of the battle, and that which was least engaged, in the first half of the day. But Shamlu knew much more of the Abdali side than Kashiraj from the inside, just as Kashiraj naturally knew more of the Maratha side. Shamlu's remark that Ahmad Shah drove away the Shindes from the banks of the river Attock and pursued them as far as Burya and Sarangpur (p. 146) is helpful in pointing out the farthest line of Maratha advance in the Panjab. It had not stopped at the Chinab as Sir Jadunath says,[15] but had reached the Indus itself as can now be proved by other contemporary material. Shamlu also gives the account of the precarious passage of Abdali's army across the Jamuna by the Budhia Ghat to Sarangpur, which is also so written in Marathi papers, while later on it somehow has assumed the form of Saharanpur, which it retains today. This is one of the instances where bad pronunciation and incorrect writing has changed a purely Hindu name into a Muslim-looking one. Shamlu's account of the battle which ensued before crossing, corroborates the account in *Bhau Sahebanchi Bakhar*. He also gives the behaviour of the Abdali troops when they entered Delhi after defeating Dattaji Shinde. They looted it, notwithstanding the fact that they had come to protect the city from the Marathas, and even the earnest intercession of Malika-i-Zamani who was the chief instigator of Ahmad Shah in calling him to India was not able to stop it. Shamlu's account of Ahmad Shah's cantonment at Anupshahar is useful in visualizing the difficulties in the Doab. His account of the patrol round the Maratha camp and cutting off of Maratha parties bringing cash from Delhi, corroborates the Marathi chronicles. But Shamlu is most useful in deciding the beginning of the battle and falsifying Kashiraj in his palpably untrue statement that just before the battle in the early hours of the morning a Maratha valet of Bhau came with the last chit. Shamlu states that Ahmad Shah, after noticing "clouds of dust ascended upto heaven" ordered Shah Pasand Khan to go forth and ascertain the cause thereof. He rode through the plain between Abdali's camp and the Maratha camp by an unfrequented path and took "four hours to advance half a kos." As Shamlu was accompanying Shah Pasand Khan, there is no cause to suspect his statement as untrue though written after thirty-five years, because no man would forget such an event

---

15 *Fall* 2.76.

on such a day.[16] Shamlu's account of Ahmad Shah's arrangement of his army also supplies a clue in correctly visualizing the battle array, which seems to differ a little from Kashiraj's account. The last important point made clear from Shamlu's account is the fact of Ahmad Shah's apprehension in the first half of the day that "he would not be able to withstand" the impetuous Maratha attack led by Bhau on the Abdali centre, and his despatch of a person "to mount the ladies of his household on fleet steeds" and keep them ready for any eventualities. That shows that Ahmad Shah was not at all sure of certain victory as made out by later historians and commentators. Incidentally it shows Ahmad Shah's wisdom and precaution against any mishap. Shamlu openly says that "by Ahmad Sultan's good fortune one Zamburak ball struck Vishwasrao on the forehead and another hit Bhau on the side," meaning thereby that good fortune and accidents had not a little to do with the Maratha defeat. Shamlu also corroborates the fact of the Maratha army's sudden desertion from the battle-field and the stampede which followed. Shah Pasand Khan received the news of this central struggle through couriers (p. 154), which again shows the distance separating the various divisions on the battle-field. Shah Pasand Khan had not possibly moved much from his original place in the battle array and charged Malharrao and Janakoji only after knowing the defeat of the centre. Shamlu only shows that they fled, though Malharrao fled westwards and Janakoji eastwards. Shamlu's account of the Maratha camp after the battle when 30,000 matchlockmen were so struck with terror and consternation that they would not lift their hand to strike anybody who came amidst them for loot, is most illuminative of the psychic effect of defeat. We think that the Marathas had exhausted their ammunition and hence were helpless to do anything. They were only putting on a bold face to conceal their deficiency. Shamlu also notes that a Maratha chief had been stationed in hindmost rank of their army and was later on seen fleeing towards the south side with six or seven thousand horse, and would not meet even "three individuals," but ran away pell-mell "at the mere firing of the guns and took another direction," shows that Bhau had not, as assumed by Sir Jadunath, left his camp unprotected in the last resort. He had properly arranged everything, but everything went astray as luck would have it. Altogether we do not think of Shamlu as a worthless witness as Sir Jadunath seems to think, and have fully utilised his account for what it is worth. As Shamlu was in the latter part of his life living in India, he had ample opportunities of conversing with other survivors from the field and of refreshing his memory of the Panipat battle-field. That he had not lost interest in the affairs of the Marathas is clear from his mention of Shah Alam's return to Delhi in the company of the Marathas, and his anecdotes about Mahadaji Shinde's lameness and the skeletons of the Maratha horses at the caravanserai of Sonepat—incidents which he only relates.

31. Sayyid Nuruddin Hasan Khan's *Life of Najib-ud-daulah*, translation by Sir Jadunath SARKAR in the *Islamic Culture*, 1933, presents one view of the life of this unscrupulous and mischievous man in Indian history. Najib

---

[16] ELLIOT 8.152.

it was who gave a crooked turn to the whole trend of Indian politics in the middle of the 18th century. He fooled all who came into contact with him, both friend and foe. He rose as a servant of Ghazi-ud-din, the Wazir, and ultimately ruined him, by his treachery. He made use of Malharrao Holkar as a god-father and did mortal harm to the Maratha politics in the north. He brought Shuja over to the side of Abdali and sent him empty-handed back to Oudh for fear of being looted by his allies. Shuja did not think even of taking leave of Ahmad Shah Abdali before decamping! Najib had not done any good to Ahmad Shah either, through whose help he became what he was. He made use of the Shah by the argument of race and religion, and that way completely ruined the Marathas. But what permanent benefit accrued to Islam from his acts? He had misinformed Ahmad Shah about the relative strength of the political parties in India as a result of which Ahmad Shah could not reap any permanent advantage. His troops could not get even their salary from him and the forty lakhs of rupees a year which Najib promised to him from the Indian lands he had conquered were never paid. Not only that, politically at the end of the great battle Ahmad Shah had to bestow the Wazirship of the Indian Empire on the hated regicide Ghazi-ud-din, a creature of the Marathas, and not on Shuja, his ally in the late war. All this is well exemplified by this life, written by an admirer though it is.

32. Bihari Lal Munshiji's *Short Life of Najib-ud-daulah,* translated by Sir Jadunath SARKAR, in the *Islamic Culture,* 1936: Though sketchy, it still adds a few more facts to his life. It supplies details in his dealings with Dattaji Shinde, especially Najib's ruse of instructing the Afghans of Kunjpura to put on scarlet caps and move like the Persian *Qizzilbashas* in order to start the rumour of the coming of Abdali to India. This rumour makes it clear why Sabaji Shinde, the Governor of the Panjab, returned long before the actual coming of Abdali and why Govindpant Bundele is found writing, very early, letters about the Shah's coming. It had the effect of demoralizing the Maratha side. It does not add anything to our knowledge of Panipat, however.

33. *Samin:* Shaikh Ghulam Hasan's (pen-name Samin) narrative, translated by W. IRVINE in *Indian Antiquary,* 1907.

This narrative gives a vivid picture of Ahmad Shah's camp, army and political behaviour, in his Indian campaign of 1756-57. The writer is poetically minded. He possesses the journalist's facile pen supplying vivid description. He is gossipy too, introducing anecdotes and stories amidst his narrative. In fact, he tries to reproduce from memory things reported to him by others, such as Imad-ul-mulk's story. He wrote his piece in 1782 at the behest of Captain Jonathan Scott. To judge from the production, this man's memory seems to be unusually strong, but it is idle to call it a diary as is done by Sir Jadunath SARKAR (p. 293, *Fall,* Vol. 2). The picture of Ahmad Shah's army on the march, his camp discipline, etc. seem exaggerated and are more in the form of psychic vision than of sober description. His introduction of poetry at intervals exemplifies his mind. Sir Jadunath has used Samin's description of Ahmad Shah's army to contrast it with the looseness of discipline in the Maratha army. We have no quarrel with the comparison, we only wish that Sir Jadunath had also taken into account the methodology of Abdali's iron discipline and his barbarous methods in his dealings with both friends and foes, Hindus no less than Muslims, for comparison with the methods followed by "the lesser breeds beyond the law," (p. 291, *Fall*, Vol., 2) by which epithet he introduces the Marathas into the comparison. Where the Marathas found it impossible to recover even eighty lakhs proffered for their services in going through a political revolution for deposing one Emperor and his Wazir and seating others in their places, after a sojourn of eight months in the Delhi region, Ahmad Shah gained crores from the city of Delhi alone in less than a month by threatening, bastonading of a Wazir and torture to his mother, and digging of (floors) houses, two years later. The Marathas suffered historically because they stood on a different moral plane from their competitors.

34. *Ichalkaranji State History* with its original papers edited by V. V. KHARE, 1913: A few letters giving news of the Panipat campaign and after are found in this collection, which are useful for deciding the point of the Peshwa's responsibility. Abdali was intercepting the letters from Panipat to the Deccan and making use of the information for his own purpose. As the Peshwa had not received any news from the north for more than a month, his plans naturally went astray. Malharrao Holkar's line of conduct is illustrated in Govind Hari Patwardhan's letter (No. 66).

35. *The Earliest Persian Account of Panipat,* translated by Sir Jadunath SARKAR in the *Sardesai Commemoration Volume,* 1938.

The account is for the most part accurate, and not inaccurate as read by the learned translator. It correctly reports as far as it does and, what is more, supplies a few facts not noted in other documents, viz. Abdali's crossing between Bagpat and Kheora (wrongly deciphered as Khekra by Sir Jadunath, which puts him on the wrong track); Bhau's posting of troops on the farther side of the Jamuna to stop Abdali's supplies (at Bhau Fort near Isapur?); Chimaji Pandit's raid across the Jamuna; winter rains; famine; Shah's precarious position at noon; the panic caused by Bhau's getting down from elephant; slaughter and running away of the Marathas; women captives.

36. *Vad and others*—Selections from the *Peshwa Diaries*—useful for administrative details with correct dates and the itinerary.

37. *Itihasa Sangraha:* A defunct Marathi magazine, Vols. I-VIII, edited by Parasnis (1909-1917), contain a few stray but primarily important letters about the Panipat campaign, events leading to it and the aftermath. They are interspersed under various headings and parts, viz. *Aitihasika Tipane-Charcha-Sphuta Lekha-Goshti,* etc. Sir Jadunath has overlooked these letters for the most part and hence his treatment has turned defective in certain particulars. Actual references are given in the foot-notes.

38. *Parasnis—Marathyanche Parakrama—Bundelkhand Prakarana* (1895) contains casual information about Govindpant Bundele and his sons, also a worthless Panipat chronicle.

39. *Bharata Itihasa Samshodhaka Mandal Quarterly* Vols. I-XXIV, as well as its *Annuals and Conference Reports.* These also contain valuable information and discussions on the various topics connected with Panipat, its personalities and politics.

40. *Hingne Daftar* Vol. I (1945), is useful for judging the Delhi politics during the pre-Panipat as well as post-Panipat period. Unfortunately here, too, no direct evidence bearing on the campaign is forthcoming.